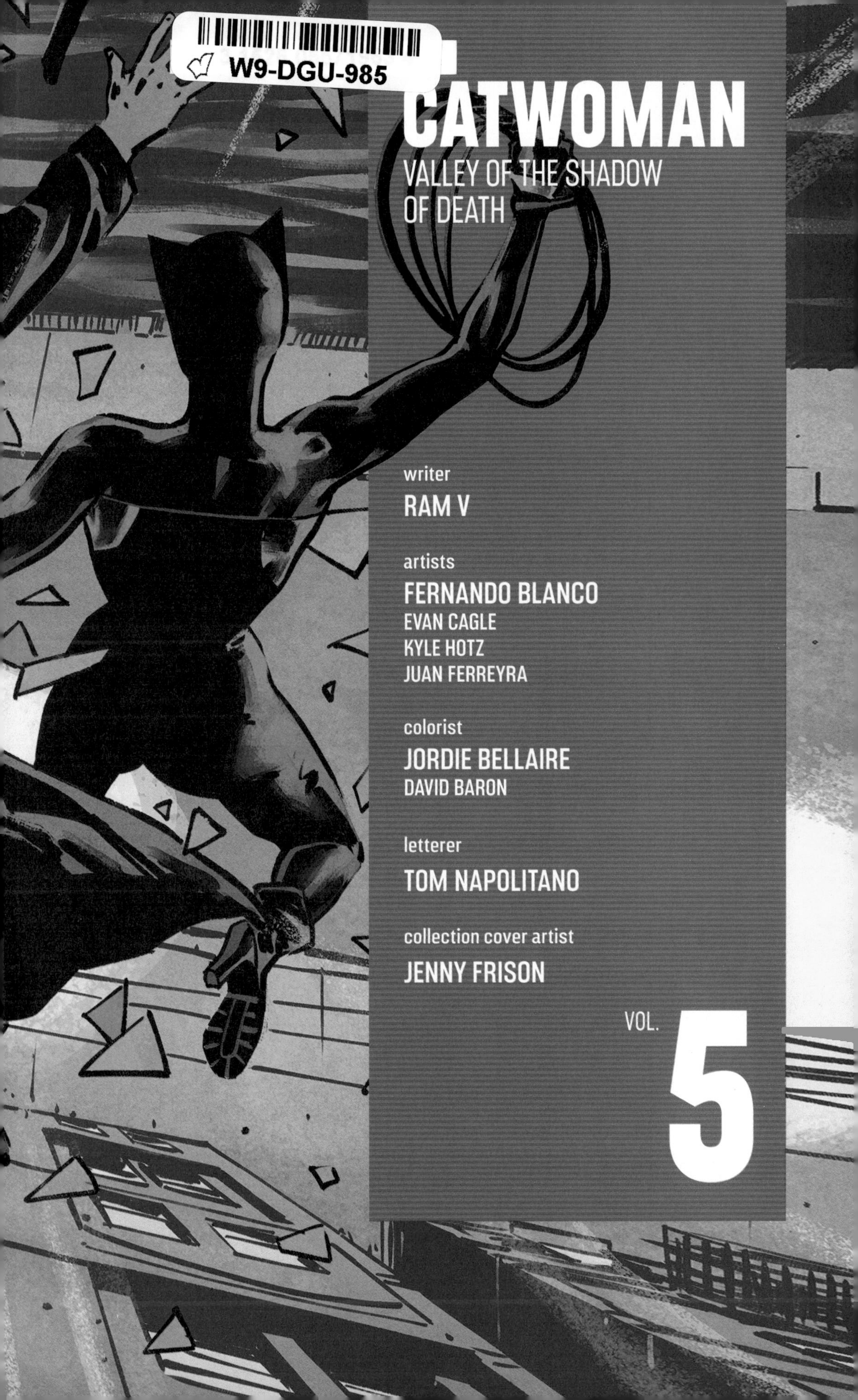

CATWOMAN

VALLEY OF THE SHADOW OF DEATH

writer
RAM V

artists
FERNANDO BLANCO
EVAN CAGLE
KYLE HOTZ
JUAN FERREYRA

colorist
JORDIE BELLAIRE
DAVID BARON

letterer
TOM NAPOLITANO

collection cover artist
JENNY FRISON

VOL. 5

JESSICA CHEN   Editor – Original Series & Collected Edition
BEN MEARES   Assistant Editor – Original Series
STEVE COOK   Design Director – Books
                          & Publication Design
CHRISTY SAWYER   Publication Production

MARIE JAVINS   Editor-in-Chief, DC Comics

DANIEL CHERRY III   Senior VP – General Manager
JIM LEE   Publisher & Chief Creative Officer
JOEN CHOE   VP – Global Brand & Creative Services
DON FALLETTI   VP – Manufacturing Operations & Workflow Management
LAWRENCE GANEM   VP – Talent Services
ALISON GILL   Senior VP – Manufacturing & Operations
NICK J. NAPOLITANO   VP – Manufacturing Administration & Design
NANCY SPEARS   VP – Revenue

CATWOMAN VOL. 5: VALLEY OF THE SHADOW OF DEATH

Published by DC Comics. Compilation and all new material Copyright © 2021 DC Comics. All Rights Reserved. Originally published in single magazine form in *Catwoman* 29-32, *Catwoman 2021 Annual* 1. Copyright © 2021 DC Comics. All Rights Reserved. All characters, their distinctive likenesses, and related elements featured in this publication are trademarks of DC Comics. The stories, characters, and incidents featured in this publication are entirely fictional. DC Comics does not read or accept unsolicited submissions of ideas, stories, or artwork. DC – a WarnerMedia Company.

DC Comics, 2900 West Alameda Ave., Burbank, CA 91505
Printed by LSC Communications, Owensville, MO, USA. 10/08/21. First Printing.
ISBN: 978-1-77951-263-5

Library of Congress Cataloging-in-Publication Data is available.

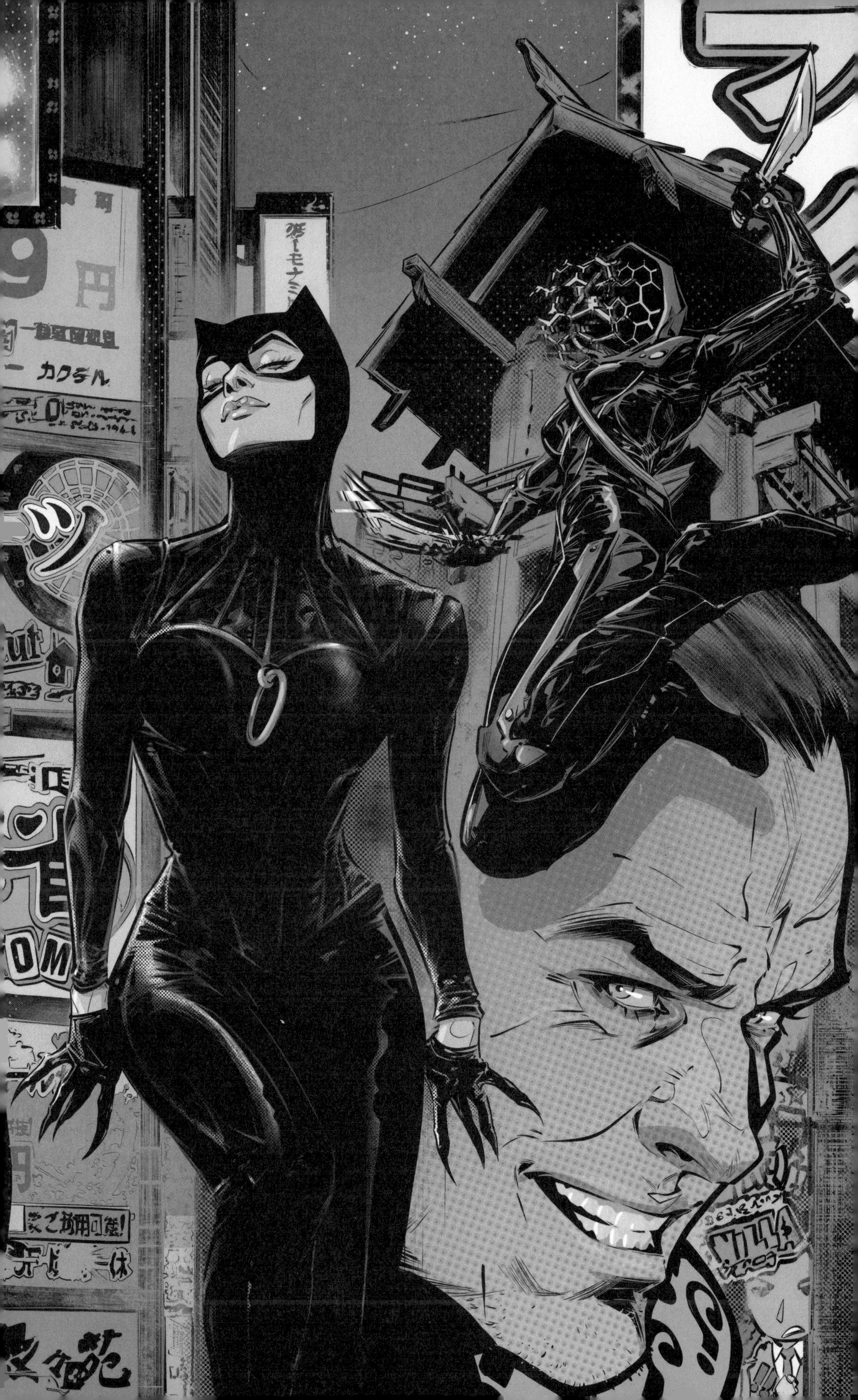
カクテル

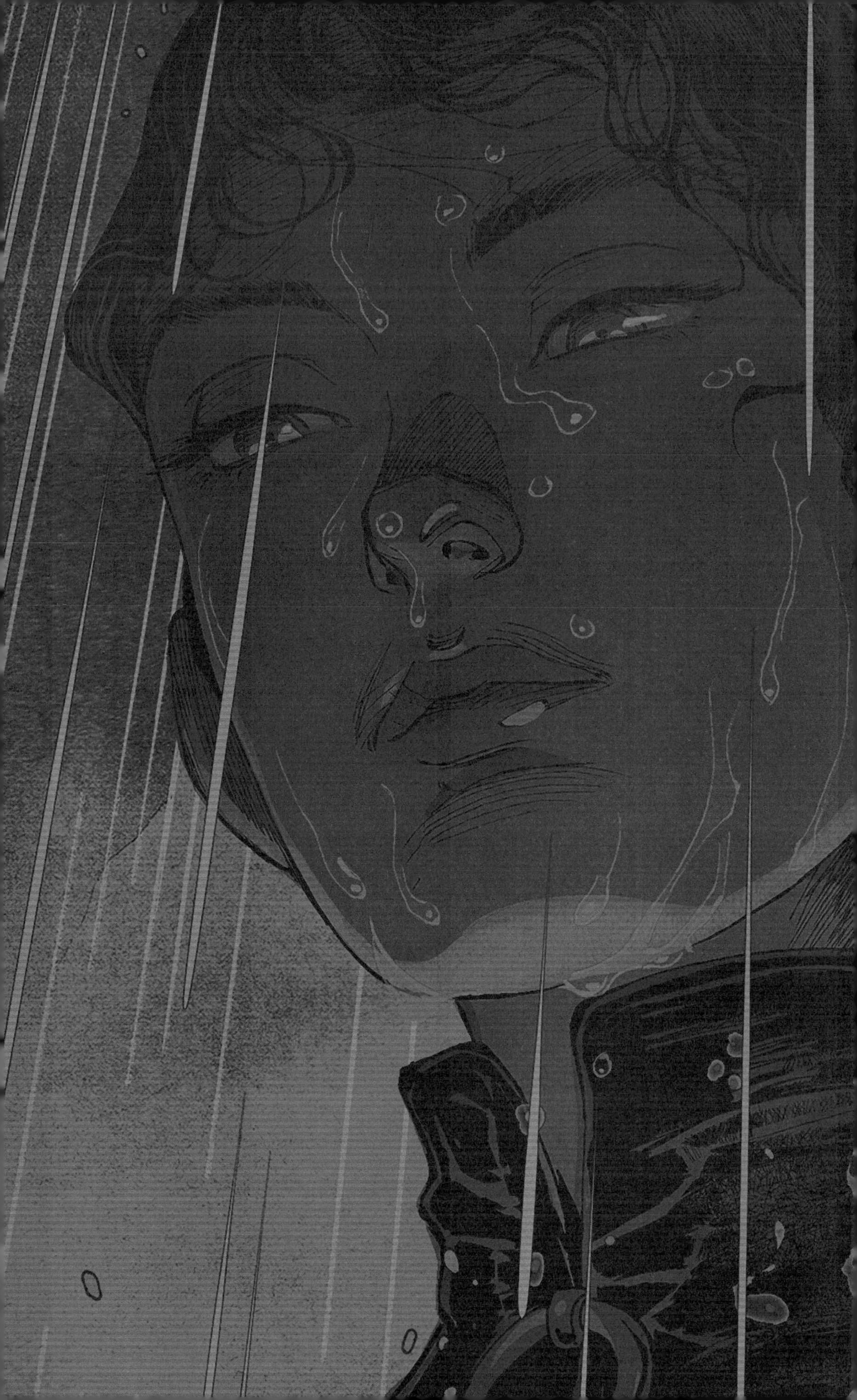

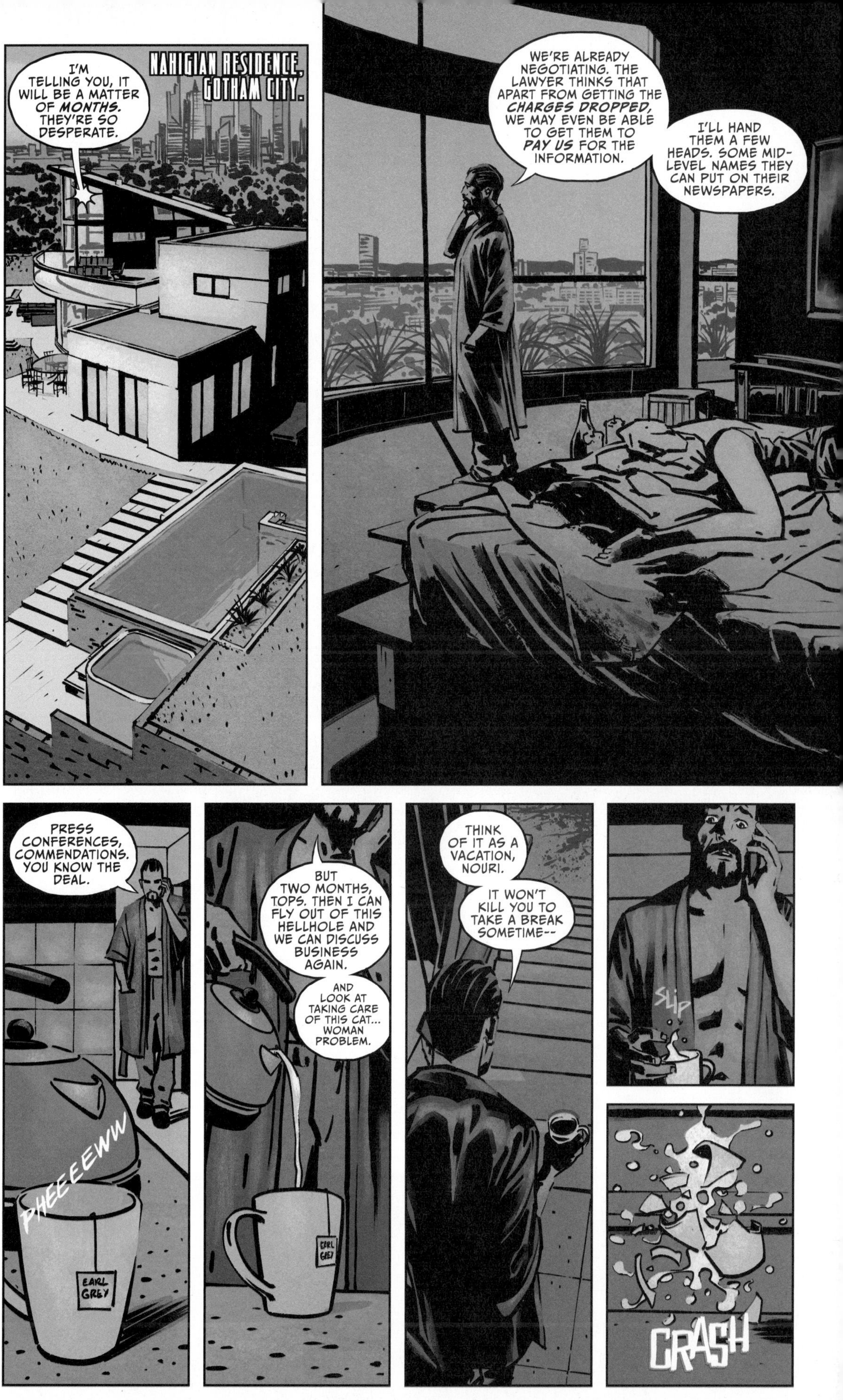
NAHIGIAN RESIDENCE, GOTHAM CITY.
I'M TELLING YOU, IT WILL BE A MATTER OF *MONTHS.* THEY'RE SO DESPERATE.
WE'RE ALREADY NEGOTIATING. THE LAWYER THINKS THAT APART FROM GETTING THE *CHARGES DROPPED,* WE MAY EVEN BE ABLE TO GET THEM TO *PAY US* FOR THE INFORMATION.
I'LL HAND THEM A FEW HEADS. SOME MID-LEVEL NAMES THEY CAN PUT ON THEIR NEWSPAPERS.
PRESS CONFERENCES, COMMENDATIONS. YOU KNOW THE DEAL.
PHEEEEWW
EARL GREY
BUT TWO MONTHS, TOPS. THEN I CAN FLY OUT OF THIS HELLHOLE AND WE CAN DISCUSS BUSINESS AGAIN.
AND LOOK AT TAKING CARE OF THIS CAT... WOMAN PROBLEM.
EARL GREY
THINK OF IT AS A VACATION, NOURI.
IT WON'T KILL YOU TO TAKE A BREAK SOMETIME--
SLIP
CRASH

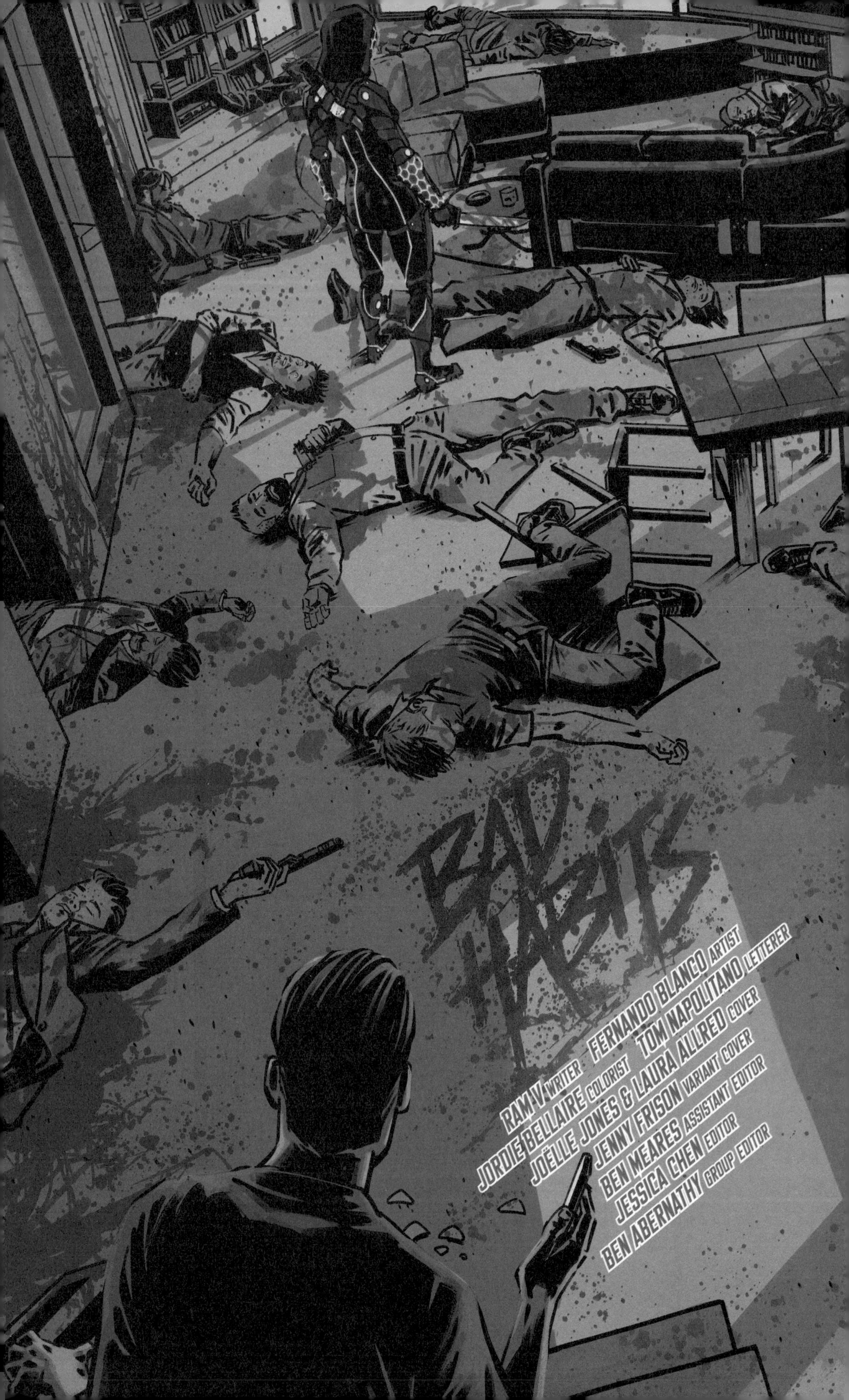
BAD HABITS
RAM V WRITER FERNANDO BLANCO ARTIST
JORDIE BELLAIRE COLORIST TOM NAPOLITANO LETTERER
JOËLLE JONES & LAURA ALLRED COVER
JENNY FRISON VARIANT COVER
BEN MEARES ASSISTANT EDITOR
JESSICA CHEN EDITOR
BEN ABERNATHY GROUP EDITOR

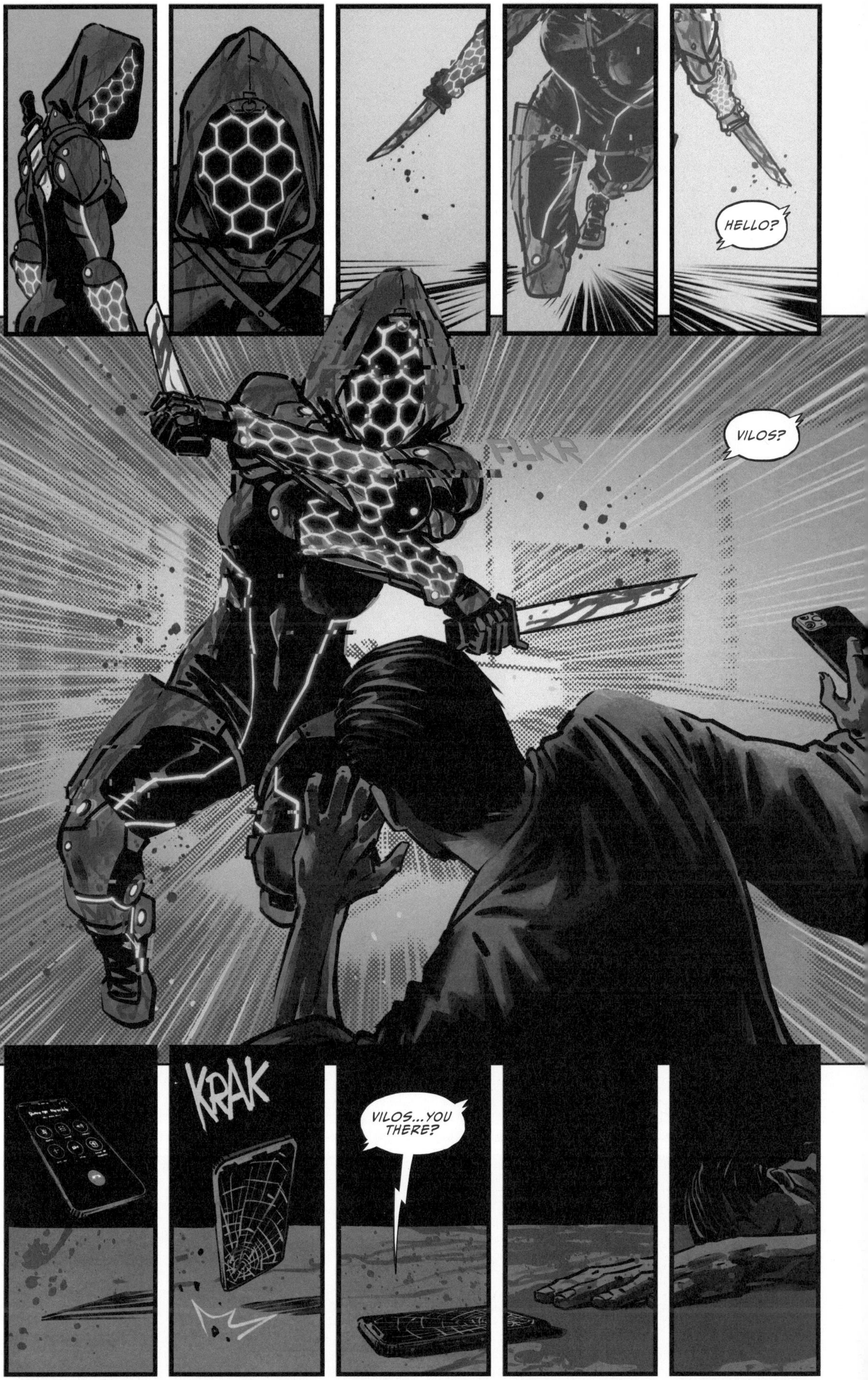
HELLO?
VILOS?
FLKR
KRAK
VILOS...YOU THERE?

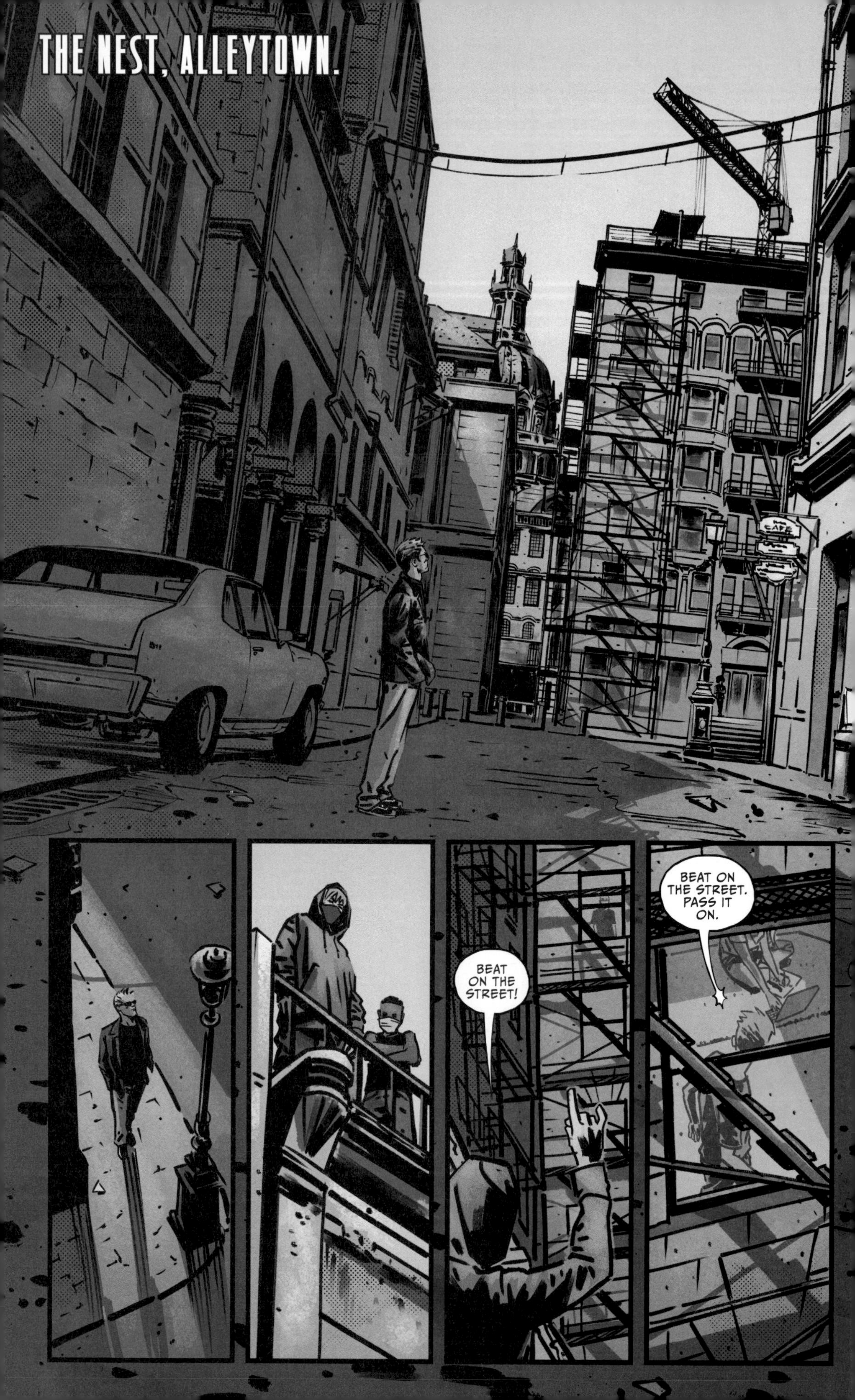
THE NEST, ALLEYTOWN.
BEAT ON THE STREET!
BEAT ON THE STREET. PASS IT ON.

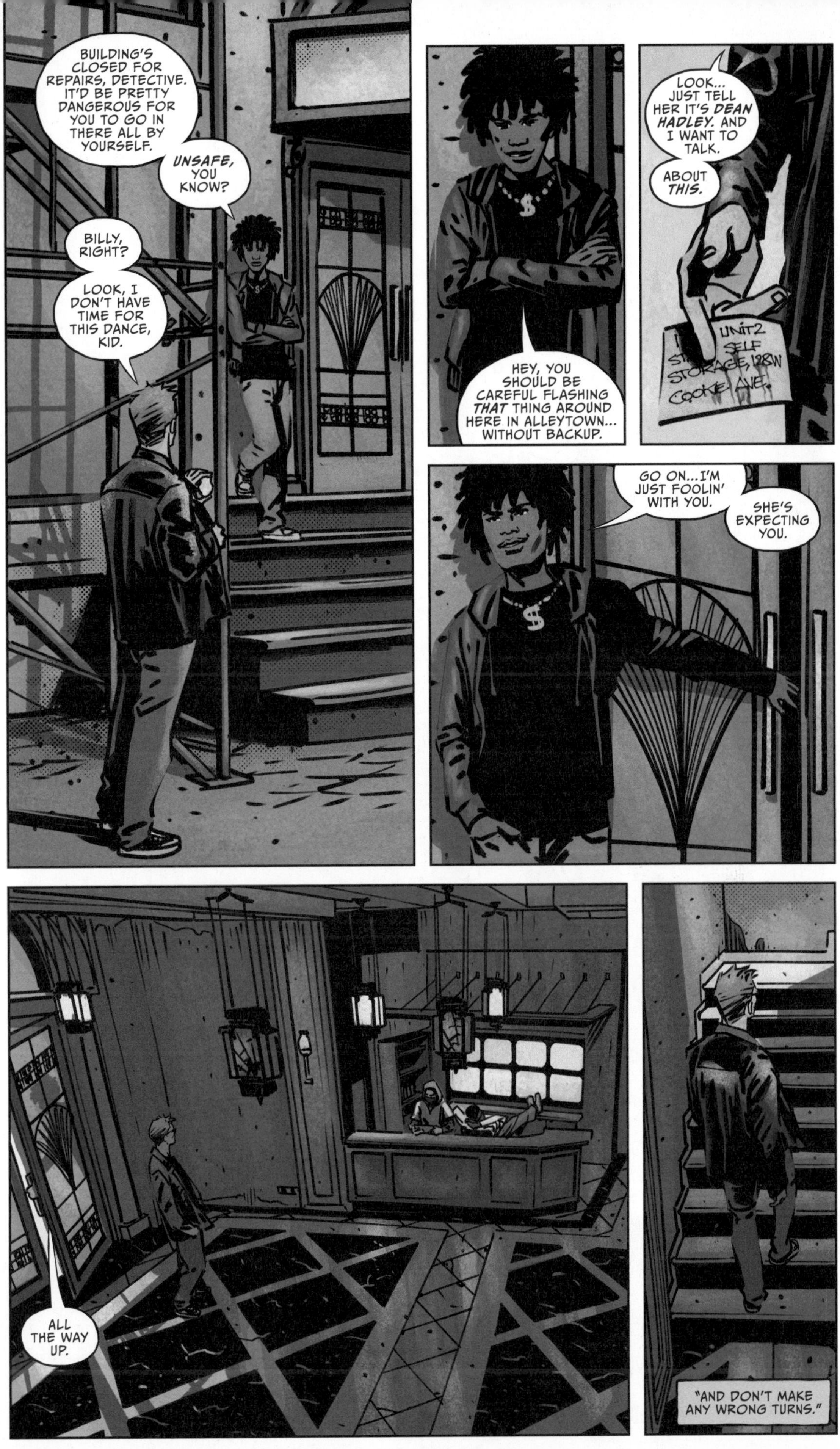
BUILDING'S CLOSED FOR REPAIRS, DETECTIVE. IT'D BE PRETTY DANGEROUS FOR YOU TO GO IN THERE ALL BY YOURSELF.
UNSAFE, YOU KNOW?
BILLY, RIGHT?
LOOK, I DON'T HAVE TIME FOR THIS DANCE, KID.
HEY, YOU SHOULD BE CAREFUL FLASHING THAT THING AROUND HERE IN ALLEYTOWN... WITHOUT BACKUP.
LOOK... JUST TELL HER IT'S DEAN HADLEY. AND I WANT TO TALK.
ABOUT THIS.
UNIT2
SELF
STORAGE, 128W
COOKE AVE.
GO ON...I'M JUST FOOLIN' WITH YOU.
SHE'S EXPECTING YOU.
ALL THE WAY UP.
"AND DON'T MAKE ANY WRONG TURNS."

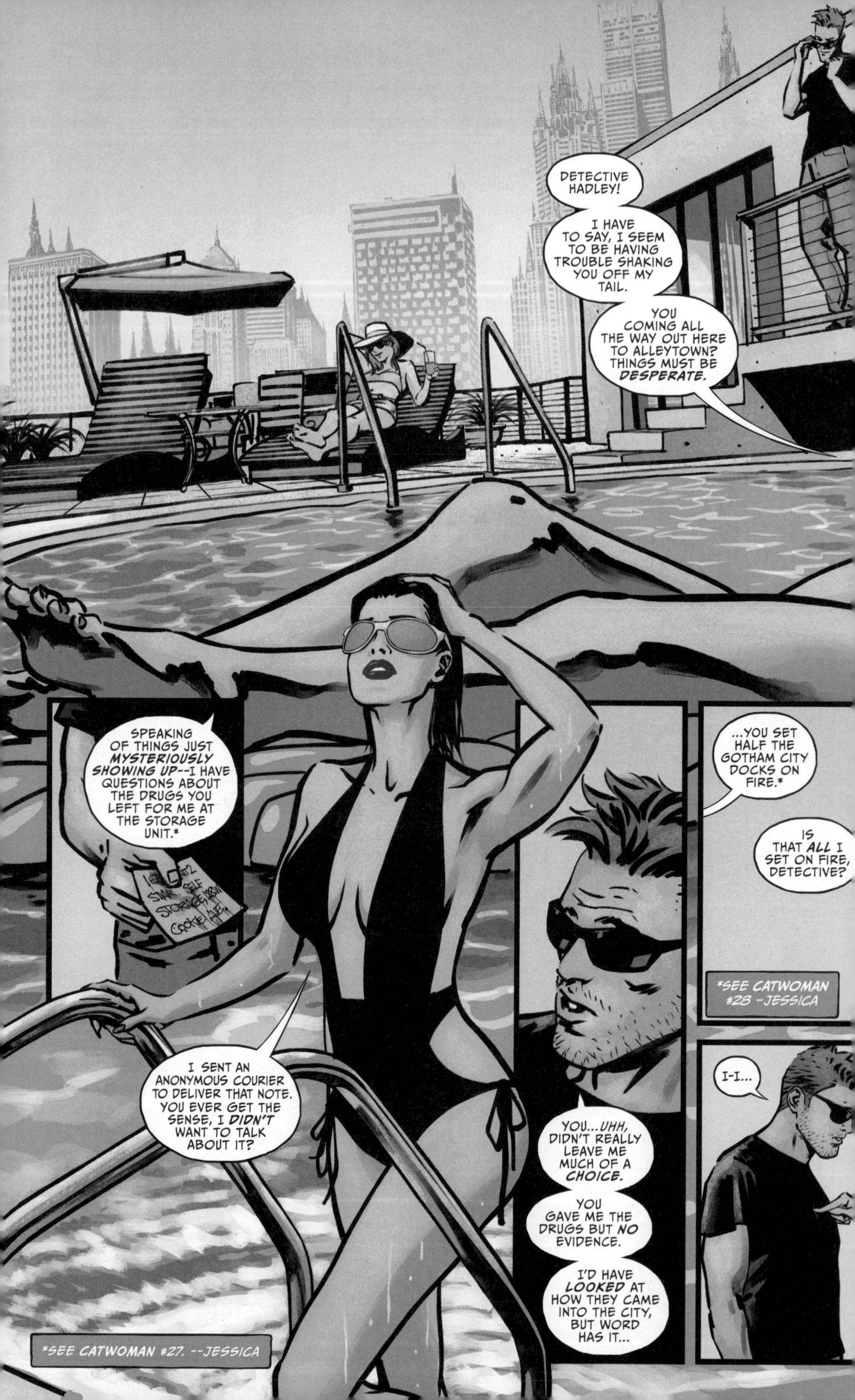
DETECTIVE HADLEY!
I HAVE TO SAY, I SEEM TO BE HAVING TROUBLE SHAKING YOU OFF MY TAIL.
YOU COMING ALL THE WAY OUT HERE TO ALLEYTOWN? THINGS MUST BE **DESPERATE.**
SPEAKING OF THINGS JUST **MYSTERIOUSLY SHOWING UP**--I HAVE QUESTIONS ABOUT THE DRUGS YOU LEFT FOR ME AT THE STORAGE UNIT.*
I SENT AN ANONYMOUS COURIER TO DELIVER THAT NOTE. YOU EVER GET THE SENSE, I ***DIDN'T*** WANT TO TALK ABOUT IT?
*SEE CATWOMAN #27. --JESSICA
YOU...*UHH*, DIDN'T REALLY LEAVE ME MUCH OF A ***CHOICE.***
YOU GAVE ME THE DRUGS BUT ***NO*** EVIDENCE.
I'D HAVE ***LOOKED*** AT HOW THEY CAME INTO THE CITY, BUT WORD HAS IT...
...YOU SET HALF THE GOTHAM CITY DOCKS ON FIRE.*
IS THAT ***ALL*** I SET ON FIRE, DETECTIVE?
*SEE CATWOMAN #28 -JESSICA
I-I...

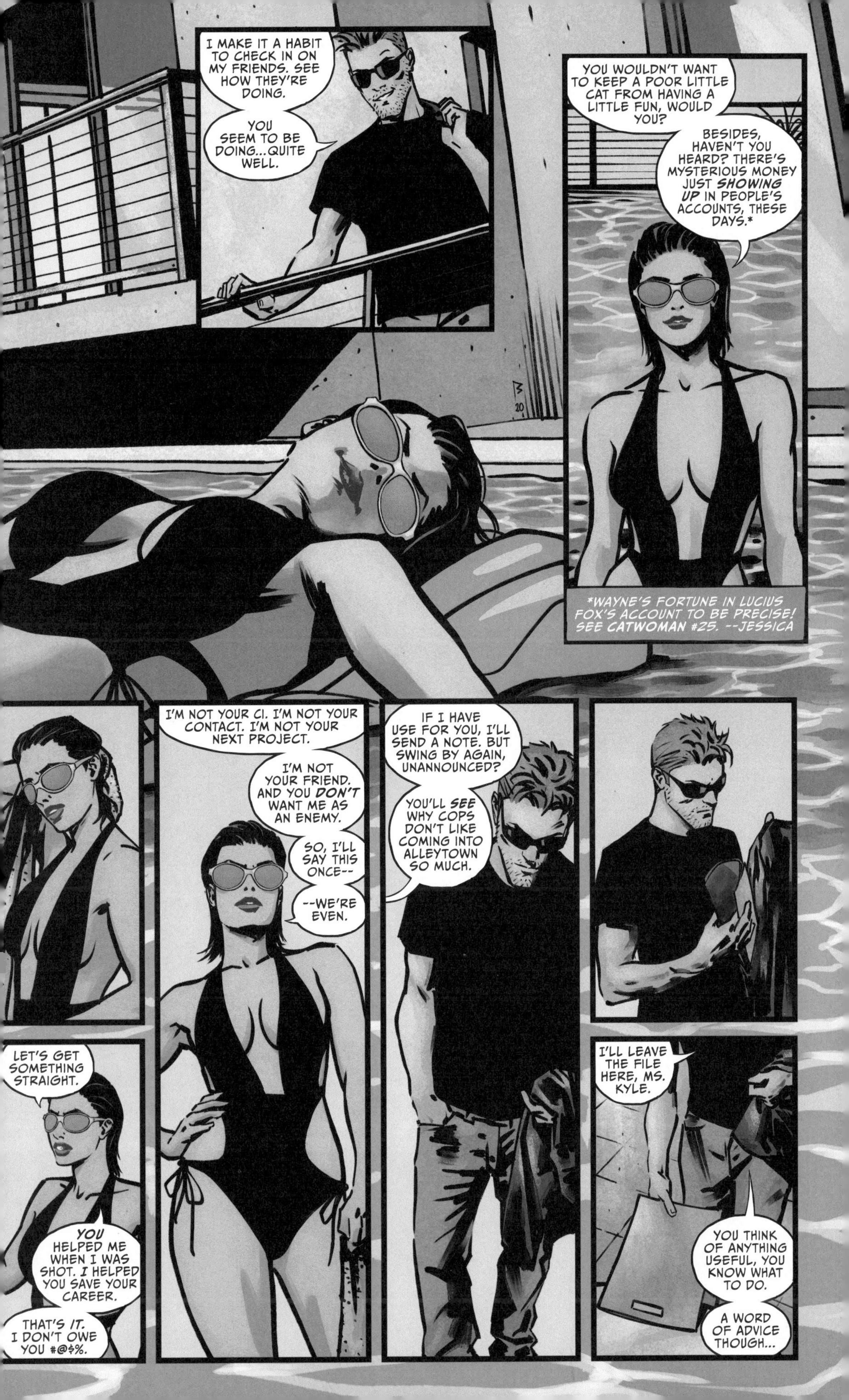
I MAKE IT A HABIT TO CHECK IN ON MY FRIENDS. SEE HOW THEY'RE DOING.
YOU SEEM TO BE DOING...QUITE WELL.
YOU WOULDN'T WANT TO KEEP A POOR LITTLE CAT FROM HAVING A LITTLE FUN, WOULD YOU?
BESIDES, HAVEN'T YOU HEARD? THERE'S MYSTERIOUS MONEY JUST SHOWING UP IN PEOPLE'S ACCOUNTS, THESE DAYS.*
*WAYNE'S FORTUNE IN LUCIUS FOX'S ACCOUNT TO BE PRECISE! SEE CATWOMAN #25. --JESSICA
LET'S GET SOMETHING STRAIGHT.
YOU HELPED ME WHEN I WAS SHOT. I HELPED YOU SAVE YOUR CAREER.
THAT'S IT. I DON'T OWE YOU #@$%.
I'M NOT YOUR CI. I'M NOT YOUR CONTACT. I'M NOT YOUR NEXT PROJECT.
I'M NOT YOUR FRIEND. AND YOU DON'T WANT ME AS AN ENEMY.
SO, I'LL SAY THIS ONCE--
--WE'RE EVEN.
IF I HAVE USE FOR YOU, I'LL SEND A NOTE. BUT SWING BY AGAIN, UNANNOUNCED?
YOU'LL SEE WHY COPS DON'T LIKE COMING INTO ALLEYTOWN SO MUCH.
I'LL LEAVE THE FILE HERE, MS. KYLE.
YOU THINK OF ANYTHING USEFUL, YOU KNOW WHAT TO DO.
A WORD OF ADVICE THOUGH...

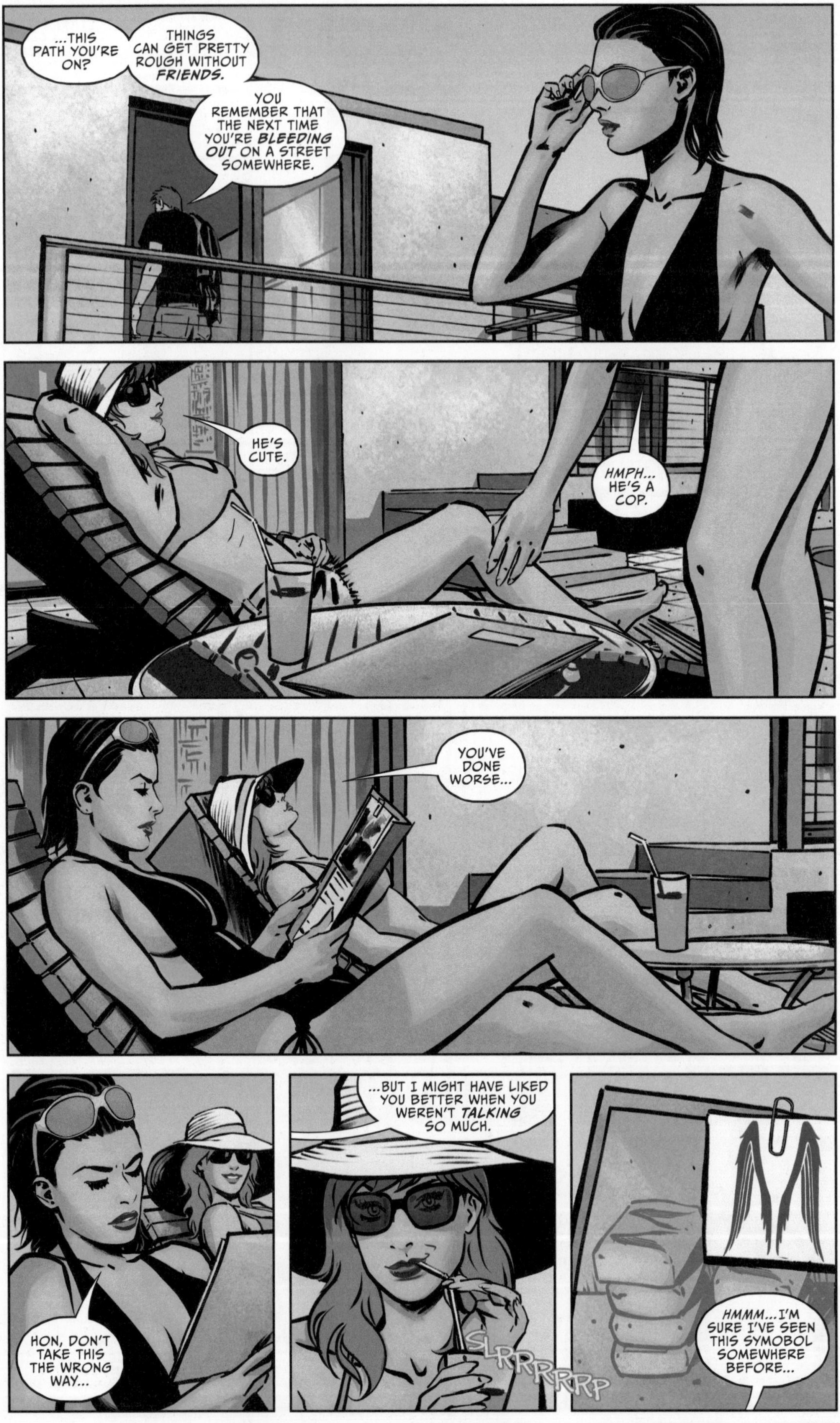
...THIS PATH YOU'RE ON?
THINGS CAN GET PRETTY ROUGH WITHOUT FRIENDS.
YOU REMEMBER THAT THE NEXT TIME YOU'RE BLEEDING OUT ON A STREET SOMEWHERE.
HE'S CUTE.
HMPH... HE'S A COP.
YOU'VE DONE WORSE...
HON, DON'T TAKE THIS THE WRONG WAY...
...BUT I MIGHT HAVE LIKED YOU BETTER WHEN YOU WEREN'T TALKING SO MUCH.
SLRRRRRRP
HMMM...I'M SURE I'VE SEEN THIS SYMOBOL SOMEWHERE BEFORE...

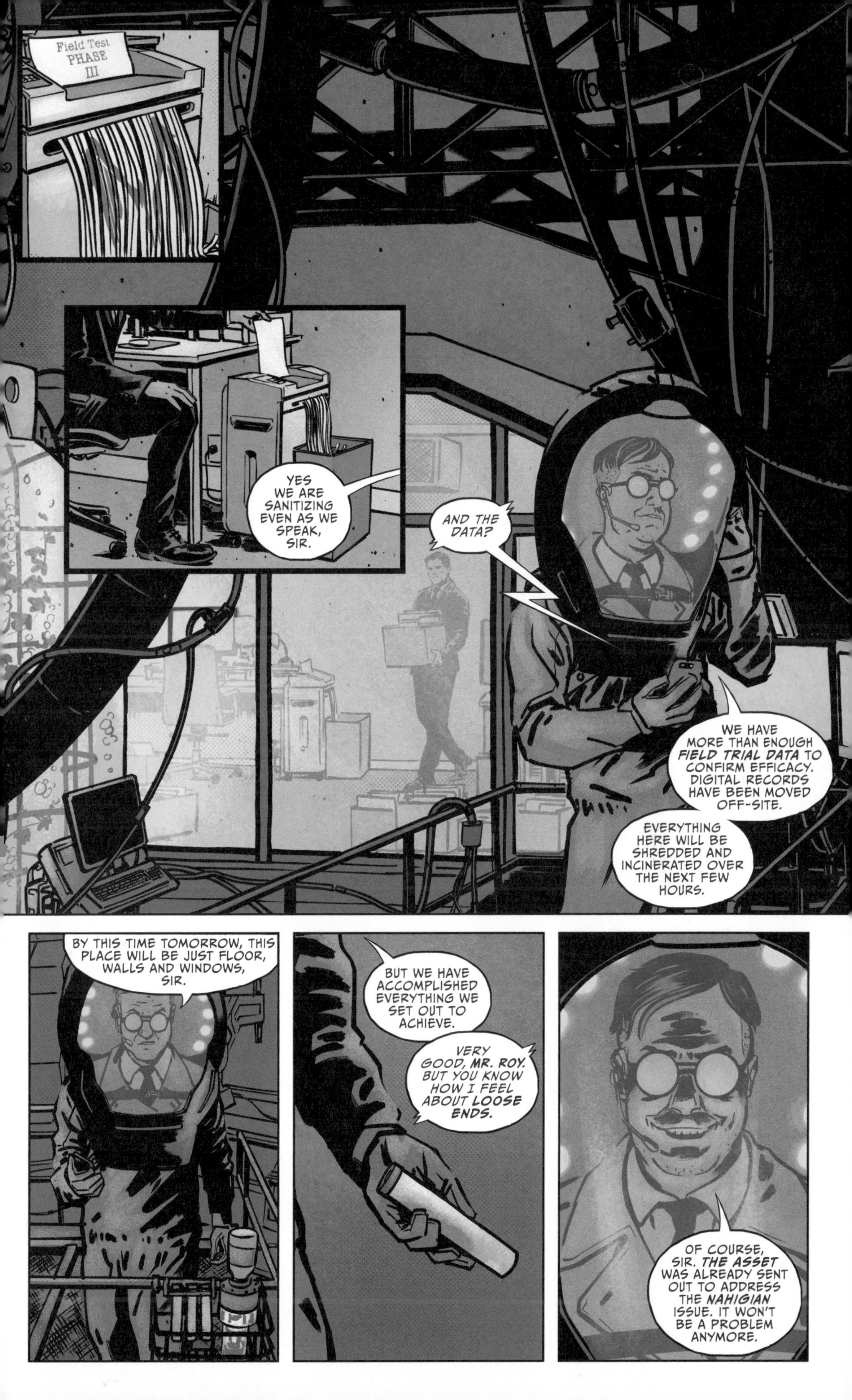
Field Test PHASE III
YES WE ARE SANITIZING EVEN AS WE SPEAK, SIR.
AND THE DATA?
WE HAVE MORE THAN ENOUGH FIELD TRIAL DATA TO CONFIRM EFFICACY. DIGITAL RECORDS HAVE BEEN MOVED OFF-SITE.
EVERYTHING HERE WILL BE SHREDDED AND INCINERATED OVER THE NEXT FEW HOURS.
BY THIS TIME TOMORROW, THIS PLACE WILL BE JUST FLOOR, WALLS AND WINDOWS, SIR.
BUT WE HAVE ACCOMPLISHED EVERYTHING WE SET OUT TO ACHIEVE.
VERY GOOD, MR. ROY. BUT YOU KNOW HOW I FEEL ABOUT LOOSE ENDS.
OF COURSE, SIR. THE ASSET WAS ALREADY SENT OUT TO ADDRESS THE NAHIGIAN ISSUE. IT WON'T BE A PROBLEM ANYMORE.

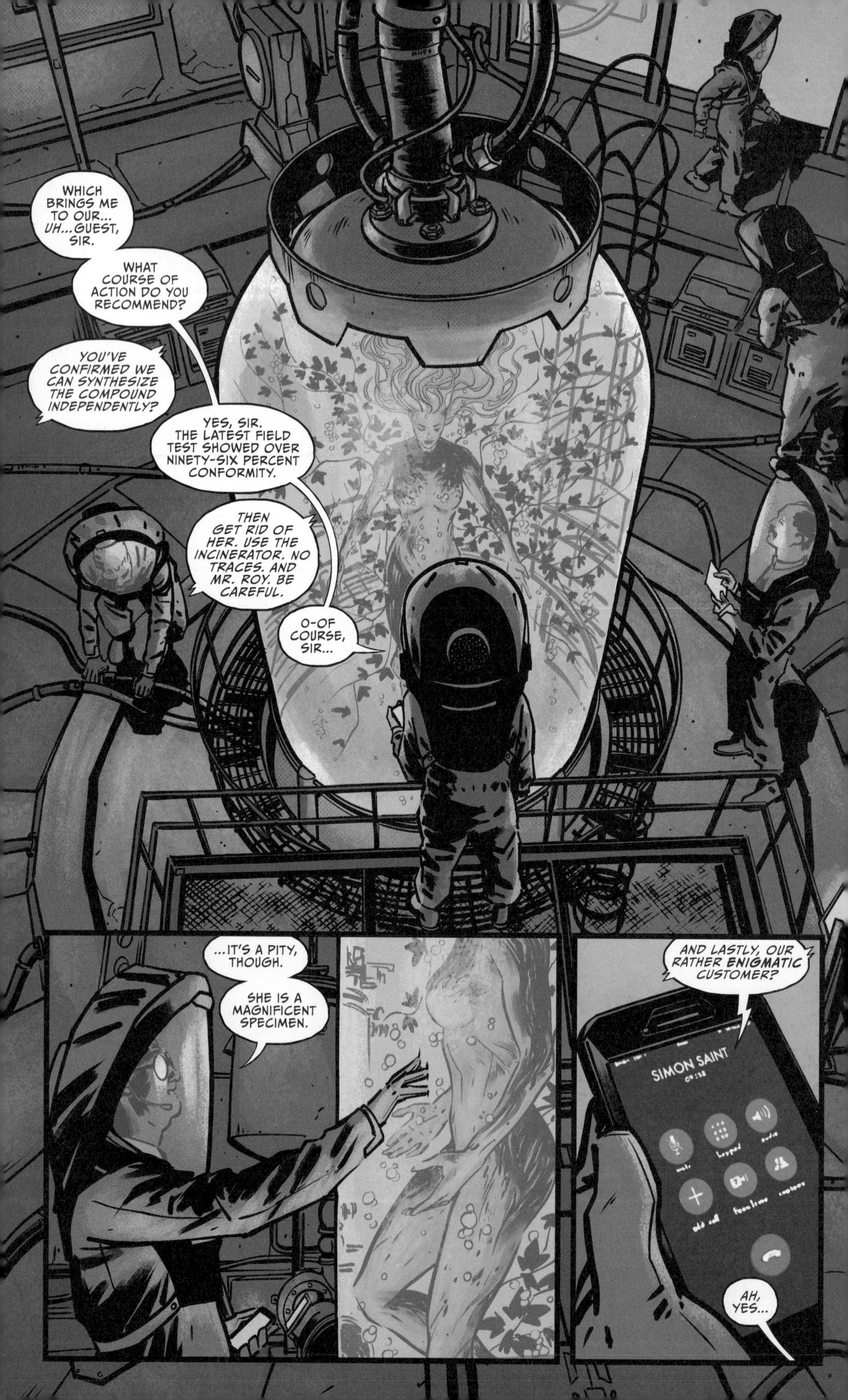
WHICH BRINGS ME TO OUR... UH...GUEST, SIR.
WHAT COURSE OF ACTION DO YOU RECOMMEND?
YOU'VE CONFIRMED WE CAN SYNTHESIZE THE COMPOUND INDEPENDENTLY?
YES, SIR. THE LATEST FIELD TEST SHOWED OVER NINETY-SIX PERCENT CONFORMITY.
THEN GET RID OF HER. USE THE INCINERATOR. NO TRACES. AND MR. ROY. BE CAREFUL.
O-OF COURSE, SIR...
...IT'S A PITY, THOUGH.
SHE IS A MAGNIFICENT SPECIMEN.
AND LASTLY, OUR RATHER ENIGMATIC CUSTOMER?
SIMON SAINT
AH, YES...

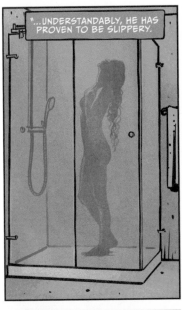

"...UNDERSTANDABLY, HE HAS PROVEN TO BE SLIPPERY.

"BUT IT'S BEEN A WEEK SINCE *WE CUT HIM OFF* AND SURVEILLANCE HAS TRACED HIS LOCATION.

"I'VE REASSIGNED *THE ASSET.*"

"ASSET PERFORMANCE IS STABLE SO FAR?"

"SHE'S BEEN IMPRESSIVE. PERFECT COMPLIANCE AND YET HAS SHOWN A REMARKABLE ABILITY TO IMPROVISE IN THE FIELD.

FLKR

"SHE'S ADAPTED TO HER META-ABILITIES WELL."

VRROOOM

"GOOD...THE *WIGHT WITCH* IS OUR STAR, ROY. TAKE GOOD CARE OF HER AND KEEP ME APPRAISED.

"MR. *NYGMA,* EVEN IN HIS *TROUBLED STATE,* SHOULD PROVIDE AN INTERESTING CHALLENGE."

VRRRRRMMM

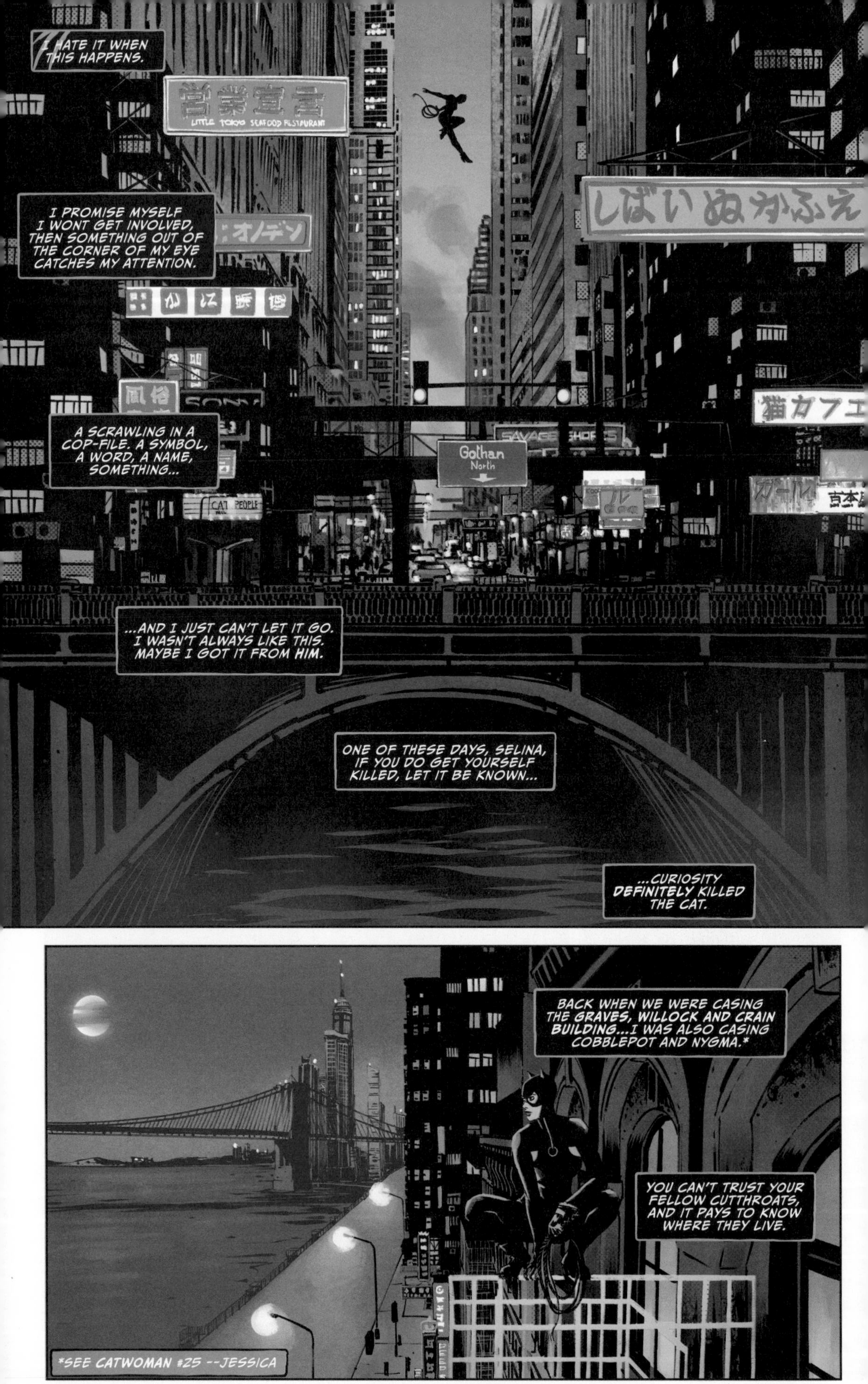
I HATE IT WHEN THIS HAPPENS.
LITTLE TOKYO SEAFOOD RESTAURANT
しばいぬかふぇ
I PROMISE MYSELF I WONT GET INVOLVED, THEN SOMETHING OUT OF THE CORNER OF MY EYE CATCHES MY ATTENTION.
猫カフェ
A SCRAWLING IN A COP-FILE. A SYMBOL, A WORD, A NAME, SOMETHING...
Gotham North
...AND I JUST CAN'T LET IT GO. I WASN'T ALWAYS LIKE THIS. MAYBE I GOT IT FROM HIM.
ONE OF THESE DAYS, SELINA, IF YOU DO GET YOURSELF KILLED, LET IT BE KNOWN...
...CURIOSITY DEFINITELY KILLED THE CAT.
BACK WHEN WE WERE CASING THE GRAVES, WILLOCK AND CRAIN BUILDING...I WAS ALSO CASING COBBLEPOT AND NYGMA.*
YOU CAN'T TRUST YOUR FELLOW CUTTHROATS, AND IT PAYS TO KNOW WHERE THEY LIVE.
*SEE CATWOMAN #25 --JESSICA

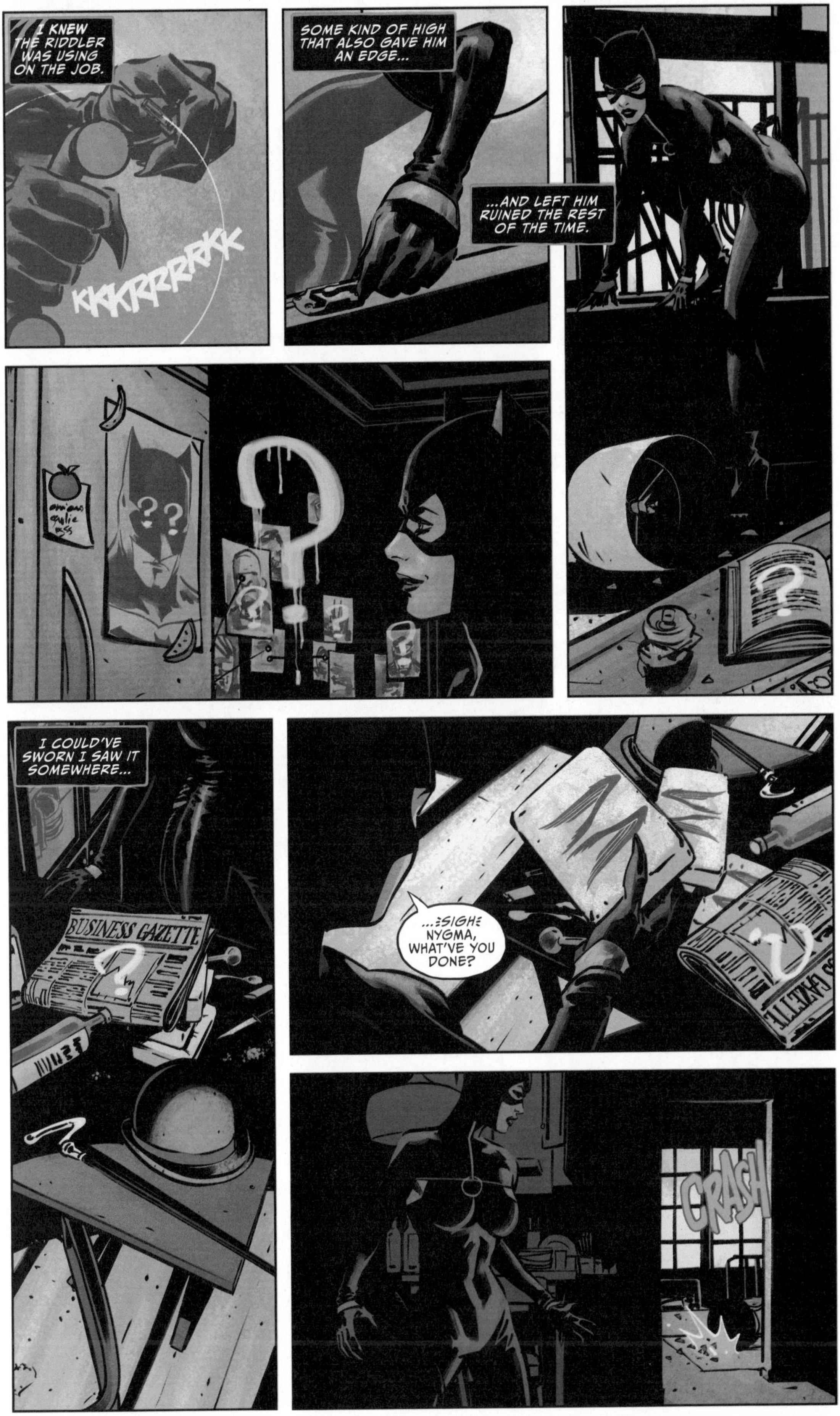
I KNEW THE RIDDLER WAS USING ON THE JOB.
KKKRRRRKK
SOME KIND OF HIGH THAT ALSO GAVE HIM AN EDGE...
...AND LEFT HIM RUINED THE REST OF THE TIME.
I COULD'VE SWORN I SAW IT SOMEWHERE...
BUSINESS GAZETTE
...SIGH... NYGMA, WHAT'VE YOU DONE?
CRASH

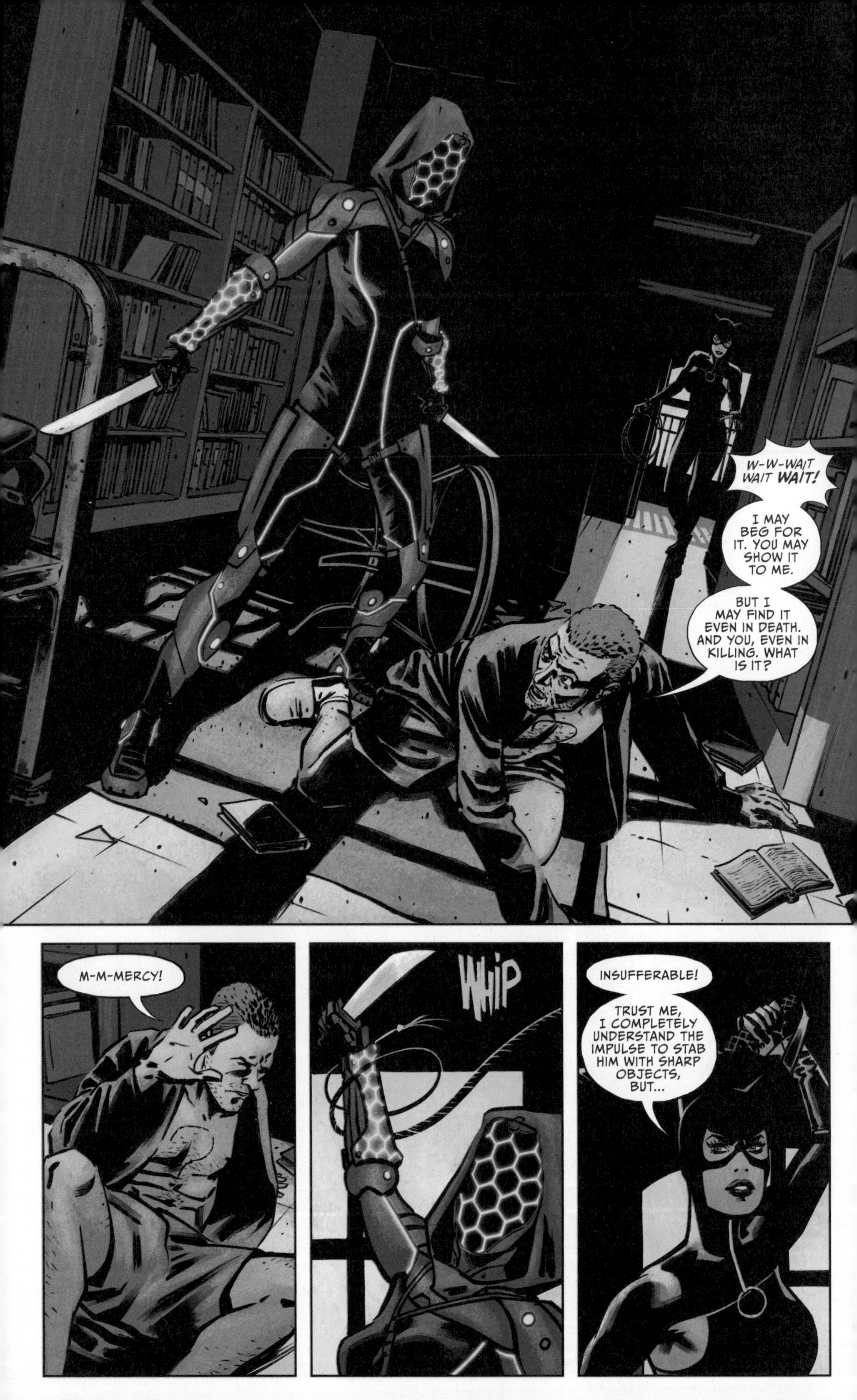
W-W-WAIT WAIT WAIT!
I MAY BEG FOR IT. YOU MAY SHOW IT TO ME.
BUT I MAY FIND IT EVEN IN DEATH. AND YOU, EVEN IN KILLING. WHAT IS IT?
M-M-MERCY!
WHIP
INSUFFERABLE!
TRUST ME, I COMPLETELY UNDERSTAND THE IMPULSE TO STAB HIM WITH SHARP OBJECTS, BUT...

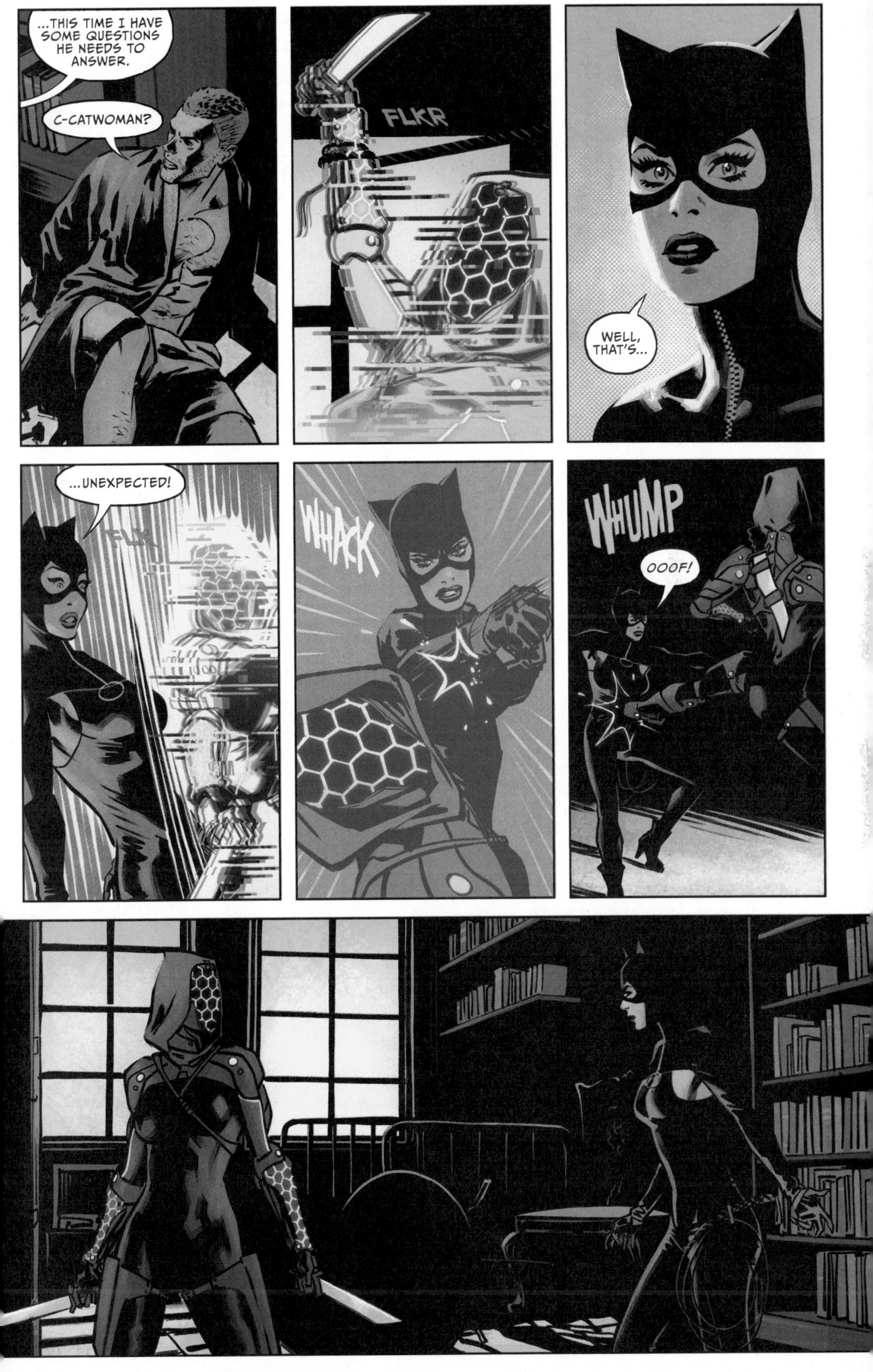
...THIS TIME I HAVE SOME QUESTIONS HE NEEDS TO ANSWER.
C-CATWOMAN?
FLKR
WELL, THAT'S...
...UNEXPECTED!
FLKR
WHACK
WHUMP
OOOF!

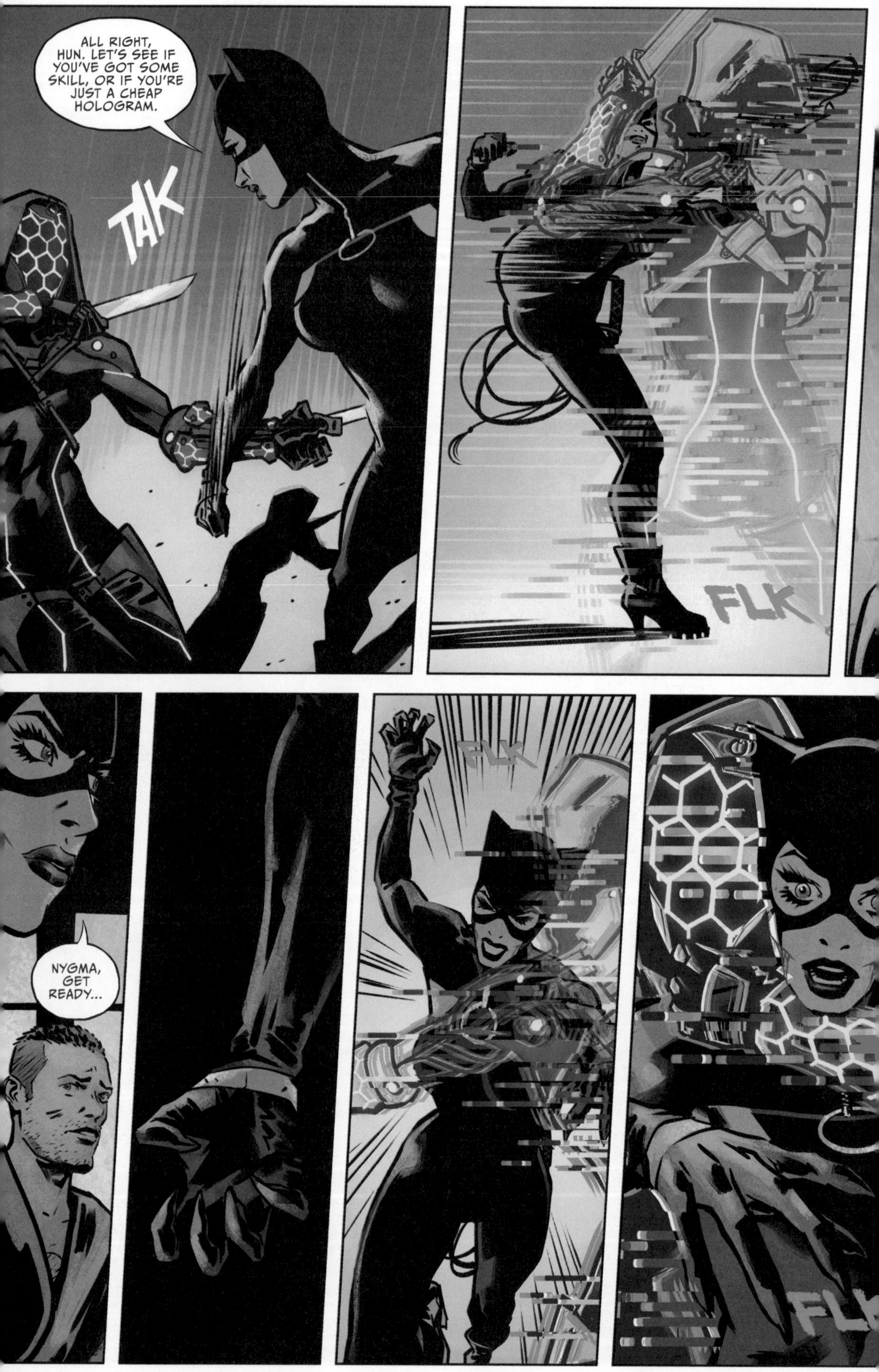
ALL RIGHT, HUN. LET'S SEE IF YOU'VE GOT SOME SKILL, OR IF YOU'RE JUST A CHEAP HOLOGRAM.
TAK
FLK
NYGMA, GET READY...
FLK

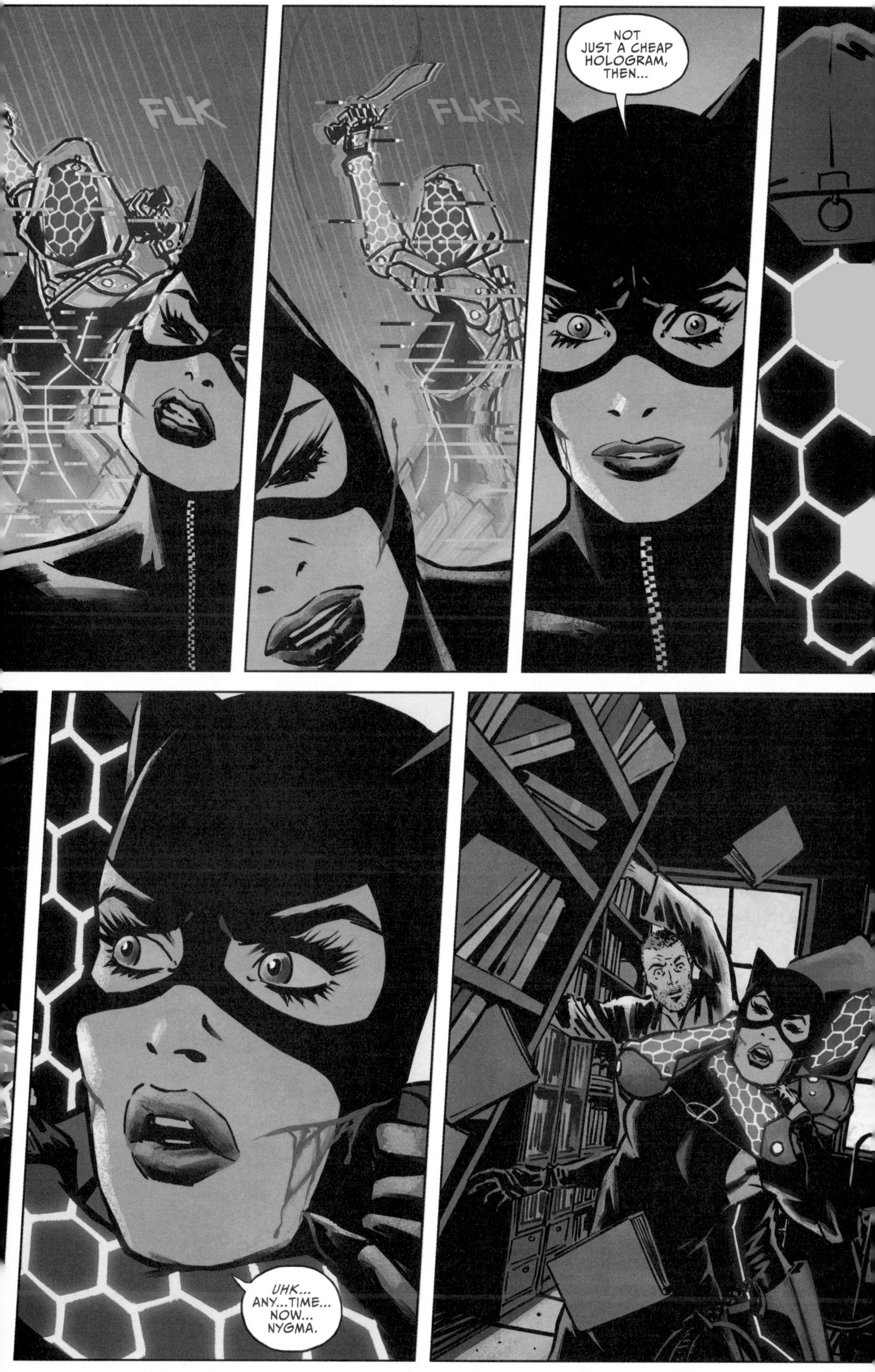
FLK
FLKR
NOT JUST A CHEAP HOLOGRAM, THEN...
UHK... ANY...TIME... NOW... NYGMA.

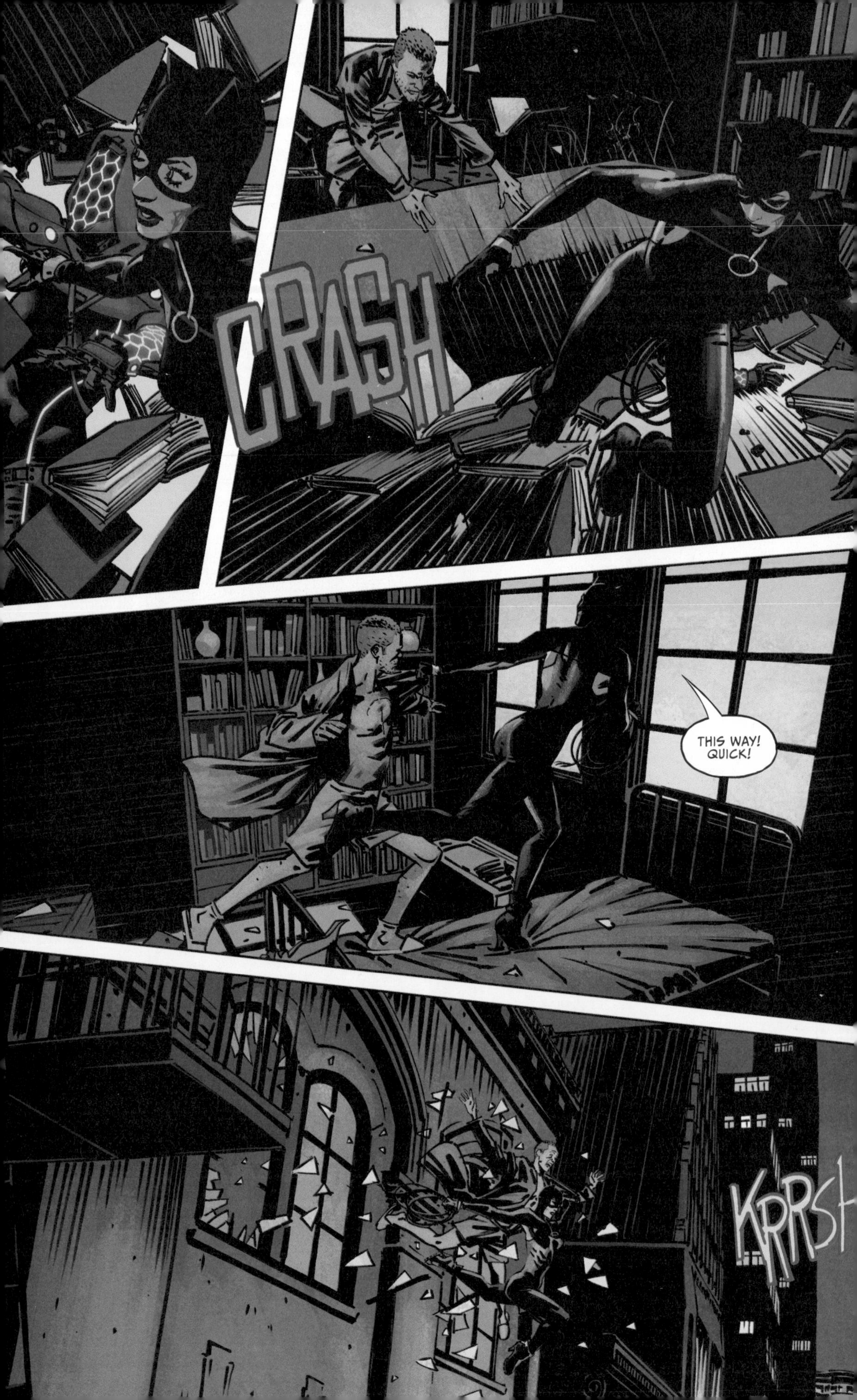
CRASH
THIS WAY! QUICK!
KRRSH

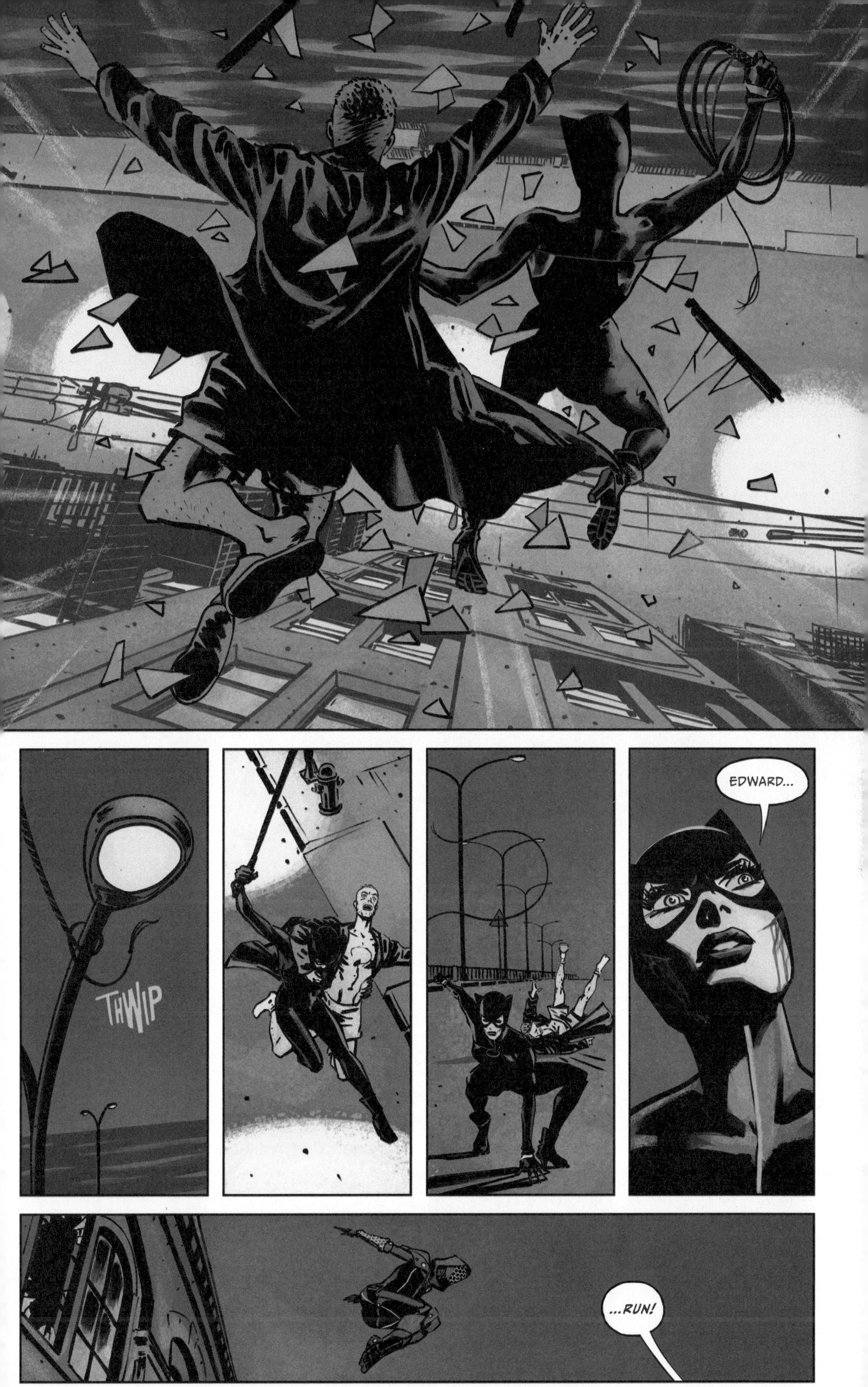
THWIP
EDWARD...
...RUN!

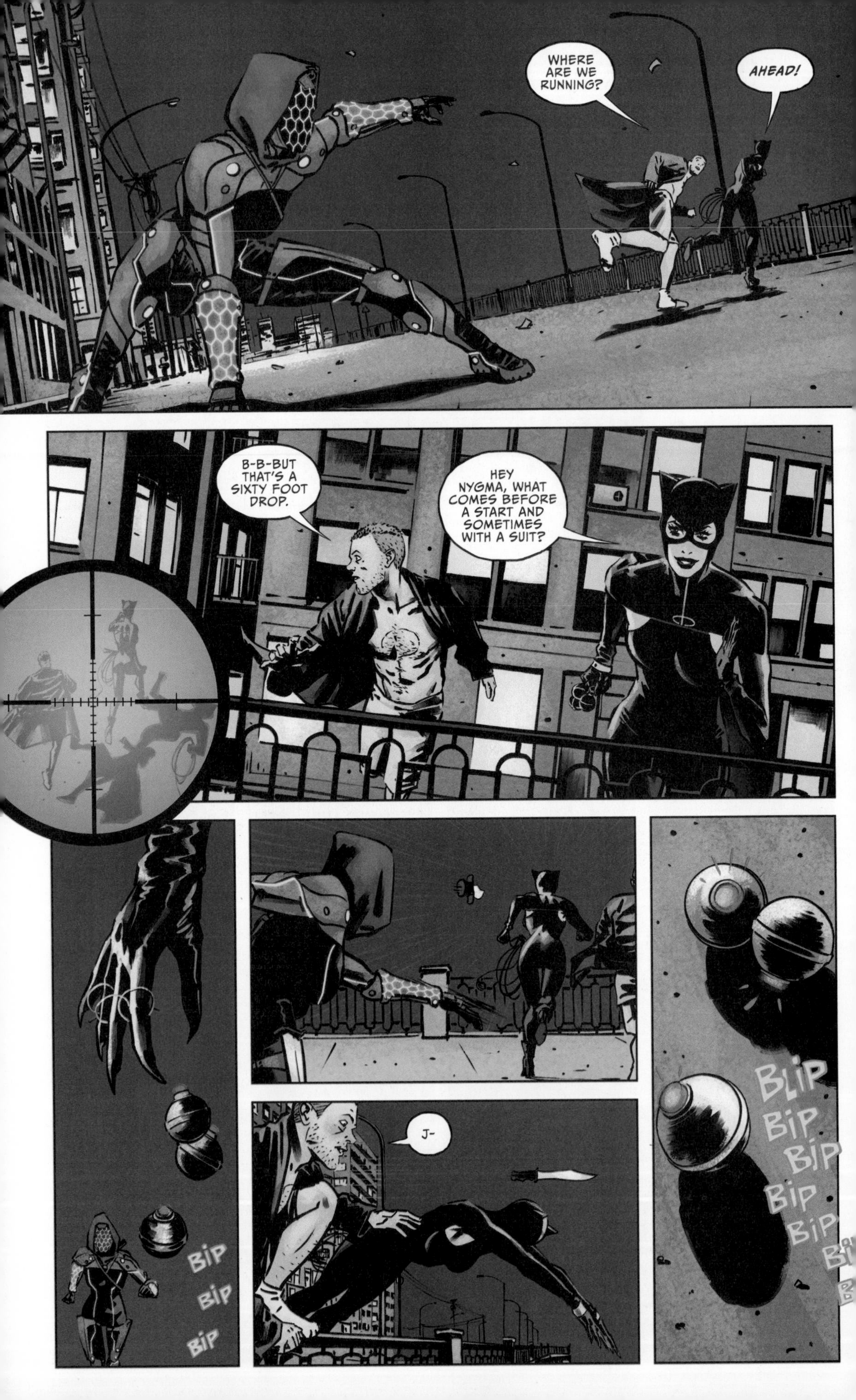
WHERE ARE WE RUNNING?
AHEAD!
B-B-BUT THAT'S A SIXTY FOOT DROP.
HEY NYGMA, WHAT COMES BEFORE A START AND SOMETIMES WITH A SUIT?
BIP BIP BIP
J-
BLIP BIP BIP BIP BIP

KF WOOOM

--JUMP?!

KA-KRAK

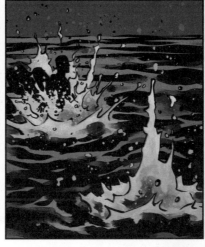

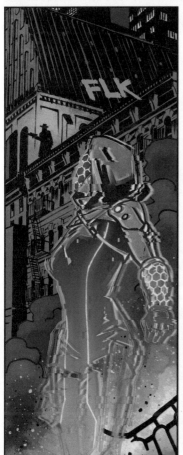

FLK

"I KILL AND I MAKE ALIVE; I WOUND, AND I HEAL; AND THERE IS NONE THAT CAN DELIVER YOU OUT OF MY HAND."

DEUTERONOMY THIRTY TWO, THIRTY NINE.

WHAT CURIOUS THINGS THE CAT DRAGS HOME. PERHAPS YOU AND I SHALL MEET IN BLOOD AND FURY.

BUT NOT TODAY...

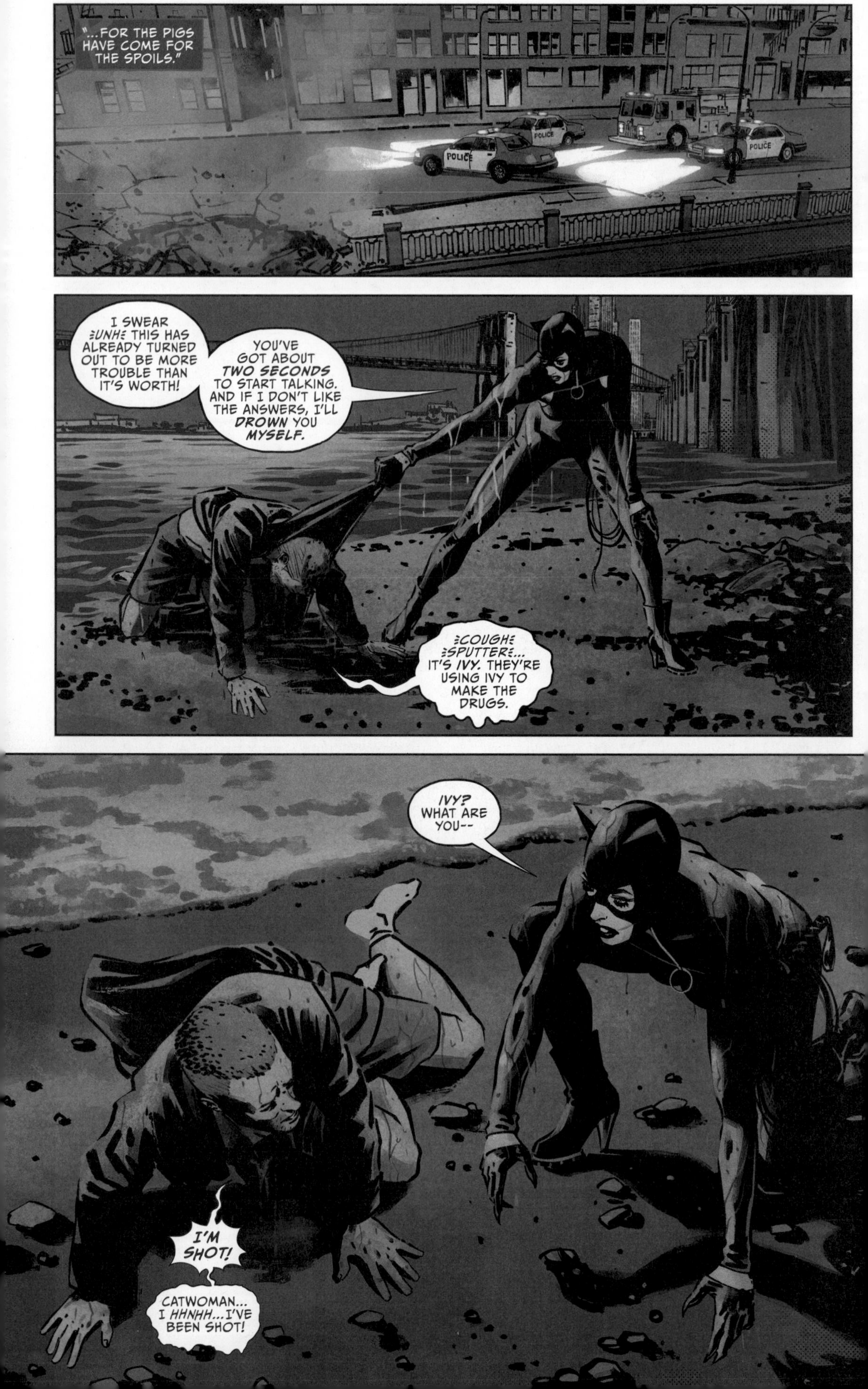
"...FOR THE PIGS HAVE COME FOR THE SPOILS."
POLICE
POLICE
POLICE
I SWEAR ≡UNH≡ THIS HAS ALREADY TURNED OUT TO BE MORE TROUBLE THAN IT'S WORTH!
YOU'VE GOT ABOUT TWO SECONDS TO START TALKING. AND IF I DON'T LIKE THE ANSWERS, I'LL DROWN YOU MYSELF.
≡COUGH≡ ≡SPUTTER≡... IT'S IVY. THEY'RE USING IVY TO MAKE THE DRUGS.
IVY? WHAT ARE YOU--
I'M SHOT!
CATWOMAN... I HHNHH... I'VE BEEN SHOT!

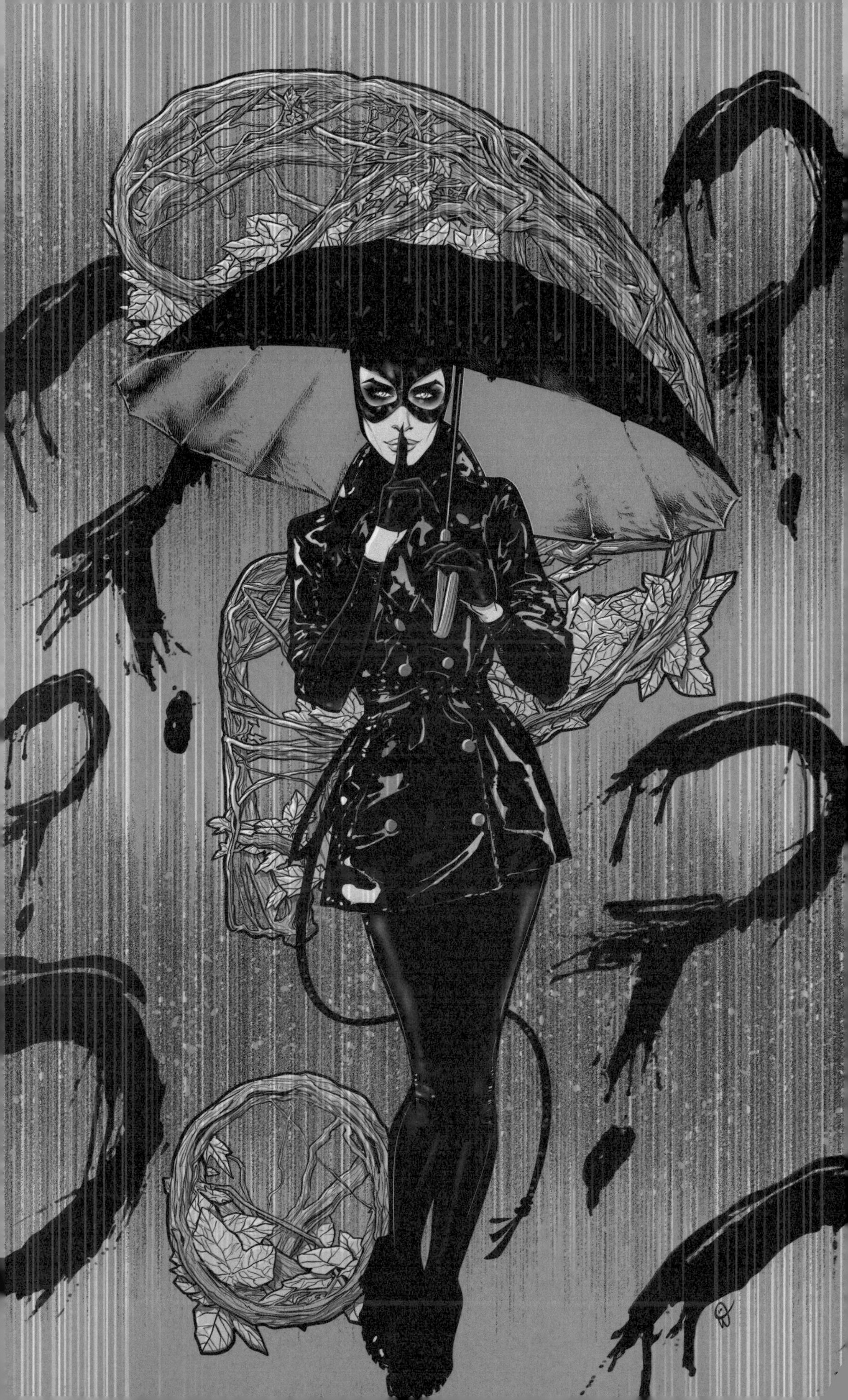

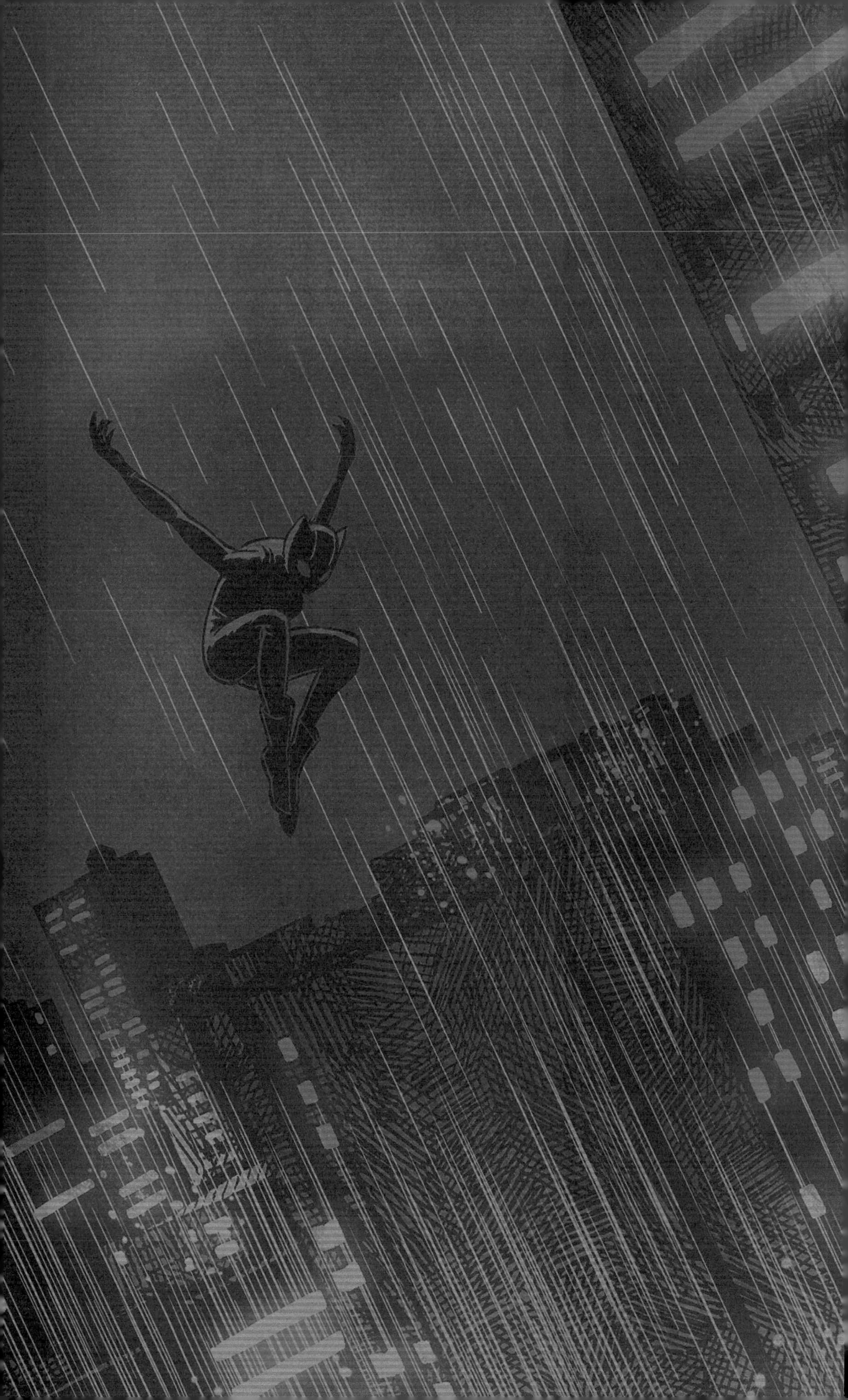

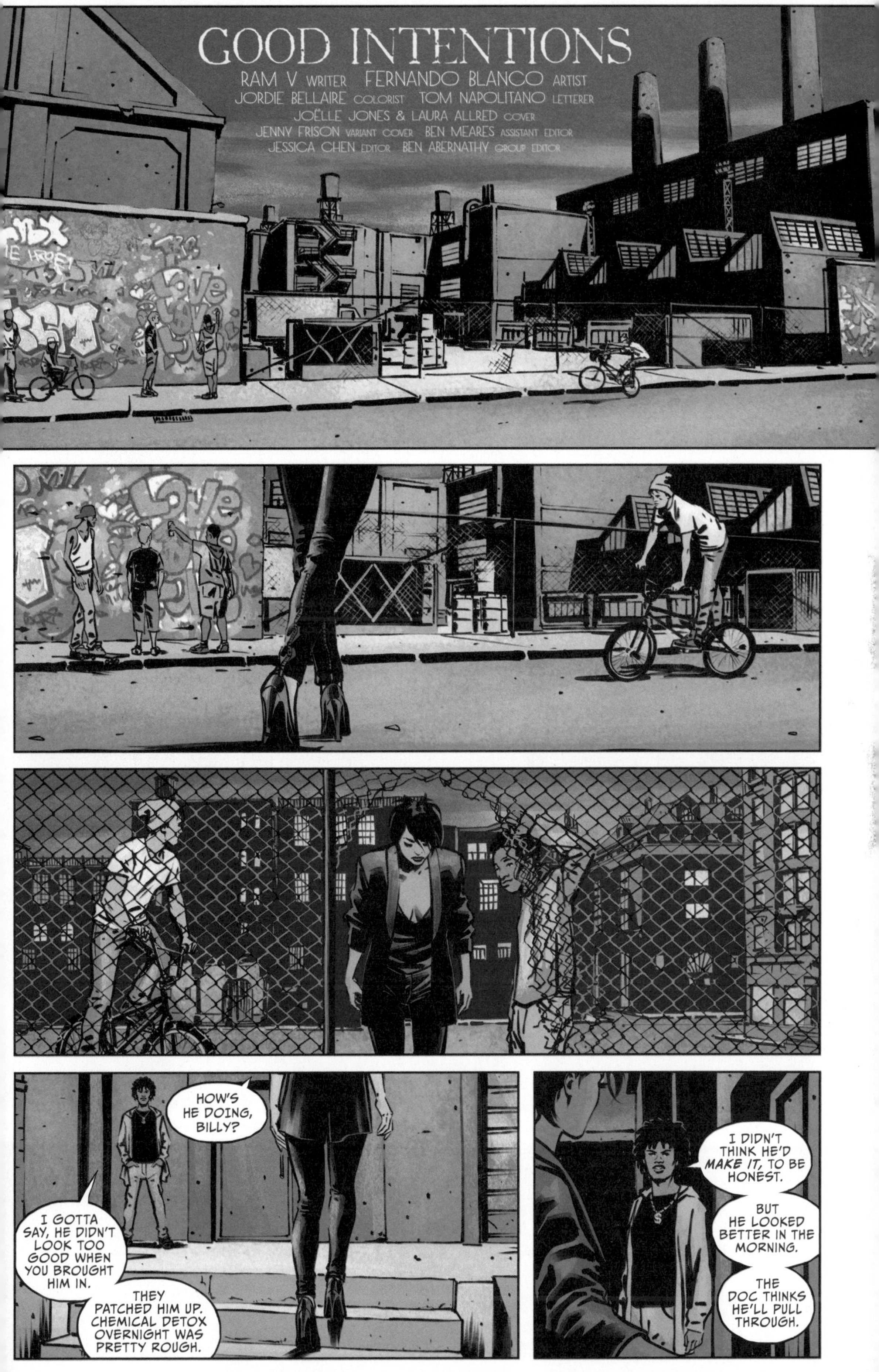
GOOD INTENTIONS
RAM V WRITER FERNANDO BLANCO ARTIST
JORDIE BELLAIRE COLORIST TOM NAPOLITANO LETTERER
JOËLLE JONES & LAURA ALLRED COVER
JENNY FRISON VARIANT COVER BEN MEARES ASSISTANT EDITOR
JESSICA CHEN EDITOR BEN ABERNATHY GROUP EDITOR
HOW'S HE DOING, BILLY?
I GOTTA SAY, HE DIDN'T LOOK TOO GOOD WHEN YOU BROUGHT HIM IN.
THEY PATCHED HIM UP. CHEMICAL DETOX OVERNIGHT WAS PRETTY ROUGH.
I DIDN'T THINK HE'D *MAKE IT*, TO BE HONEST.
BUT HE LOOKED BETTER IN THE MORNING.
THE DOC THINKS HE'LL PULL THROUGH.

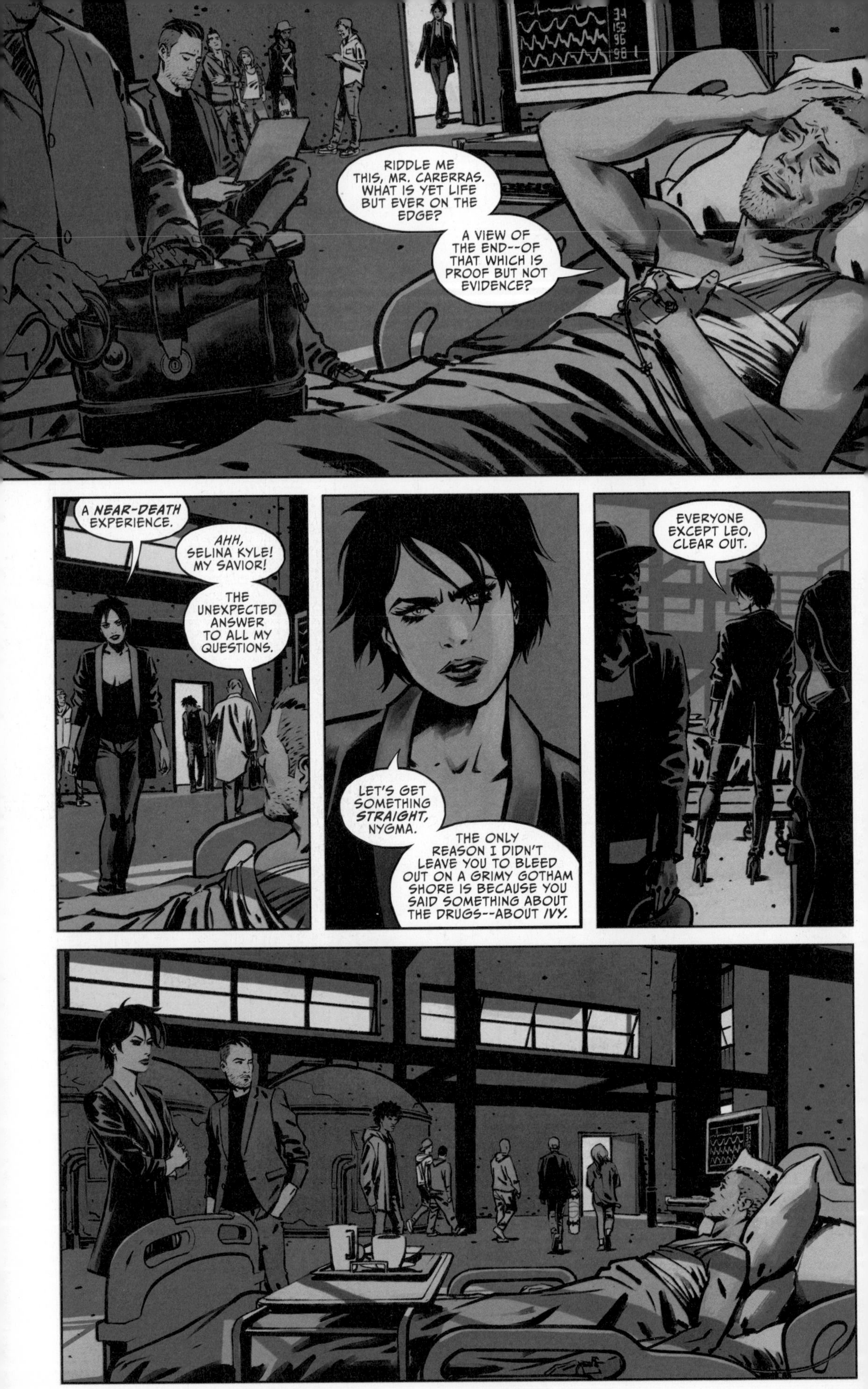
RIDDLE ME THIS, MR. CARERRAS. WHAT IS YET LIFE BUT EVER ON THE EDGE?
A VIEW OF THE END--OF THAT WHICH IS PROOF BUT NOT EVIDENCE?
A NEAR-DEATH EXPERIENCE.
AHH, SELINA KYLE! MY SAVIOR!
THE UNEXPECTED ANSWER TO ALL MY QUESTIONS.
LET'S GET SOMETHING STRAIGHT, NYGMA.
THE ONLY REASON I DIDN'T LEAVE YOU TO BLEED OUT ON A GRIMY GOTHAM SHORE IS BECAUSE YOU SAID SOMETHING ABOUT THE DRUGS--ABOUT IVY.
EVERYONE EXCEPT LEO, CLEAR OUT.

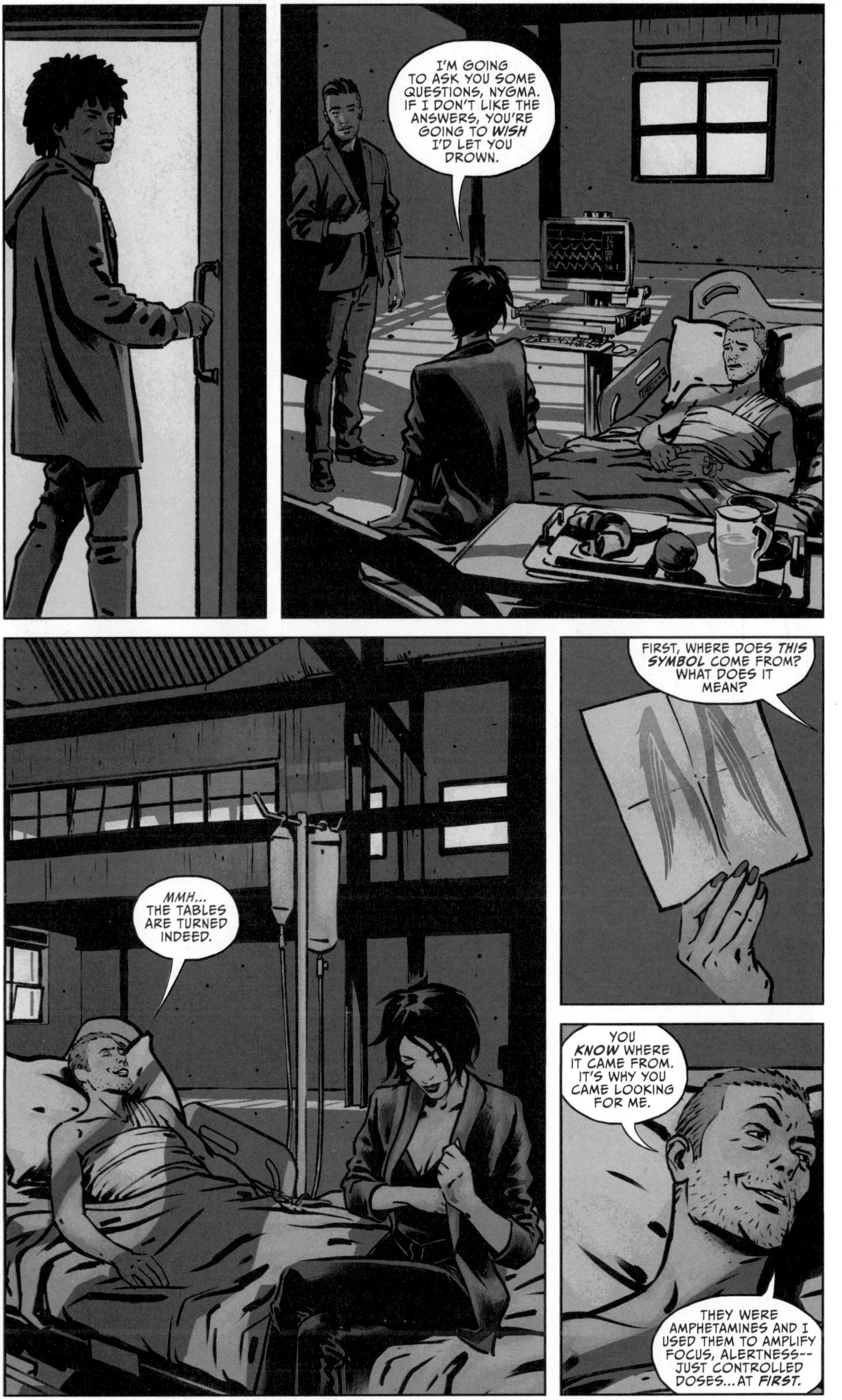
I'M GOING TO ASK YOU SOME QUESTIONS, NYGMA. IF I DON'T LIKE THE ANSWERS, YOU'RE GOING TO WISH I'D LET YOU DROWN.
FIRST, WHERE DOES THIS SYMBOL COME FROM? WHAT DOES IT MEAN?
MMH... THE TABLES ARE TURNED INDEED.
YOU KNOW WHERE IT CAME FROM. IT'S WHY YOU CAME LOOKING FOR ME.
THEY WERE AMPHETAMINES AND I USED THEM TO AMPLIFY FOCUS, ALERTNESS-- JUST CONTROLLED DOSES...AT FIRST.

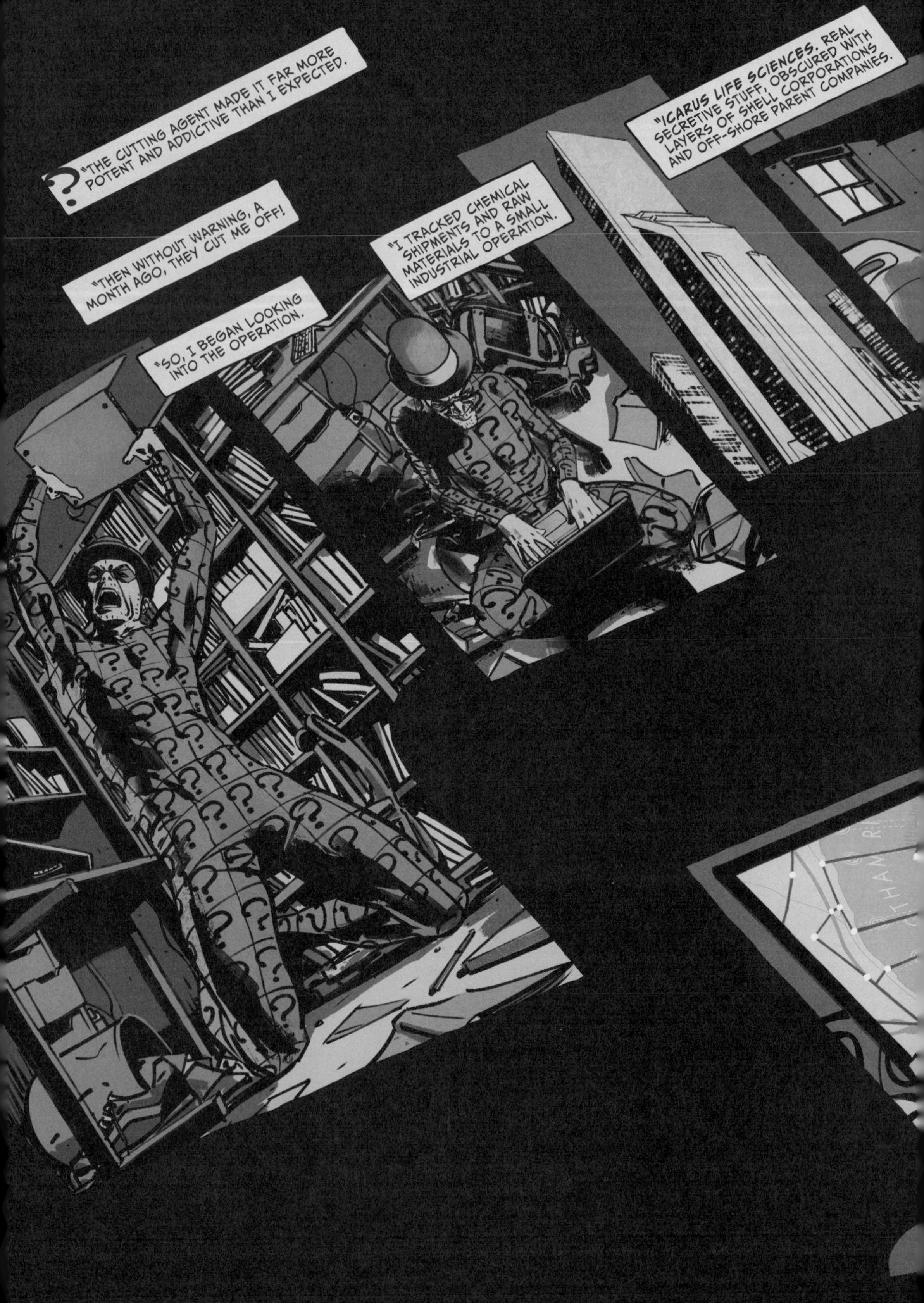
"THE CUTTING AGENT MADE IT FAR MORE POTENT AND ADDICTIVE THAN I EXPECTED.
"THEN WITHOUT WARNING, A MONTH AGO, THEY CUT ME OFF!
"SO, I BEGAN LOOKING INTO THE OPERATION.
"I TRACKED CHEMICAL SHIPMENTS AND RAW MATERIALS TO A SMALL INDUSTRIAL OPERATION.
"ICARUS LIFE SCIENCES. REAL SECRETIVE STUFF, OBSCURED WITH LAYERS OF SHELL CORPORATIONS AND OFF-SHORE PARENT COMPANIES.

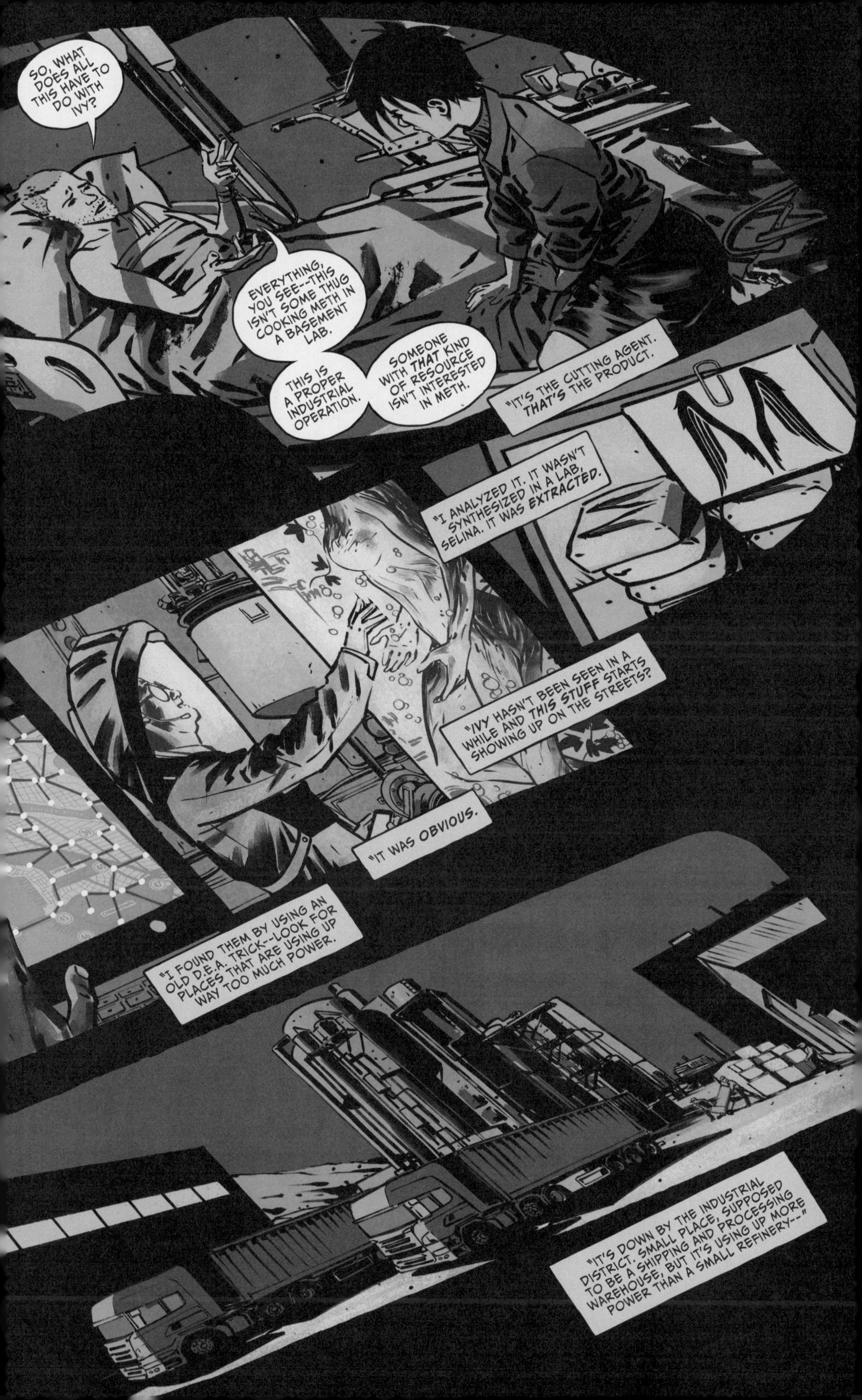

SO, WHAT DOES ALL THIS HAVE TO DO WITH IVY?
EVERYTHING, YOU SEE--THIS ISN'T SOME THUG COOKING METH IN A BASEMENT LAB.
THIS IS A PROPER INDUSTRIAL OPERATION.
SOMEONE WITH THAT KIND OF RESOURCE ISN'T INTERESTED IN METH.
"IT'S THE CUTTING AGENT. THAT'S THE PRODUCT.
"I ANALYZED IT. IT WASN'T SYNTHESIZED IN A LAB, SELINA. IT WAS EXTRACTED.
"IVY HASN'T BEEN SEEN IN A WHILE AND THIS STUFF STARTS SHOWING UP ON THE STREETS?
"IT WAS OBVIOUS.
"I FOUND THEM BY USING AN OLD D.E.A. TRICK--LOOK FOR PLACES THAT ARE USING UP WAY TOO MUCH POWER.
"IT'S DOWN BY THE INDUSTRIAL DISTRICT. SMALL PLACE, SUPPOSED TO BE A SHIPPING AND PROCESSING WAREHOUSE, BUT IT'S USING UP MORE POWER THAN A SMALL REFINERY--"

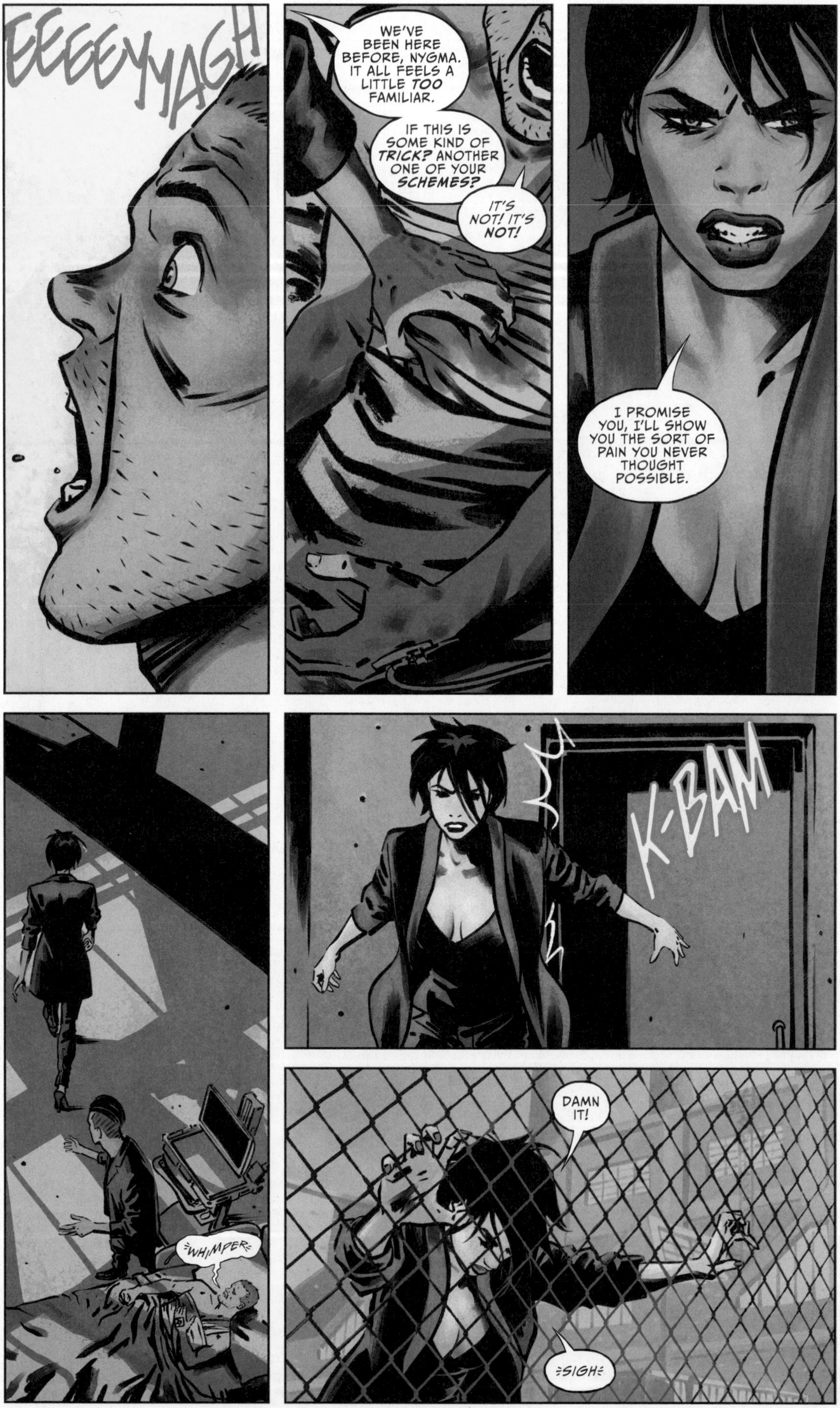
EEEEEYYAGH
WE'VE BEEN HERE BEFORE, NYGMA. IT ALL FEELS A LITTLE TOO FAMILIAR.
IF THIS IS SOME KIND OF TRICK? ANOTHER ONE OF YOUR SCHEMES?
IT'S NOT! IT'S NOT!
I PROMISE YOU, I'LL SHOW YOU THE SORT OF PAIN YOU NEVER THOUGHT POSSIBLE.
WHIMPER
K-BAM
DAMN IT!
SIGH

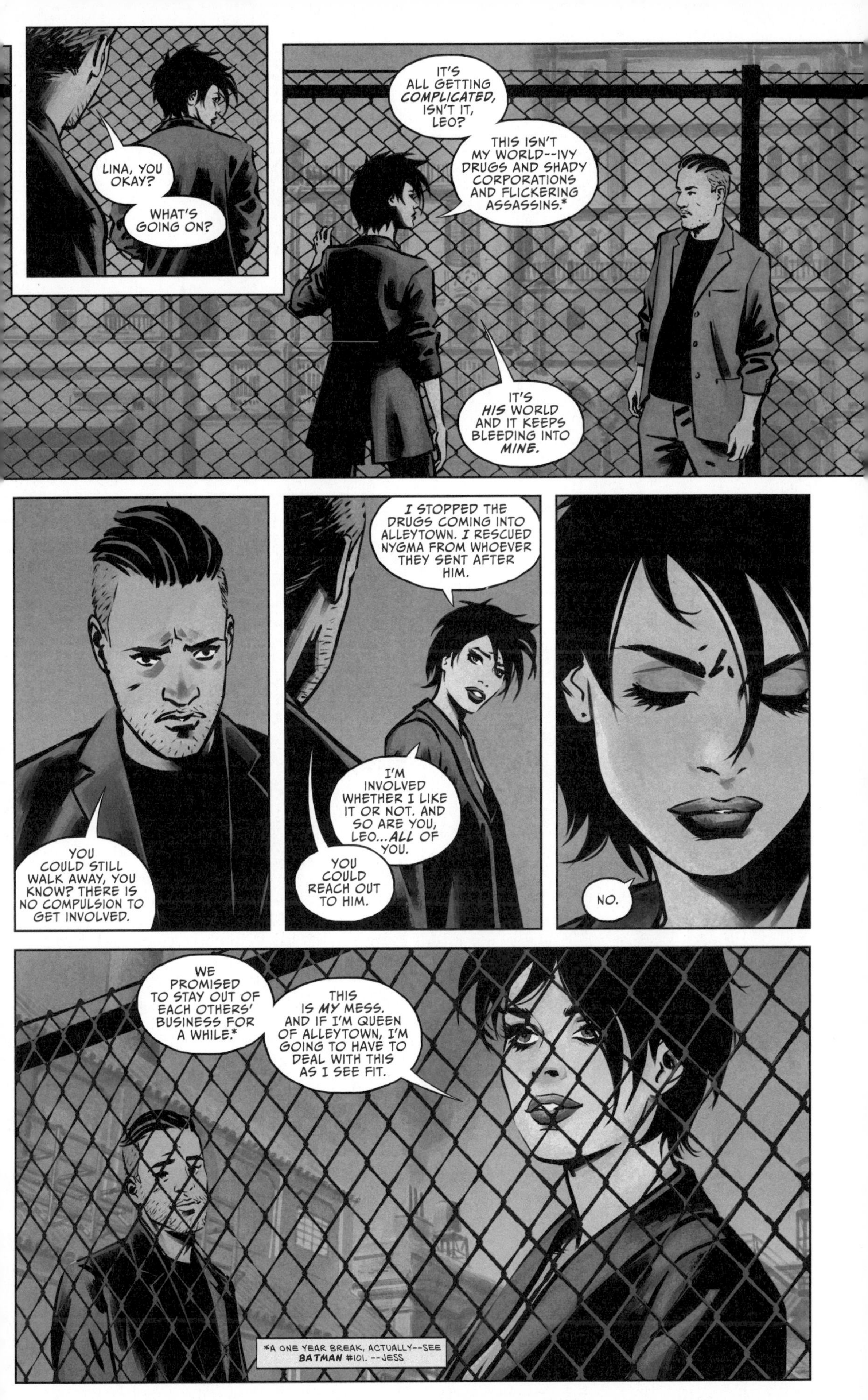
LINA, YOU OKAY?
WHAT'S GOING ON?
IT'S ALL GETTING *COMPLICATED,* ISN'T IT, LEO?
THIS ISN'T MY WORLD--IVY DRUGS AND SHADY CORPORATIONS AND FLICKERING ASSASSINS.*
IT'S *HIS* WORLD AND IT KEEPS BLEEDING INTO *MINE.*
YOU COULD STILL WALK AWAY, YOU KNOW? THERE IS NO COMPULSION TO GET INVOLVED.
I STOPPED THE DRUGS COMING INTO ALLEYTOWN. *I* RESCUED NYGMA FROM WHOEVER THEY SENT AFTER HIM.
I'M INVOLVED WHETHER I LIKE IT OR NOT. AND SO ARE YOU, LEO...*ALL* OF YOU.
YOU COULD REACH OUT TO HIM.
NO.
WE PROMISED TO STAY OUT OF EACH OTHERS' BUSINESS FOR A WHILE.*
THIS IS *MY* MESS. AND IF I'M QUEEN OF ALLEYTOWN, I'M GOING TO HAVE TO DEAL WITH THIS AS I SEE FIT.
*A ONE YEAR BREAK, ACTUALLY--SEE **BATMAN** #101. --JESS

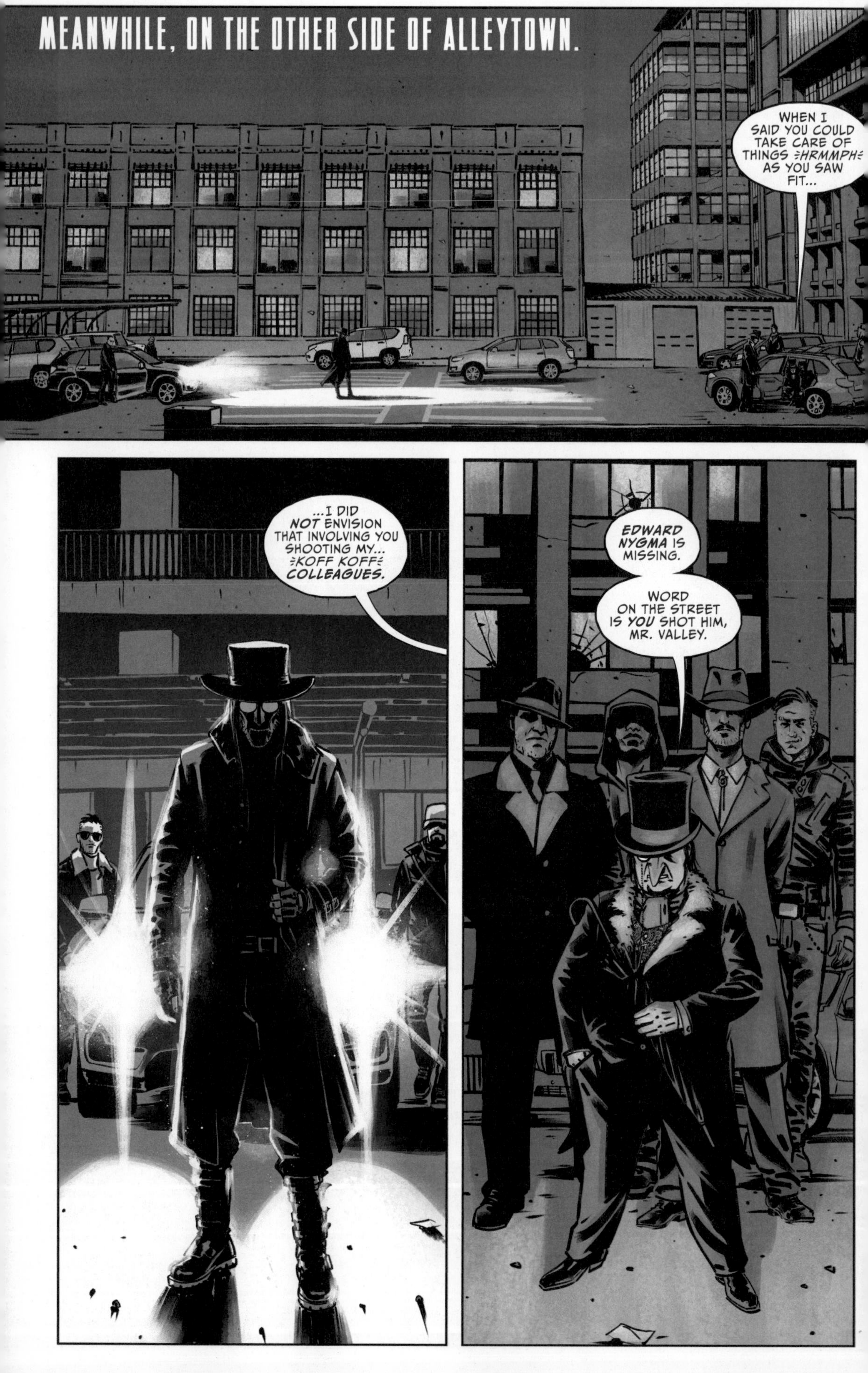
MEANWHILE, ON THE OTHER SIDE OF ALLEYTOWN.
WHEN I SAID YOU COULD TAKE CARE OF THINGS =HRMMPH= AS YOU SAW FIT...
...I DID NOT ENVISION THAT INVOLVING YOU SHOOTING MY... =KOFF KOFF= COLLEAGUES.
EDWARD NYGMA IS MISSING.
WORD ON THE STREET IS YOU SHOT HIM, MR. VALLEY.

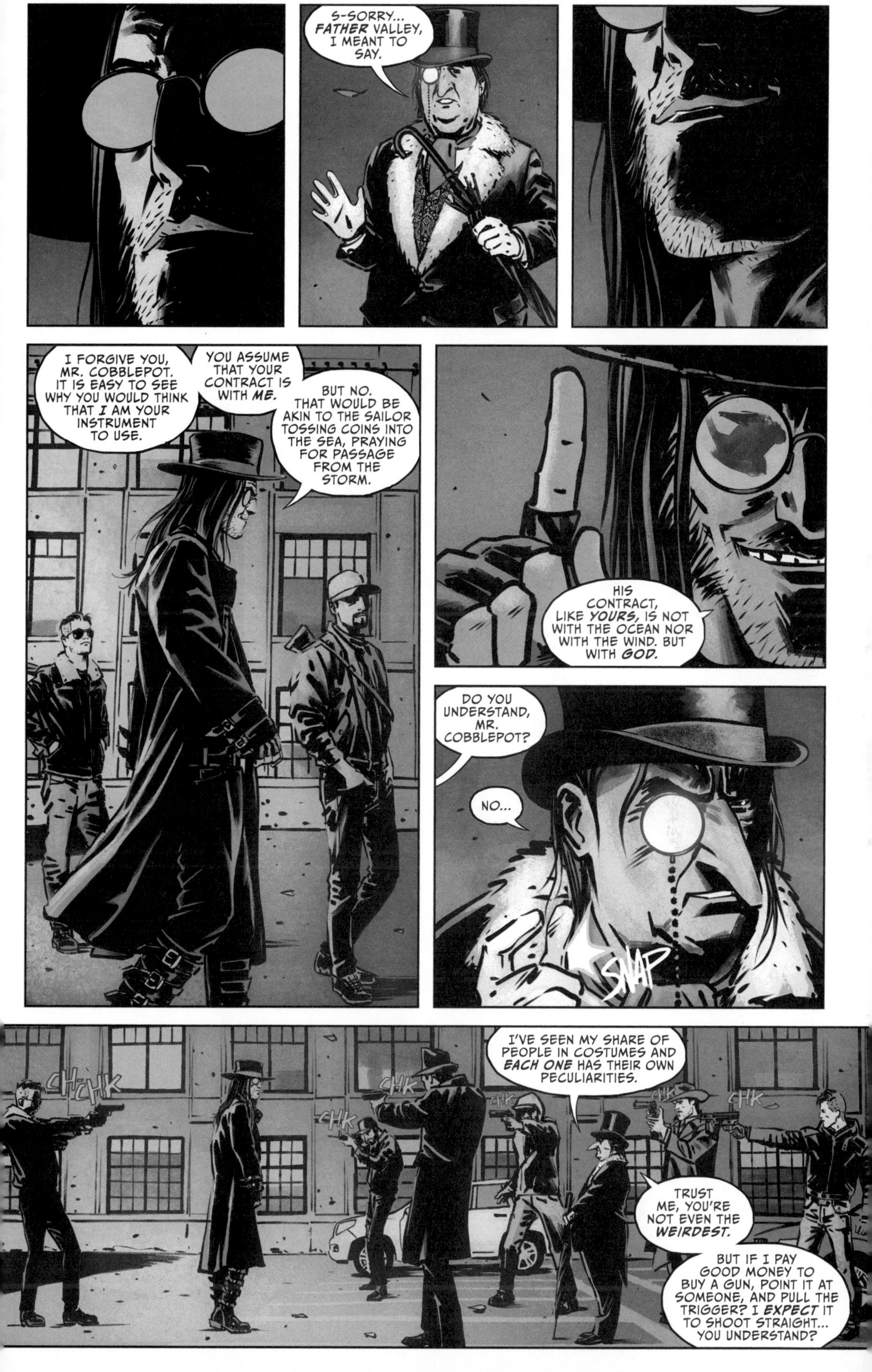
S-SORRY... FATHER VALLEY, I MEANT TO SAY.
I FORGIVE YOU, MR. COBBLEPOT. IT IS EASY TO SEE WHY YOU WOULD THINK THAT I AM YOUR INSTRUMENT TO USE.
YOU ASSUME THAT YOUR CONTRACT IS WITH ME.
BUT NO. THAT WOULD BE AKIN TO THE SAILOR TOSSING COINS INTO THE SEA, PRAYING FOR PASSAGE FROM THE STORM.
HIS CONTRACT, LIKE YOURS, IS NOT WITH THE OCEAN NOR WITH THE WIND. BUT WITH GOD.
DO YOU UNDERSTAND, MR. COBBLEPOT?
NO...
SNAP
CHCHK
CHK
CHK
CHK
CHK
CHK
I'VE SEEN MY SHARE OF PEOPLE IN COSTUMES AND EACH ONE HAS THEIR OWN PECULIARITIES.
TRUST ME, YOU'RE NOT EVEN THE WEIRDEST.
BUT IF I PAY GOOD MONEY TO BUY A GUN, POINT IT AT SOMEONE, AND PULL THE TRIGGER? I EXPECT IT TO SHOOT STRAIGHT... YOU UNDERSTAND?

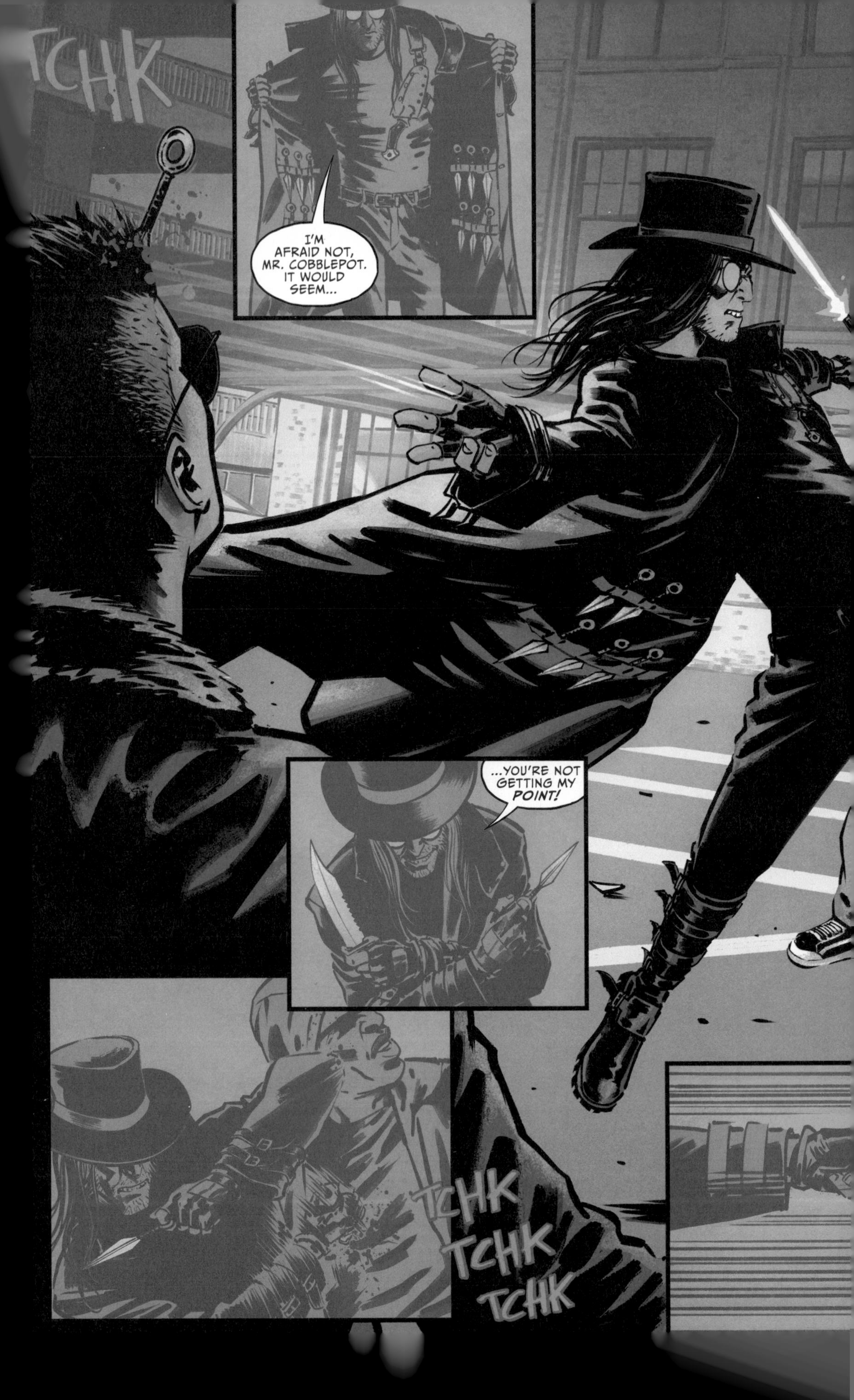
TCHK
I'M AFRAID NOT, MR. COBBLEPOT. IT WOULD SEEM...
...YOU'RE NOT GETTING MY *POINT!*
TCHK
TCHK
TCHK

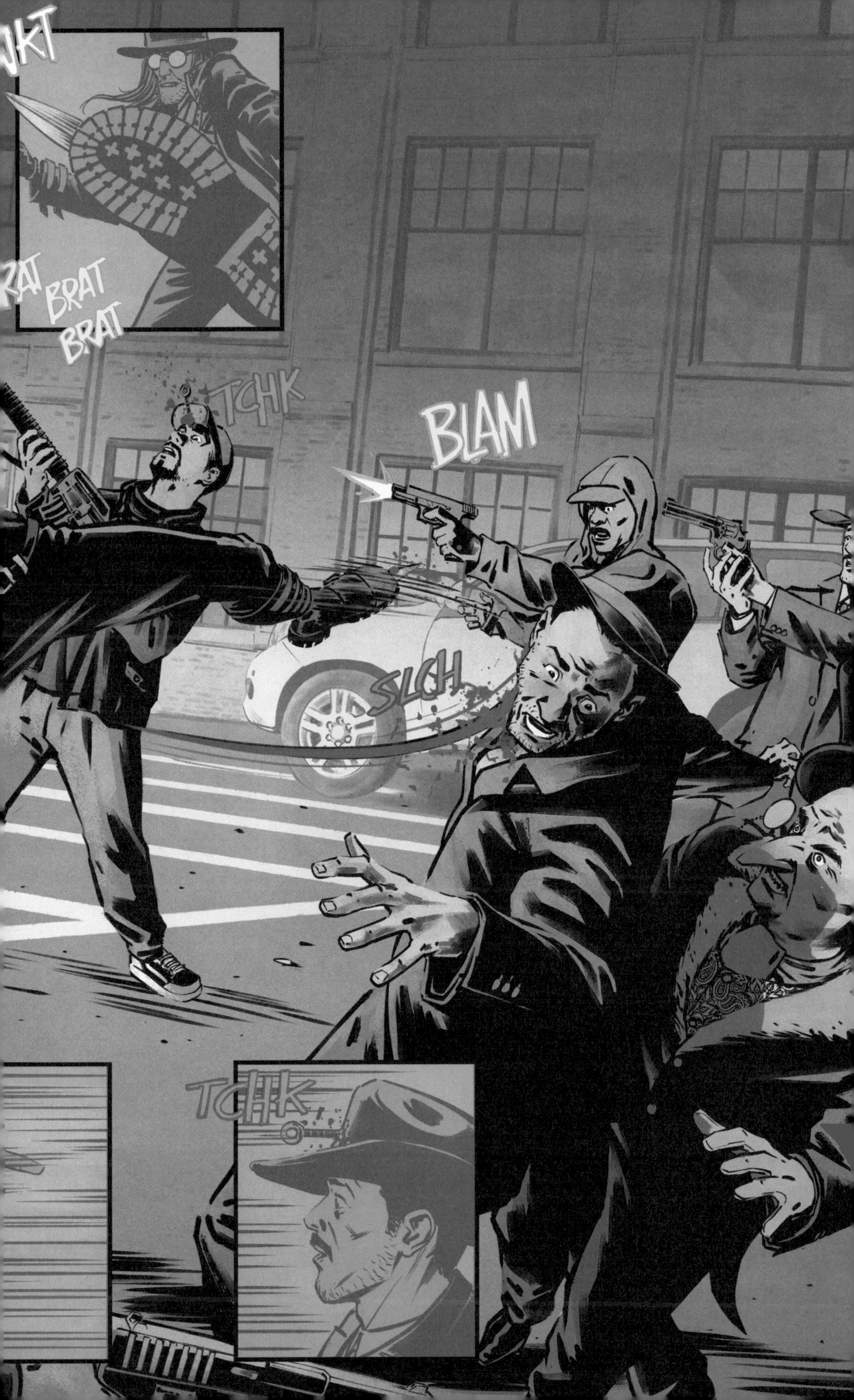

NKT
BRAT
BRAT
BRAT
TCHK
BLAM
SLCH
TCHK

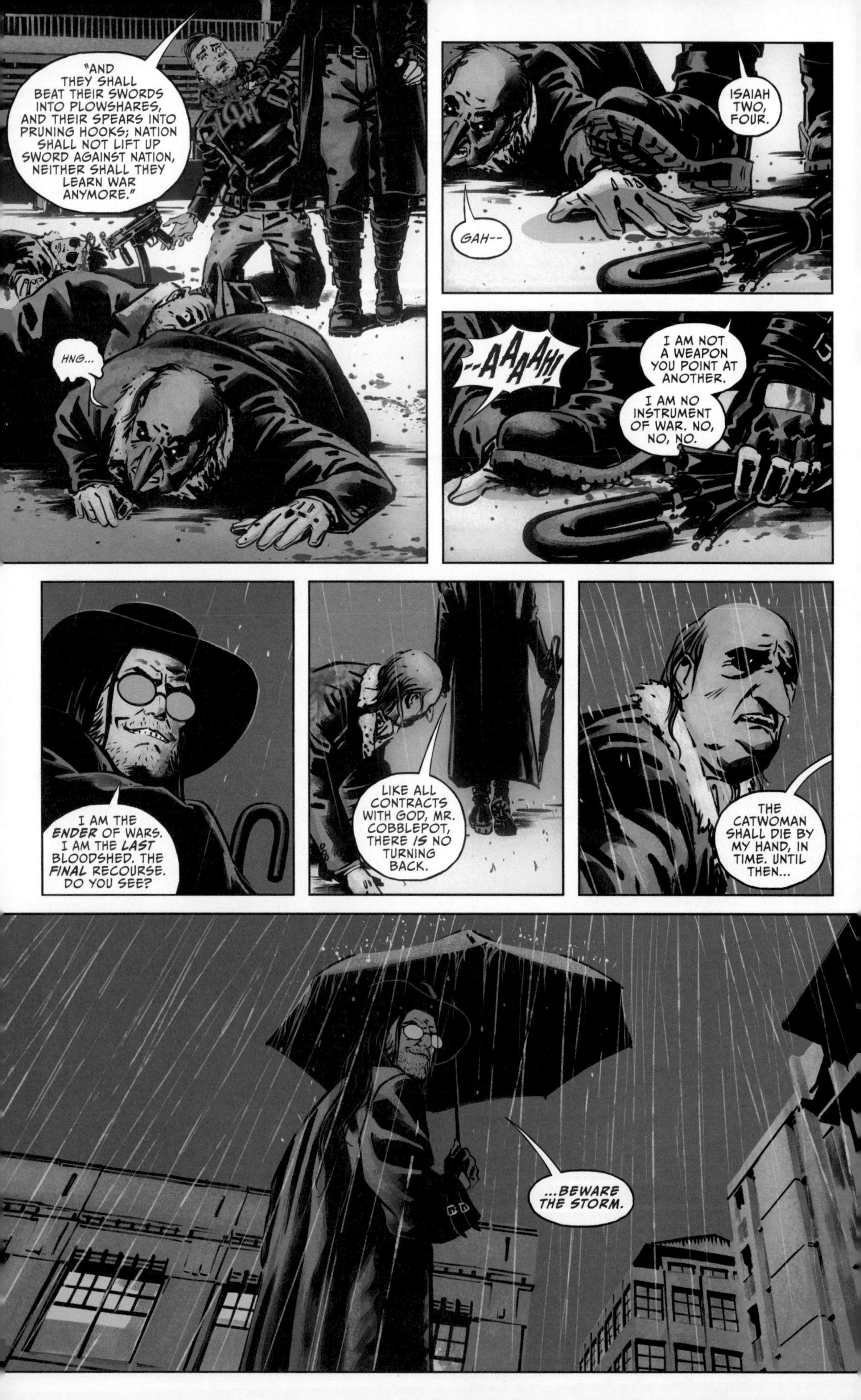
"AND THEY SHALL BEAT THEIR SWORDS INTO PLOWSHARES, AND THEIR SPEARS INTO PRUNING HOOKS; NATION SHALL NOT LIFT UP SWORD AGAINST NATION, NEITHER SHALL THEY LEARN WAR ANYMORE."
HNG...
ISAIAH TWO, FOUR.
GAH--
--AAAAH!
I AM NOT A WEAPON YOU POINT AT ANOTHER.
I AM NO INSTRUMENT OF WAR. NO, NO, NO.
I AM THE ENDER OF WARS. I AM THE LAST BLOODSHED. THE FINAL RECOURSE. DO YOU SEE?
LIKE ALL CONTRACTS WITH GOD, MR. COBBLEPOT, THERE IS NO TURNING BACK.
THE CATWOMAN SHALL DIE BY MY HAND, IN TIME. UNTIL THEN...
...BEWARE THE STORM.

FOLLOWING THE TRAIL FROM THE RIDDLER'S CONFESSIONS IS EASY.

PRRRRR

I ASKED LEO TO DIG INTO EVERYTHING ABOUT THE COMPANY.

START UNCOVERING THE LAYERS OF CORPORATE SUBTERFUGE.

MY EYES ON THE STREET TELL ME THEY'RE CLEARING OUT THE LOCATION.

TWO TRUCKLOADS HEADED TO THE INCINERATOR AT THE EDGE OF THE NARROWS.

IVY WOULD NEVER LET HERSELF BE USED TO CORPORATE ENDS.

IF THEY'RE GETTING RID OF EVIDENCE, MY BEST BET IS THAT IVY IS ON ONE OF THOSE TRUCKS.

I CAN'T STOP THINKING ABOUT WHAT LEO SAID...I SHOULDN'T GET INVOLVED.

CATS STAY IN THE SHADOWS, SELINA.

THEN AGAIN, SO DO BATS. WE SAVED IVY FROM HERSELF NOT SO LONG AGO.

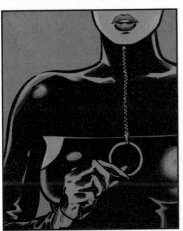

WE WERE HAPPY THEN.

MAYBE THAT'S WHAT I'M REALLY HOLDING ON TO.

PLIC PLIC PLIC

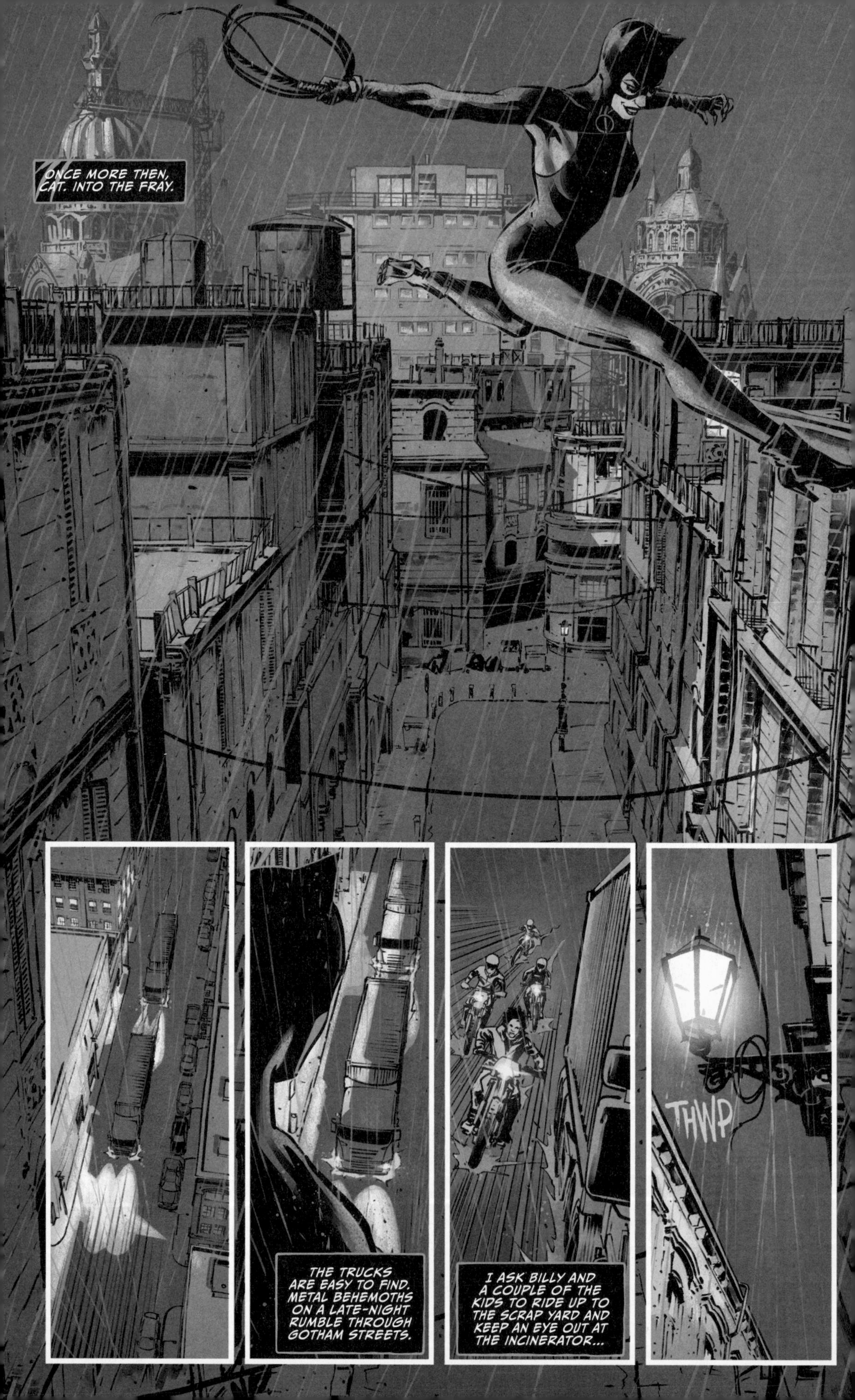
ONCE MORE THEN, CAT. INTO THE FRAY.
THE TRUCKS ARE EASY TO FIND. METAL BEHEMOTHS ON A LATE-NIGHT RUMBLE THROUGH GOTHAM STREETS.
I ASK BILLY AND A COUPLE OF THE KIDS TO RIDE UP TO THE SCRAP YARD AND KEEP AN EYE OUT AT THE INCINERATOR...
THWP

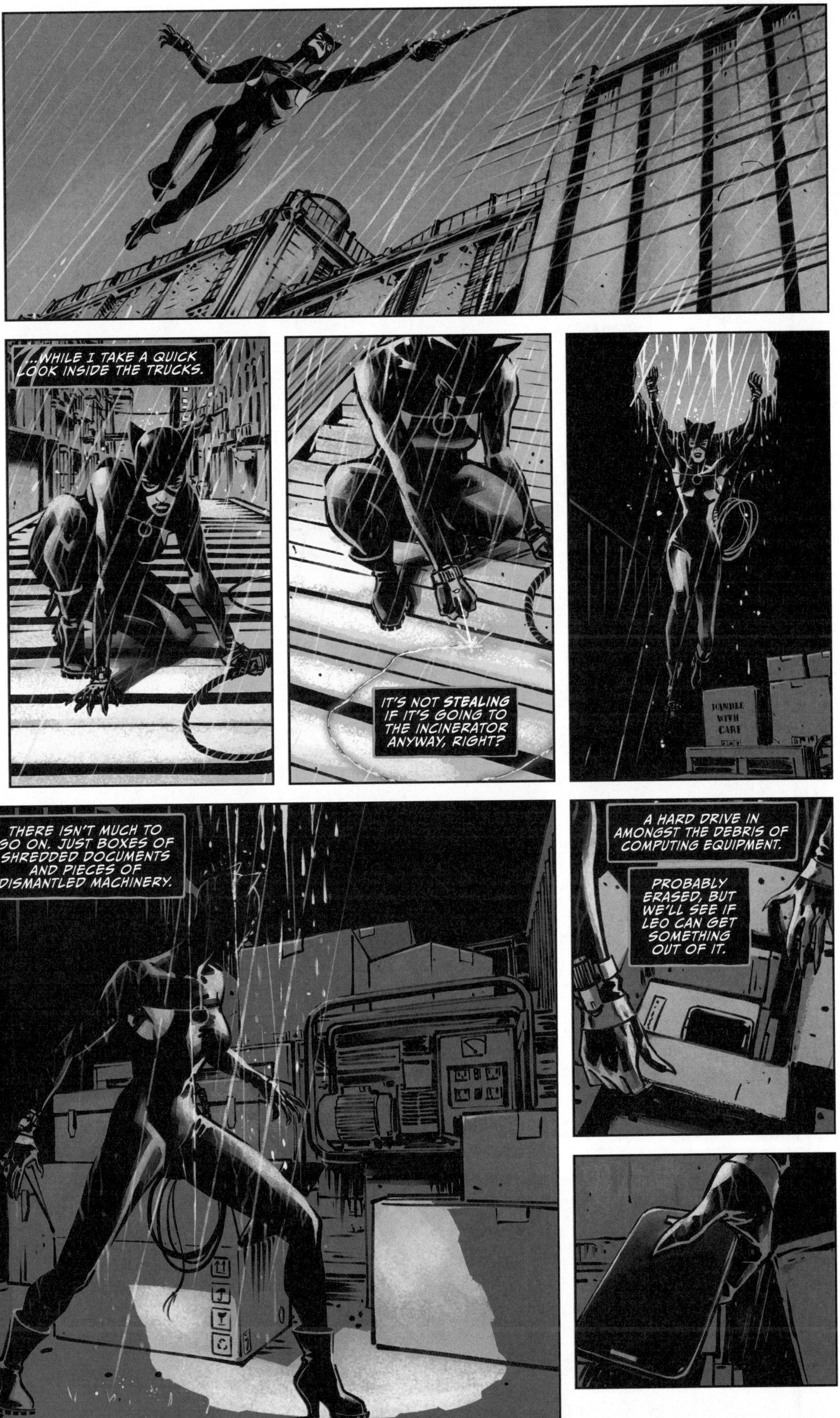
...WHILE I TAKE A QUICK LOOK INSIDE THE TRUCKS.
IT'S NOT STEALING IF IT'S GOING TO THE INCINERATOR ANYWAY, RIGHT?
THERE ISN'T MUCH TO GO ON. JUST BOXES OF SHREDDED DOCUMENTS AND PIECES OF DISMANTLED MACHINERY.
A HARD DRIVE IN AMONGST THE DEBRIS OF COMPUTING EQUIPMENT.
PROBABLY ERASED, BUT WE'LL SEE IF LEO CAN GET SOMETHING OUT OF IT.

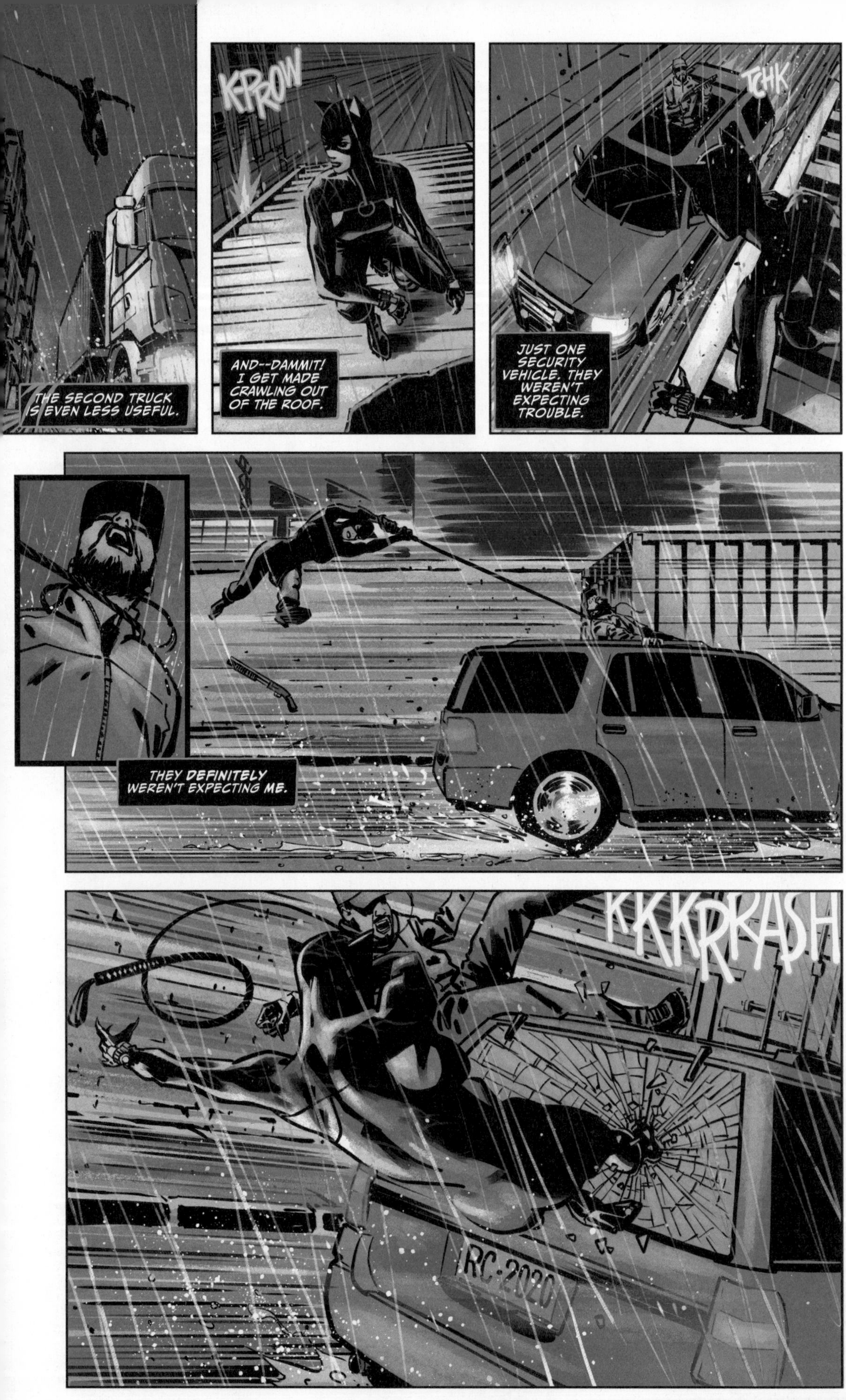
THE SECOND TRUCK IS EVEN LESS USEFUL.
K-PROW
AND--DAMMIT! I GET MADE CRAWLING OUT OF THE ROOF.
TCHK
JUST ONE SECURITY VEHICLE. THEY WEREN'T EXPECTING TROUBLE.
THEY DEFINITELY WEREN'T EXPECTING ME.
KKKRRASH
RC-2020

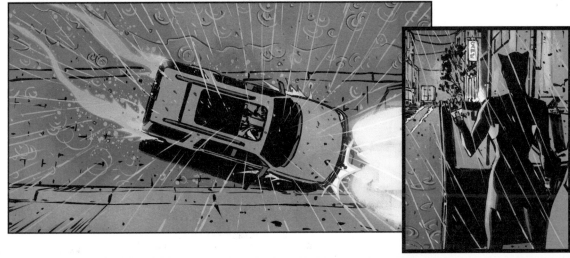

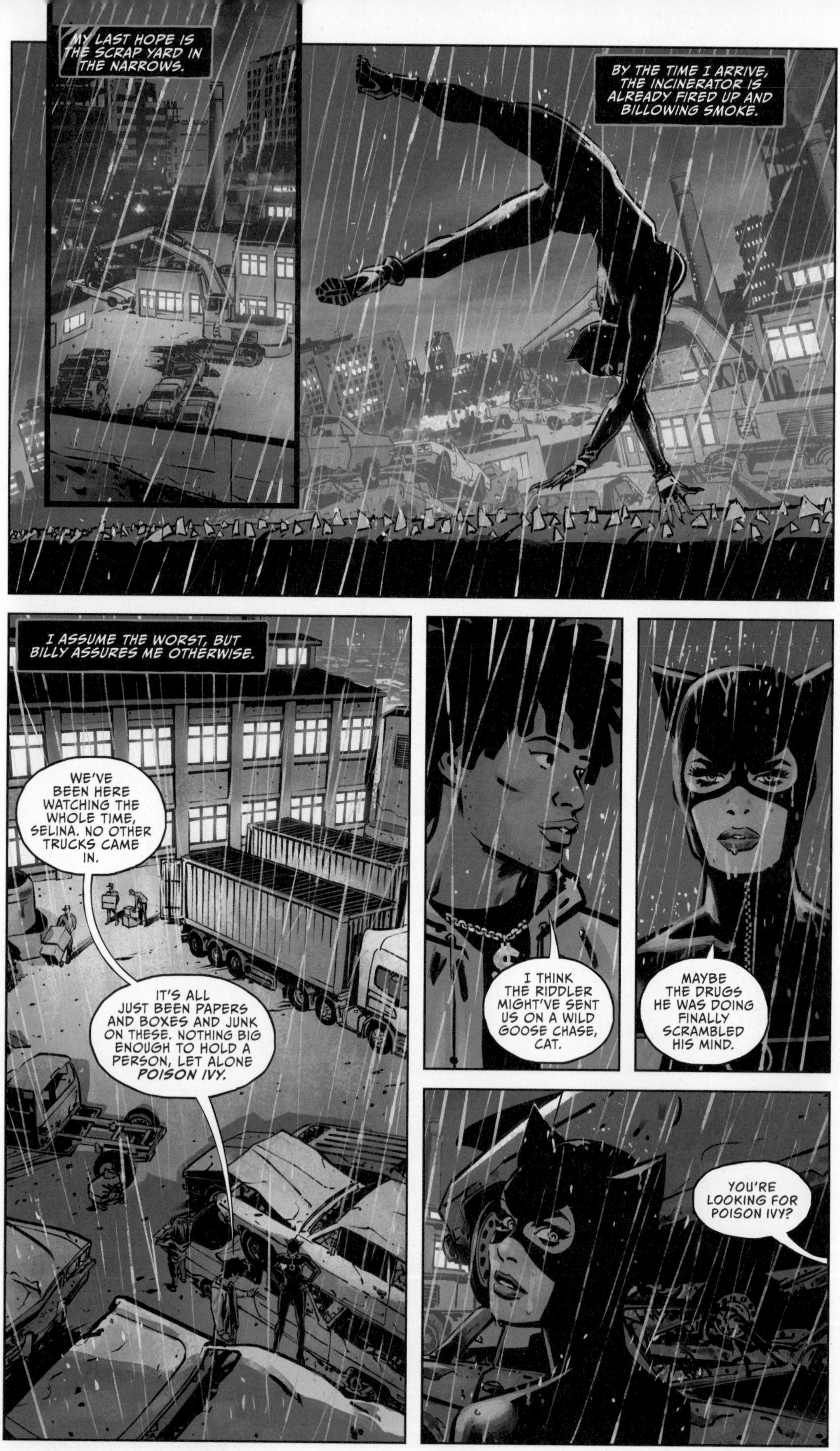
MY LAST HOPE IS THE SCRAP YARD IN THE NARROWS.
BY THE TIME I ARRIVE, THE INCINERATOR IS ALREADY FIRED UP AND BILLOWING SMOKE.
I ASSUME THE WORST, BUT BILLY ASSURES ME OTHERWISE.
WE'VE BEEN HERE WATCHING THE WHOLE TIME, SELINA. NO OTHER TRUCKS CAME IN.
IT'S ALL JUST BEEN PAPERS AND BOXES AND JUNK ON THESE. NOTHING BIG ENOUGH TO HOLD A PERSON, LET ALONE *POISON IVY.*
I THINK THE RIDDLER MIGHT'VE SENT US ON A WILD GOOSE CHASE, CAT.
MAYBE THE DRUGS HE WAS DOING FINALLY SCRAMBLED HIS MIND.
YOU'RE LOOKING FOR POISON IVY?

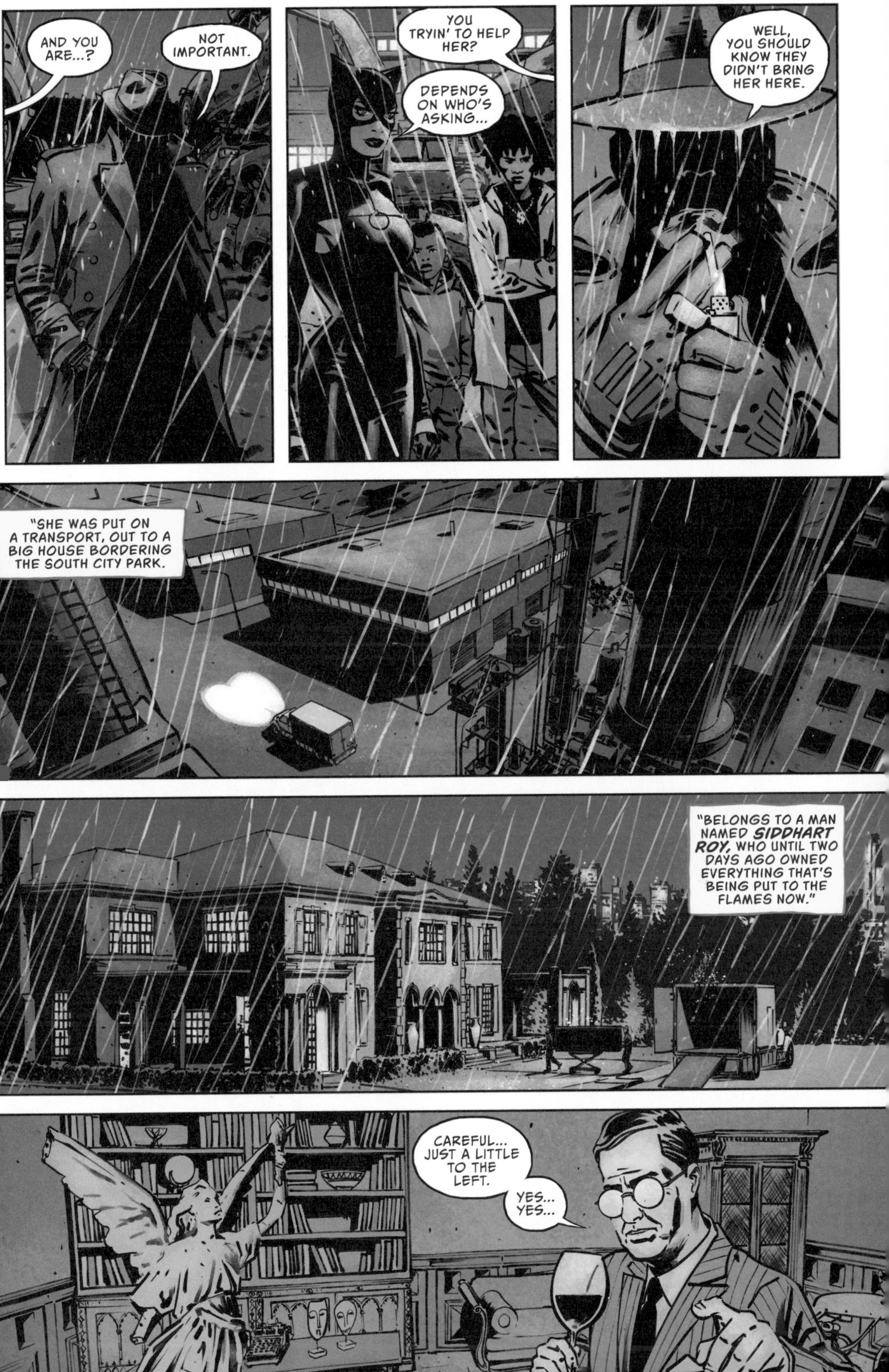
AND YOU ARE...?
NOT IMPORTANT.
YOU TRYIN' TO HELP HER?
DEPENDS ON WHO'S ASKING...
WELL, YOU SHOULD KNOW THEY DIDN'T BRING HER HERE.
"SHE WAS PUT ON A TRANSPORT, OUT TO A BIG HOUSE BORDERING THE SOUTH CITY PARK.
"BELONGS TO A MAN NAMED SIDDHART ROY, WHO UNTIL TWO DAYS AGO OWNED EVERYTHING THAT'S BEING PUT TO THE FLAMES NOW."
CAREFUL... JUST A LITTLE TO THE LEFT.
YES... YES...

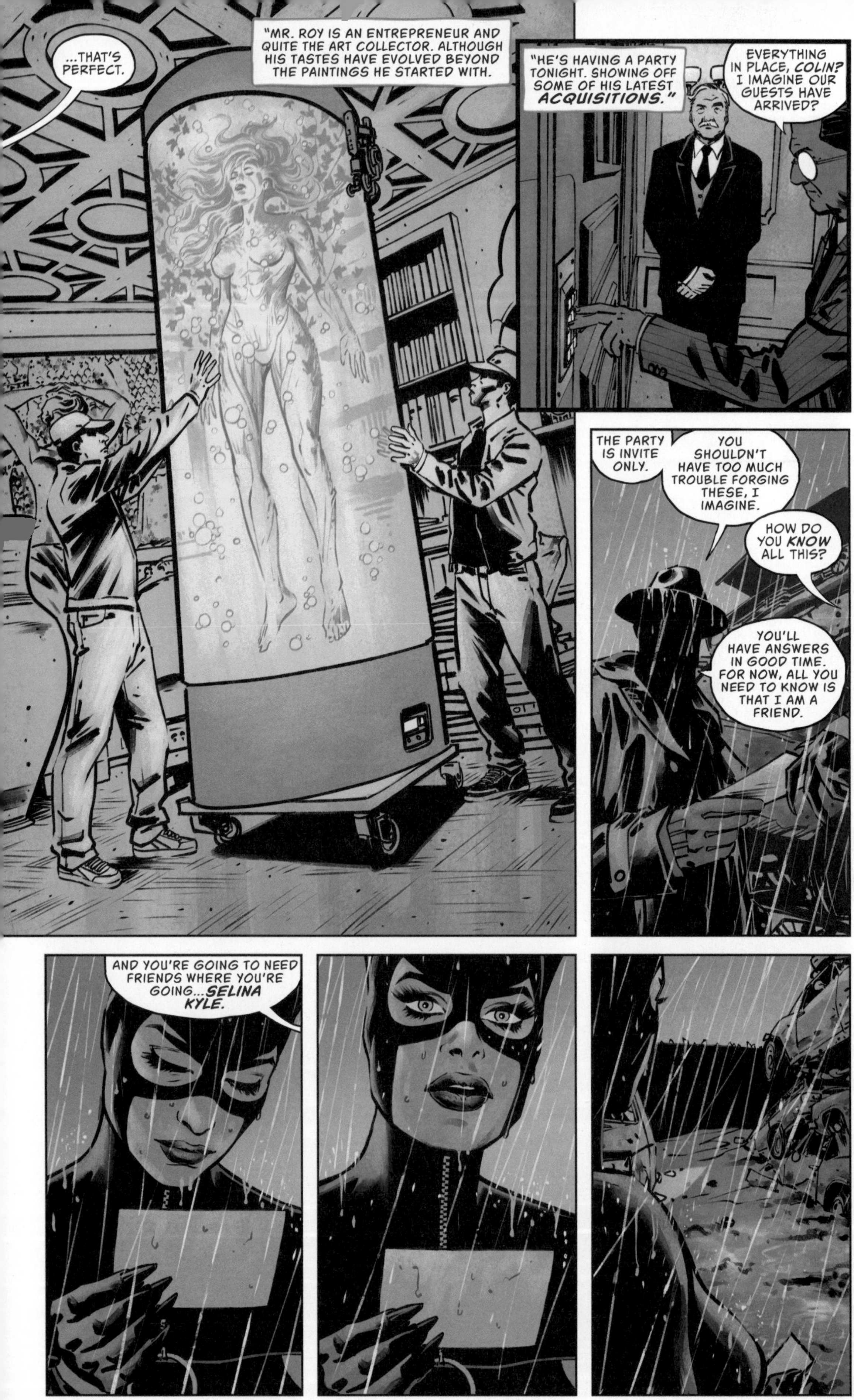
...THAT'S PERFECT.
"MR. ROY IS AN ENTREPRENEUR AND QUITE THE ART COLLECTOR. ALTHOUGH HIS TASTES HAVE EVOLVED BEYOND THE PAINTINGS HE STARTED WITH.
"HE'S HAVING A PARTY TONIGHT. SHOWING OFF SOME OF HIS LATEST ACQUISITIONS."
EVERYTHING IN PLACE, COLIN? I IMAGINE OUR GUESTS HAVE ARRIVED?
THE PARTY IS INVITE ONLY.
YOU SHOULDN'T HAVE TOO MUCH TROUBLE FORGING THESE, I IMAGINE.
HOW DO YOU KNOW ALL THIS?
YOU'LL HAVE ANSWERS IN GOOD TIME. FOR NOW, ALL YOU NEED TO KNOW IS THAT I AM A FRIEND.
AND YOU'RE GOING TO NEED FRIENDS WHERE YOU'RE GOING...SELINA KYLE.

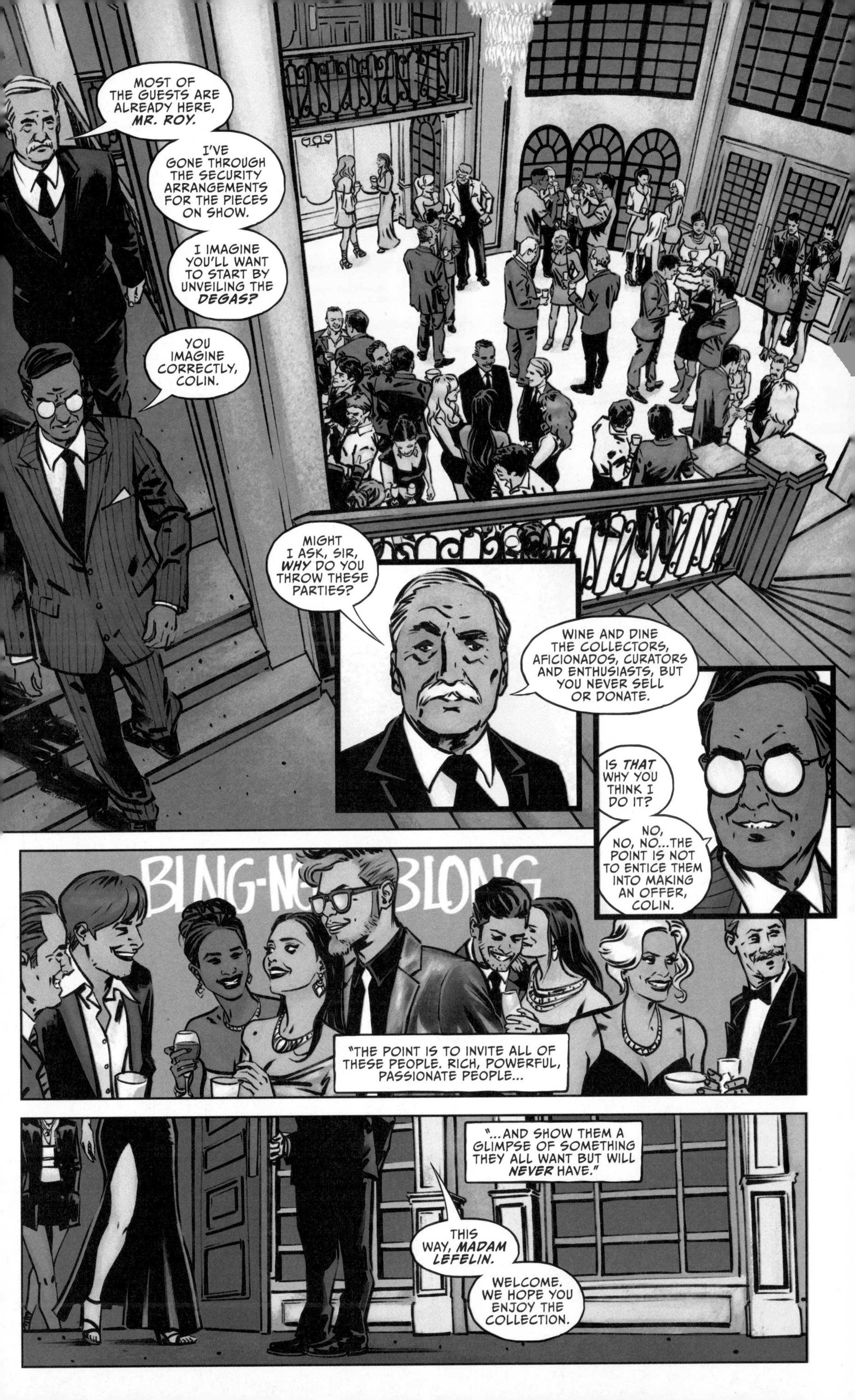
MOST OF THE GUESTS ARE ALREADY HERE, MR. ROY.
I'VE GONE THROUGH THE SECURITY ARRANGEMENTS FOR THE PIECES ON SHOW.
I IMAGINE YOU'LL WANT TO START BY UNVEILING THE DEGAS?
YOU IMAGINE CORRECTLY, COLIN.
MIGHT I ASK, SIR, WHY DO YOU THROW THESE PARTIES?
WINE AND DINE THE COLLECTORS, AFICIONADOS, CURATORS AND ENTHUSIASTS, BUT YOU NEVER SELL OR DONATE.
IS THAT WHY YOU THINK I DO IT?
NO, NO, NO...THE POINT IS NOT TO ENTICE THEM INTO MAKING AN OFFER, COLIN.
"THE POINT IS TO INVITE ALL OF THESE PEOPLE. RICH, POWERFUL, PASSIONATE PEOPLE...
"...AND SHOW THEM A GLIMPSE OF SOMETHING THEY ALL WANT BUT WILL NEVER HAVE."
THIS WAY, MADAM LEFELIN.
WELCOME. WE HOPE YOU ENJOY THE COLLECTION.

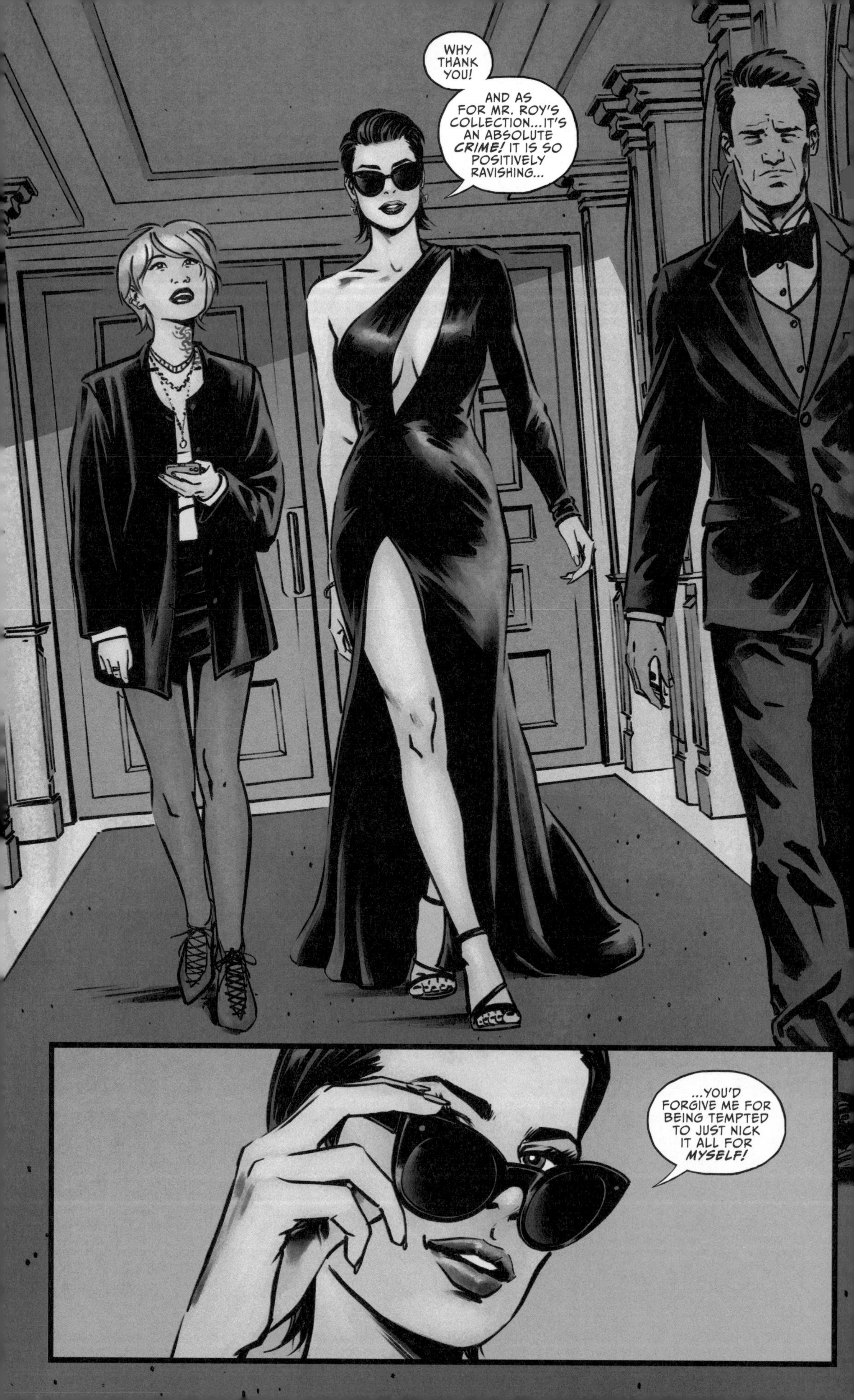

WHY THANK YOU!
AND AS FOR MR. ROY'S COLLECTION...IT'S AN ABSOLUTE CRIME! IT IS SO POSITIVELY RAVISHING...
...YOU'D FORGIVE ME FOR BEING TEMPTED TO JUST NICK IT ALL FOR MYSELF!

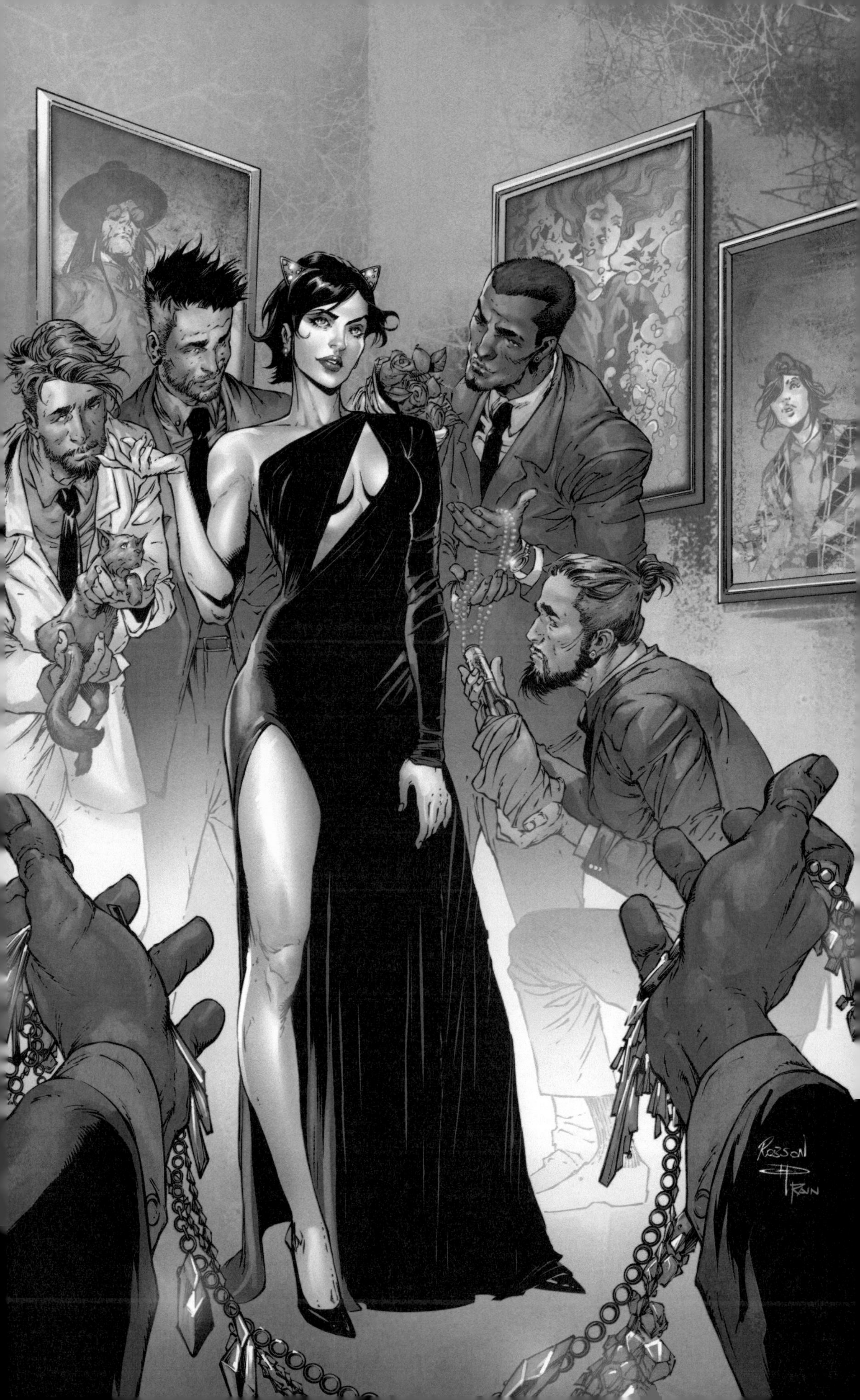

ROBSON
PRAIN

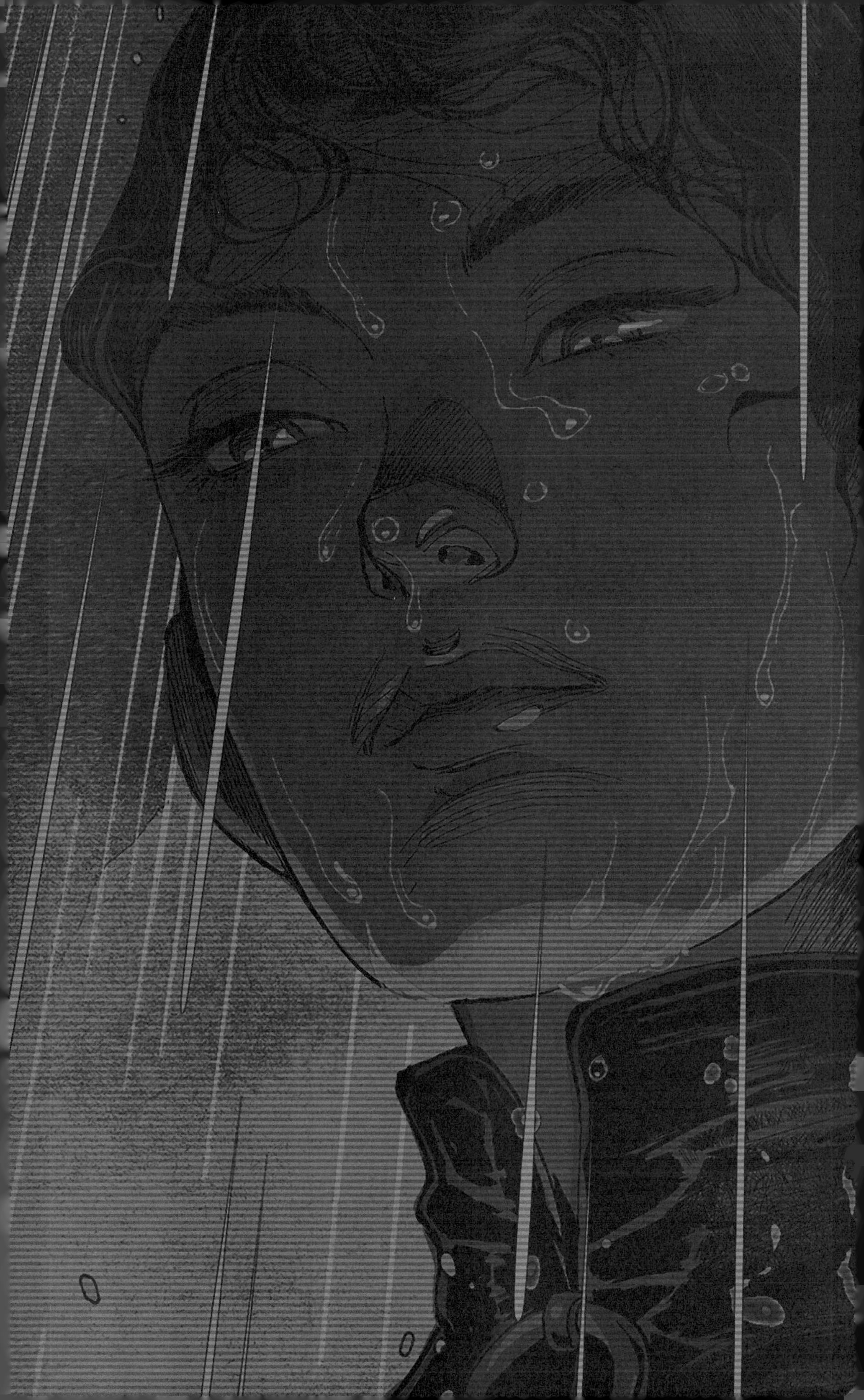

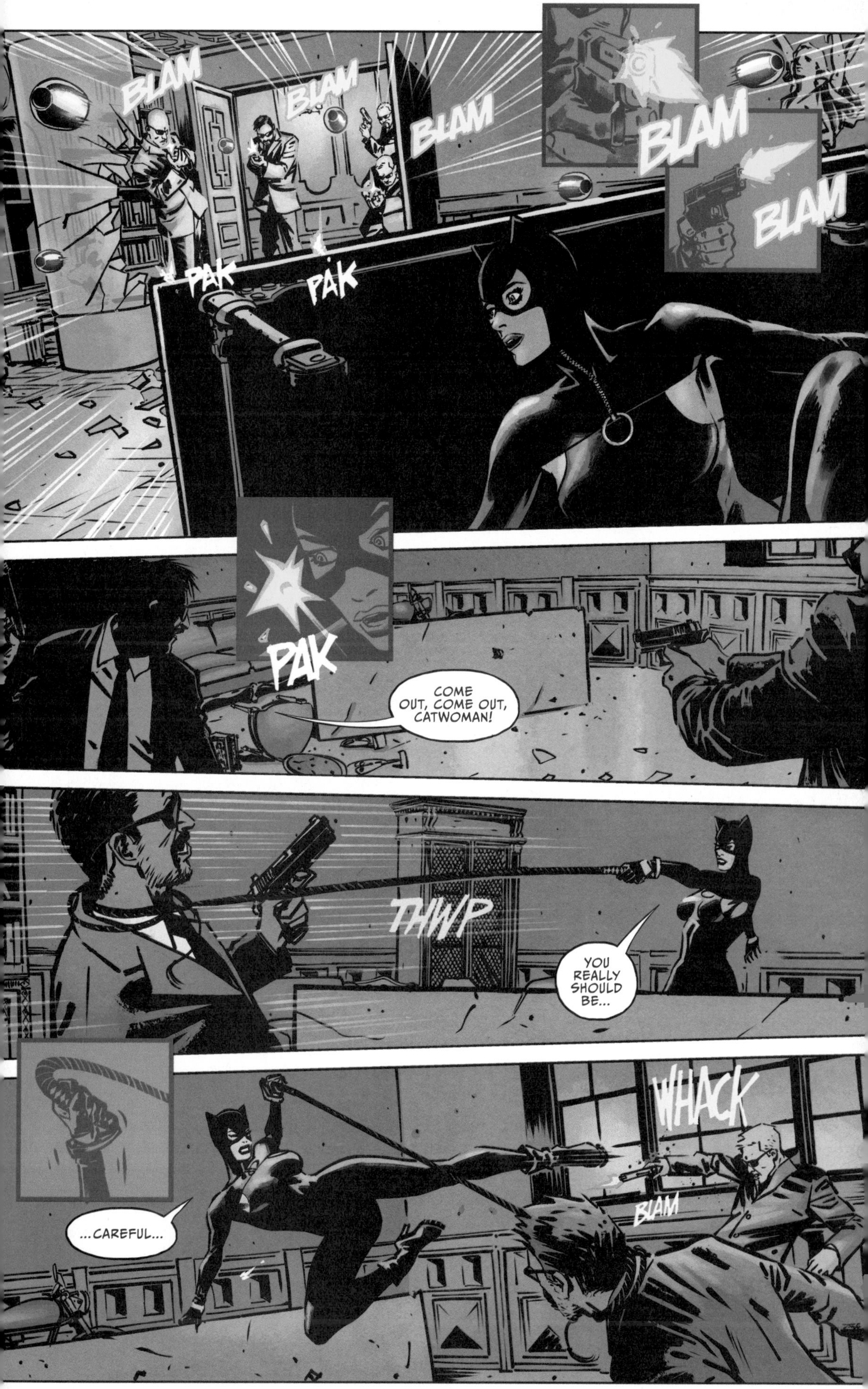
BLAM
BLAM
BLAM
BLAM
BLAM
PAK
PAK
PAK
COME OUT, COME OUT, CATWOMAN!
THWP
YOU REALLY SHOULD BE...
...CAREFUL...
WHACK
BLAM

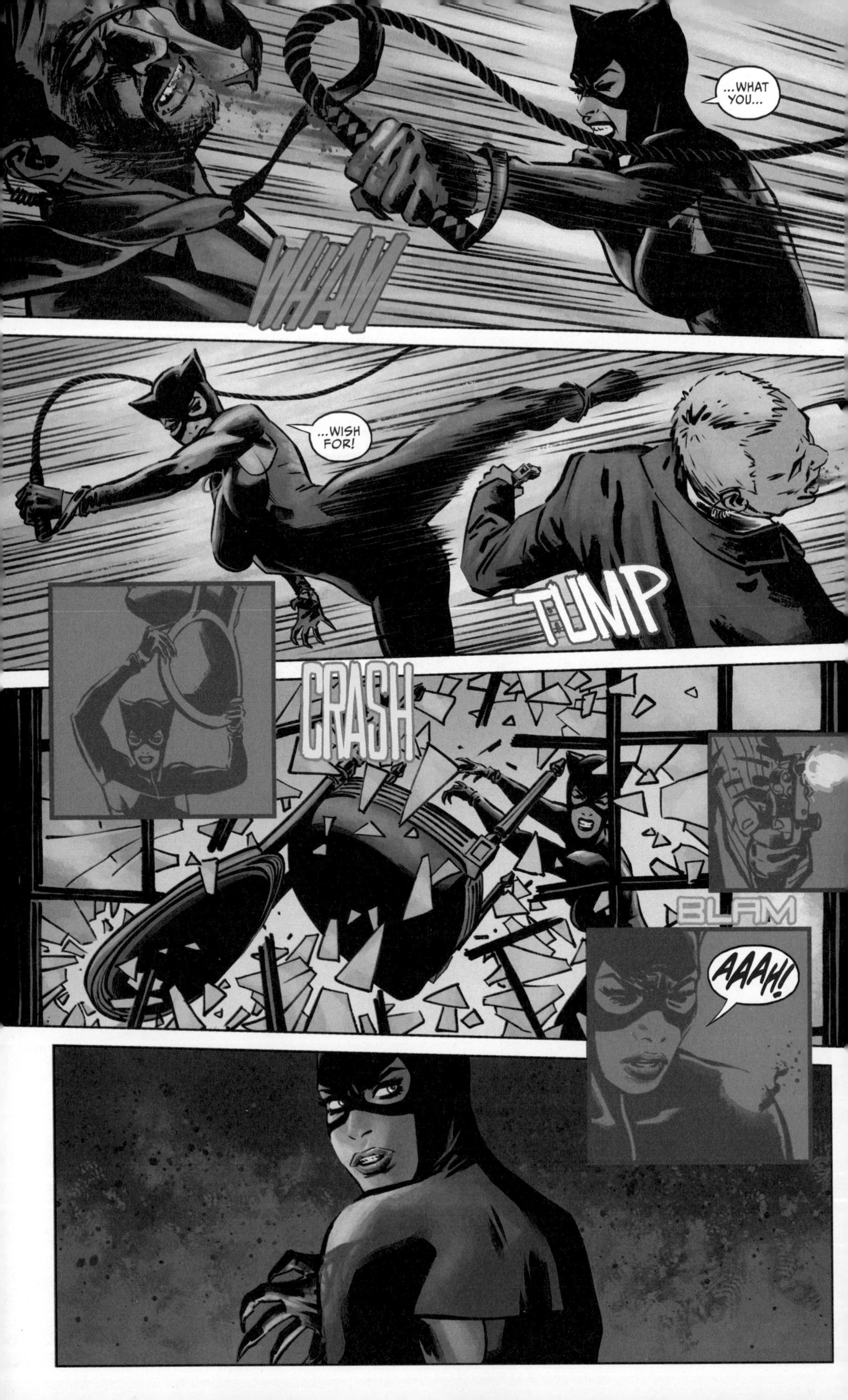
...WHAT YOU...
WHAM
...WISH FOR!
TUMP
CRASH
BLAM
AAAH!

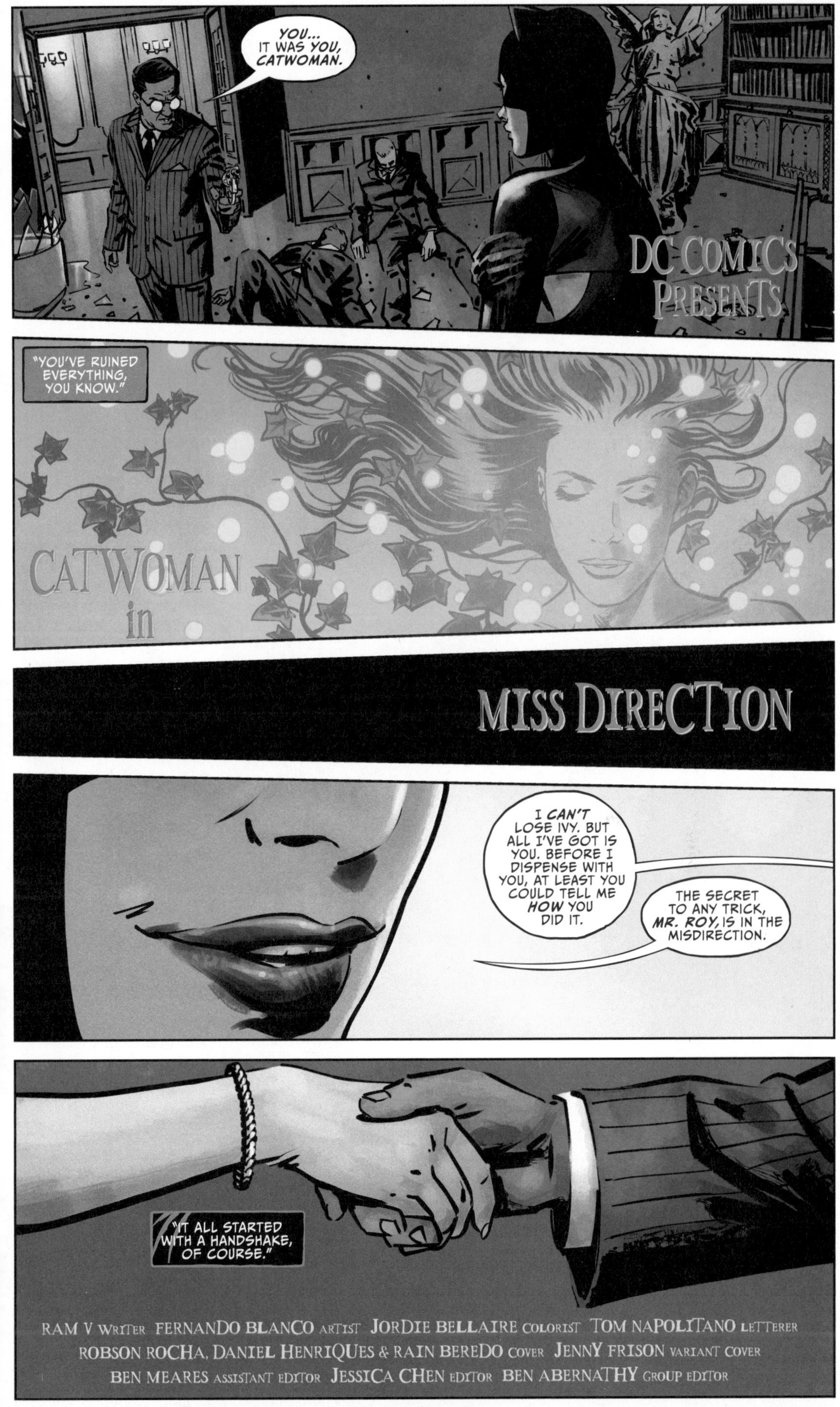

YOU... IT WAS YOU, CATWOMAN.
DC COMICS PRESENTS
"YOU'VE RUINED EVERYTHING, YOU KNOW."
CATWOMAN in
MISS DIRECTION
I CAN'T LOSE IVY. BUT ALL I'VE GOT IS YOU. BEFORE I DISPENSE WITH YOU, AT LEAST YOU COULD TELL ME HOW YOU DID IT.
THE SECRET TO ANY TRICK, MR. ROY, IS IN THE MISDIRECTION.
"IT ALL STARTED WITH A HANDSHAKE, OF COURSE."
RAM V WRITER FERNANDO BLANCO ARTIST JORDIE BELLAIRE COLORIST TOM NAPOLITANO LETTERER
ROBSON ROCHA, DANIEL HENRIQUES & RAIN BEREDO COVER JENNY FRISON VARIANT COVER
BEN MEARES ASSISTANT EDITOR JESSICA CHEN EDITOR BEN ABERNATHY GROUP EDITOR

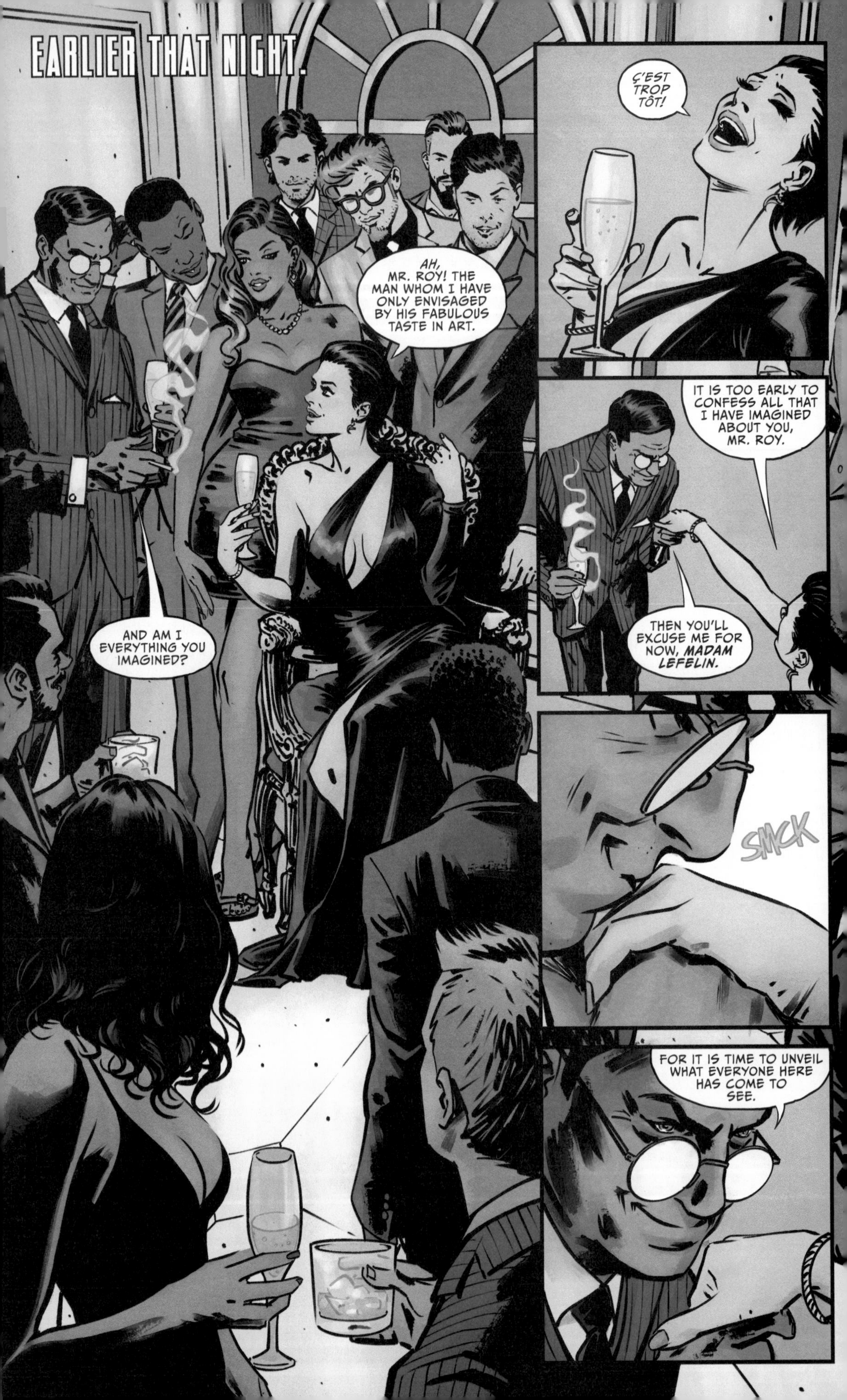
EARLIER THAT NIGHT.
AH, MR. ROY! THE MAN WHOM I HAVE ONLY ENVISAGED BY HIS FABULOUS TASTE IN ART.
AND AM I EVERYTHING YOU IMAGINED?
Ç'EST TROP TÔT!
IT IS TOO EARLY TO CONFESS ALL THAT I HAVE IMAGINED ABOUT YOU, MR. ROY.
THEN YOU'LL EXCUSE ME FOR NOW, MADAM LEFELIN.
SMCK
FOR IT IS TIME TO UNVEIL WHAT EVERYONE HERE HAS COME TO SEE.

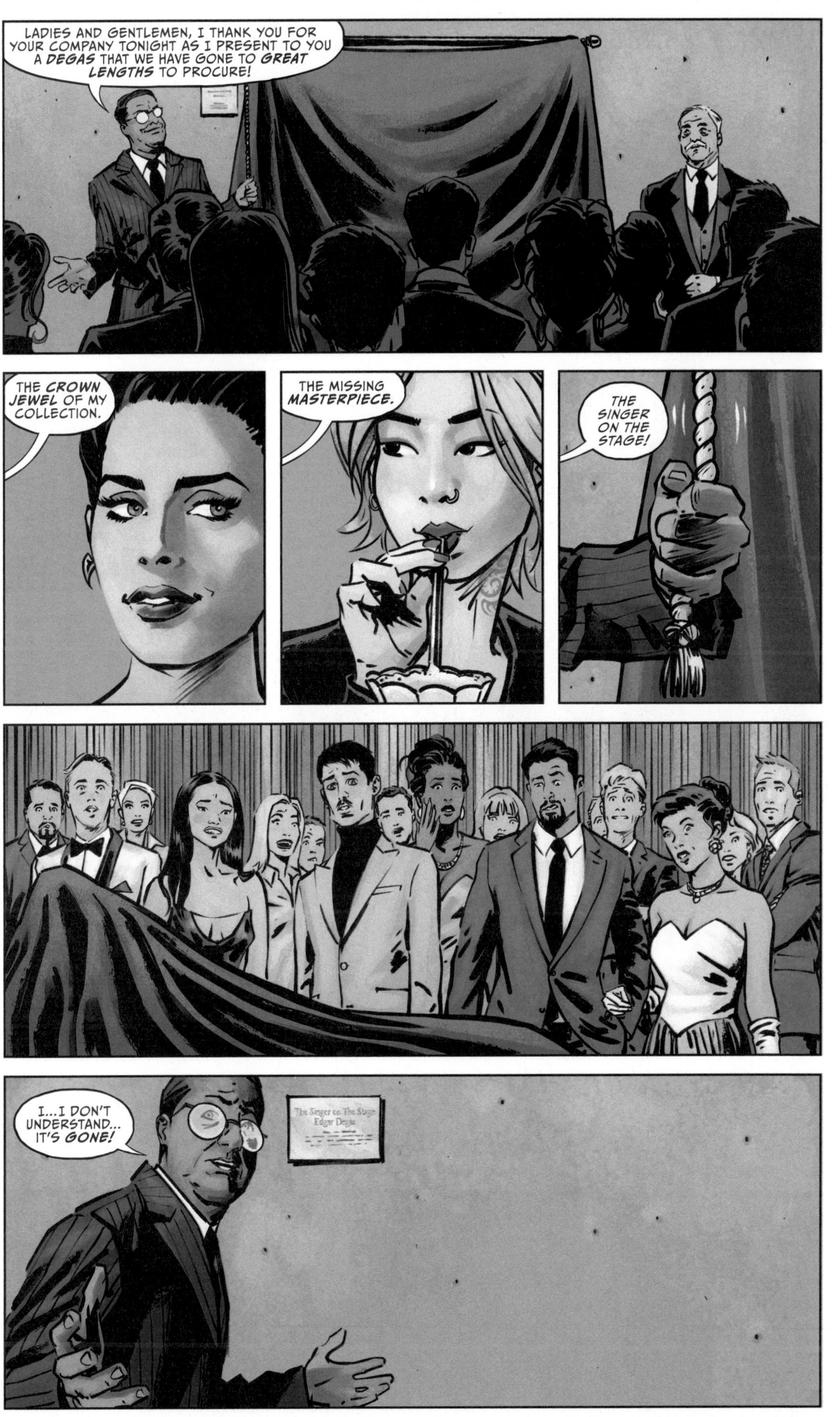
LADIES AND GENTLEMEN, I THANK YOU FOR YOUR COMPANY TONIGHT AS I PRESENT TO YOU A DEGAS THAT WE HAVE GONE TO GREAT LENGTHS TO PROCURE!
THE CROWN JEWEL OF MY COLLECTION.
THE MISSING MASTERPIECE.
THE SINGER ON THE STAGE!
I...I DON'T UNDERSTAND... IT'S GONE!
The Singer on The Stage
Edgar Degas

YES, YES... WE *KNOW* YOU STOLE THE DEGAS!

⋚TSK TSK TSK⋛ PATIENCE, MR. ROY. YOU CAN'T RUSH A GOOD STORY, YOU KNOW?

"THE DEGAS WAS GONE. YOUR SECURITY SCRAMBLED TO ACTION AND YOU PREDICTABLY RAN TO CHECK ON YOUR PRIZED POSSESSION.

"THAT'S HOW I KNEW *WHERE* YOU WERE KEEPING HER.

"AND THEN THERE WAS THE MATTER OF THE *HANDSHAKE.*

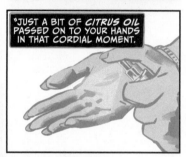

"JUST A BIT OF *CITRUS OIL* PASSED ON TO YOUR HANDS IN THAT CORDIAL MOMENT.

SMCK

"SO, WHEN *MADAM LEFELIN* SLIPPED UNNOTICED INTO THE POWDER ROOM FOR A *QUICK CHANGE*..."

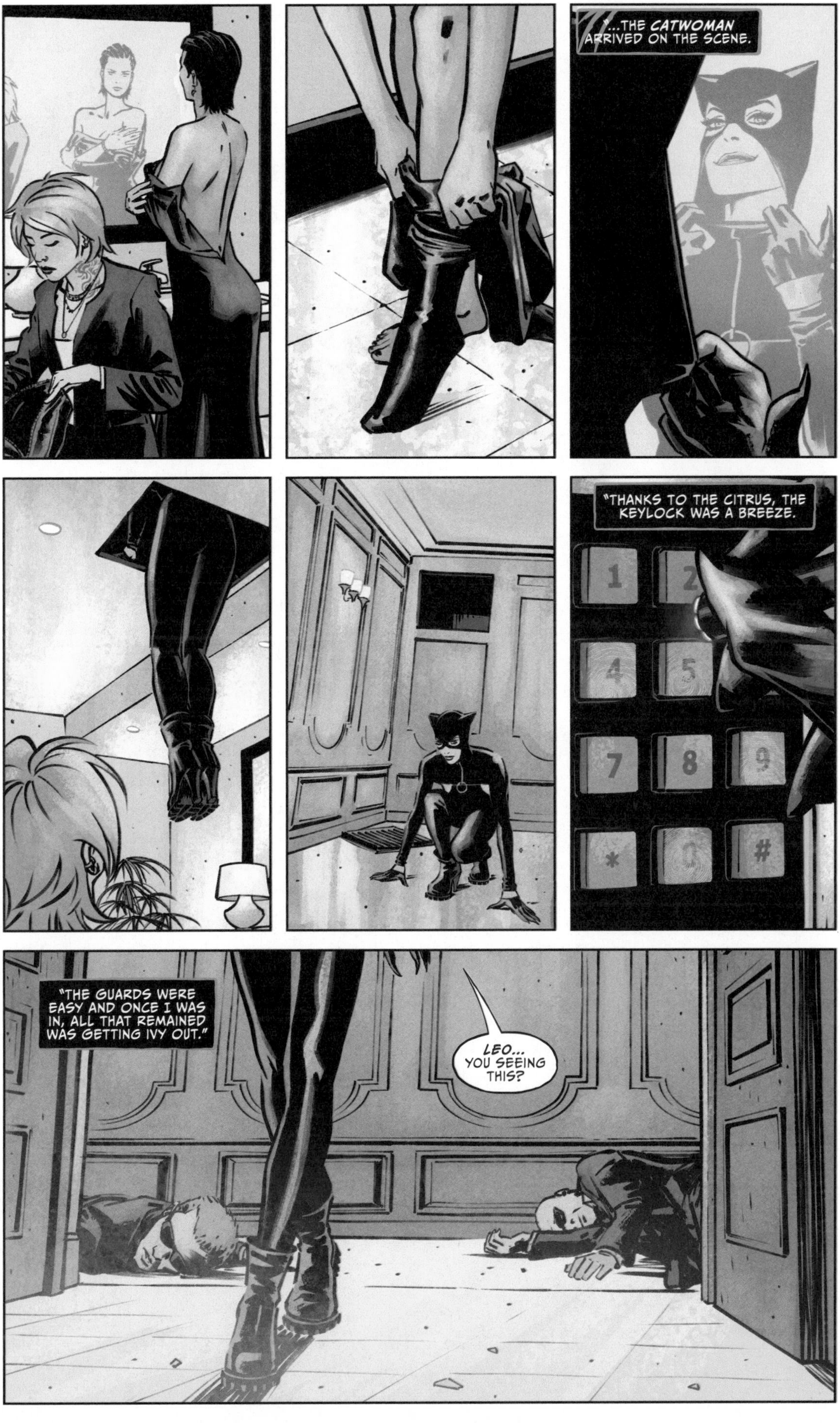
"...THE CATWOMAN ARRIVED ON THE SCENE.
"THANKS TO THE CITRUS, THE KEYLOCK WAS A BREEZE.
1 2
4 5
7 8 9
* 0 #
"THE GUARDS WERE EASY AND ONCE I WAS IN, ALL THAT REMAINED WAS GETTING IVY OUT."
LEO... YOU SEEING THIS?

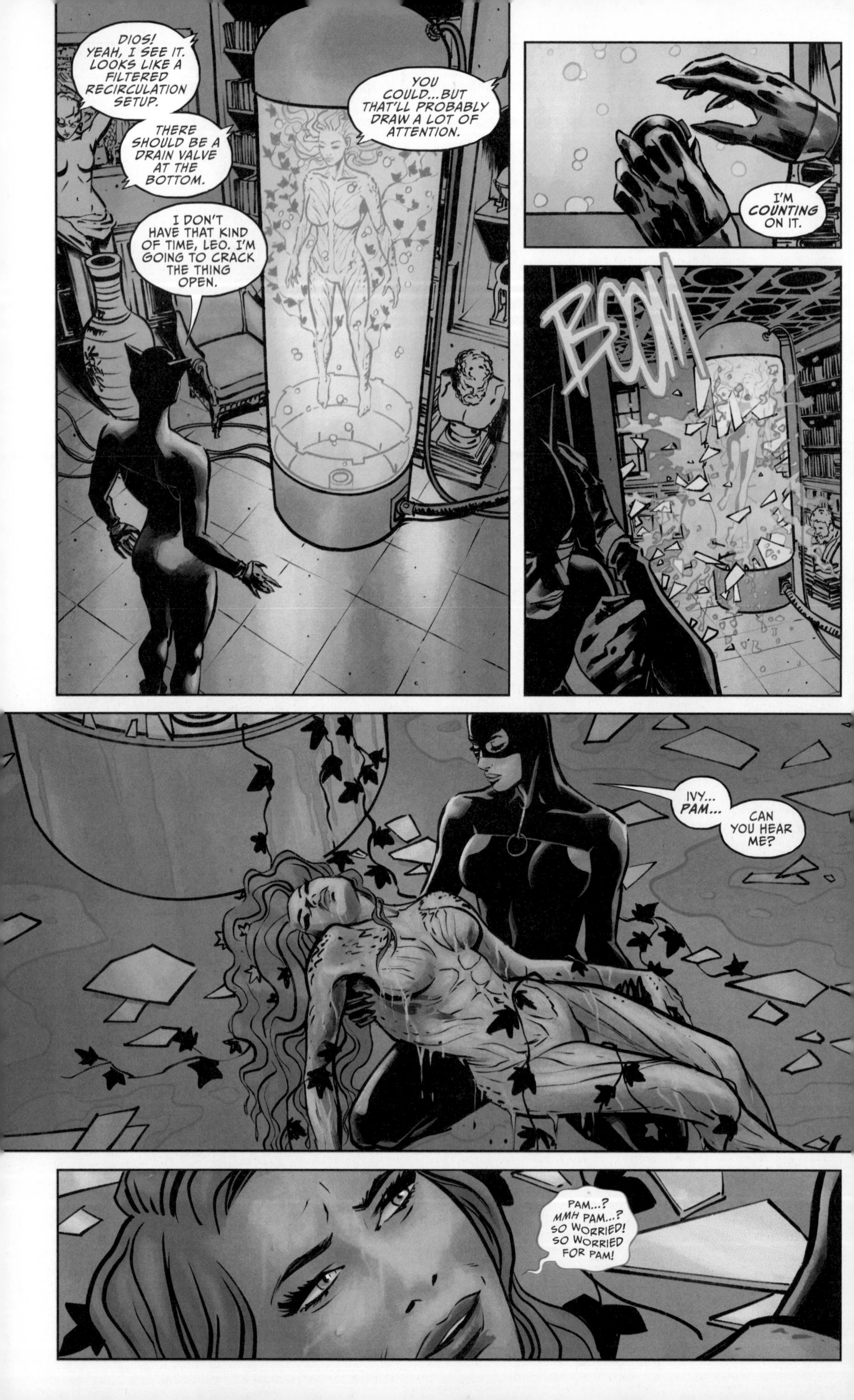
DIOS! YEAH, I SEE IT. LOOKS LIKE A FILTERED RECIRCULATION SETUP.
THERE SHOULD BE A DRAIN VALVE AT THE BOTTOM.
YOU COULD...BUT THAT'LL PROBABLY DRAW A LOT OF ATTENTION.
I DON'T HAVE THAT KIND OF TIME, LEO. I'M GOING TO CRACK THE THING OPEN.
I'M COUNTING ON IT.
BOOM
IVY... PAM...
CAN YOU HEAR ME?
PAM...? MMH PAM...? SO WORRIED! SO WORRIED FOR PAM!

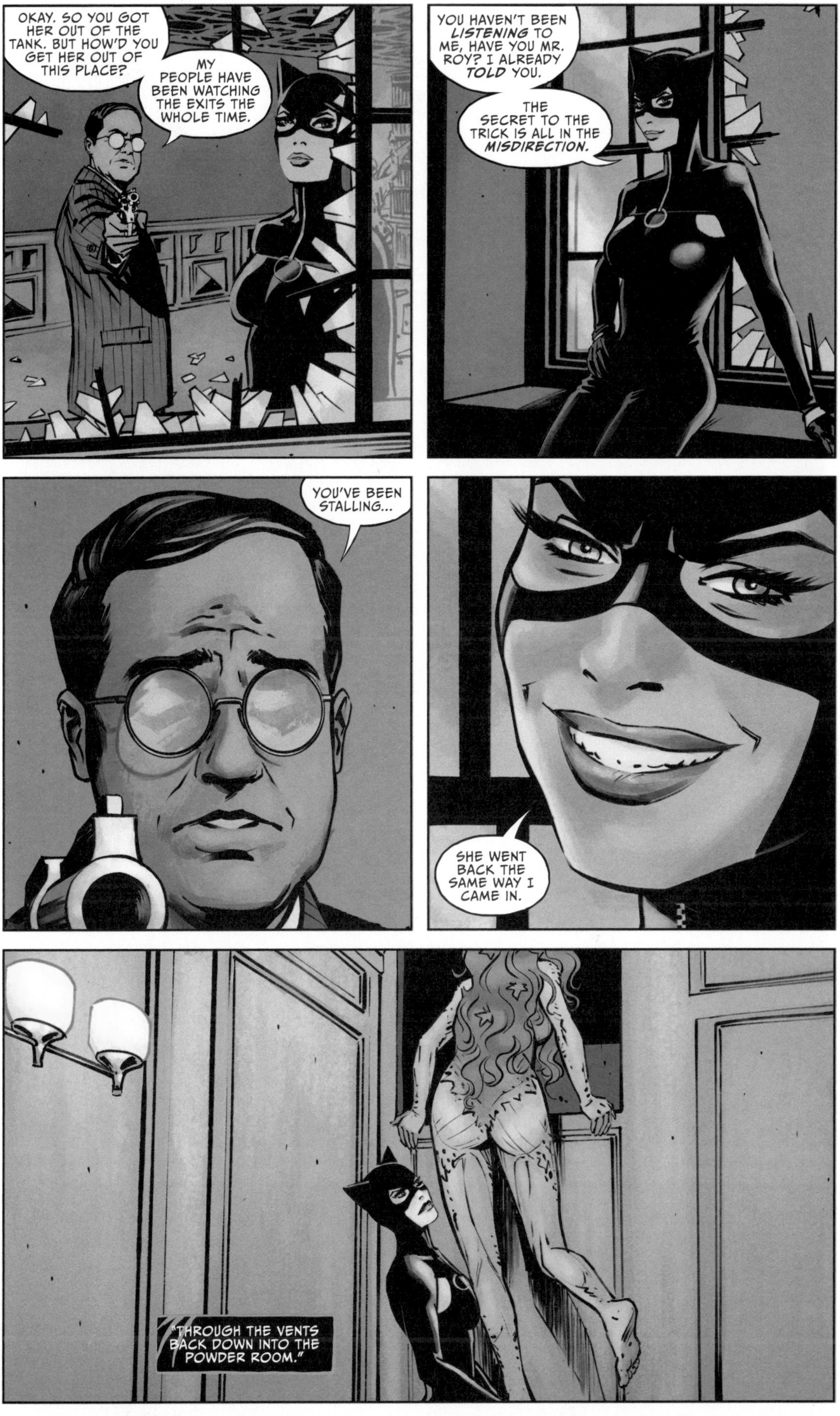

OKAY. SO YOU GOT HER OUT OF THE TANK. BUT HOW'D YOU GET HER OUT OF THIS PLACE?
MY PEOPLE HAVE BEEN WATCHING THE EXITS THE WHOLE TIME.
YOU HAVEN'T BEEN *LISTENING* TO ME, HAVE YOU MR. ROY? I ALREADY *TOLD* YOU.
THE SECRET TO THE TRICK IS ALL IN THE *MISDIRECTION.*
YOU'VE BEEN STALLING...
SHE WENT BACK THE SAME WAY I CAME IN.
"THROUGH THE VENTS BACK DOWN INTO THE POWDER ROOM."

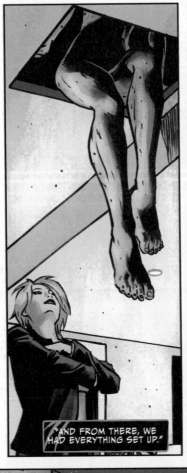

"AND FROM THERE, WE HAD EVERYTHING SET UP."

WOW... YOU *ARE* *REALLY* GREEN.

PUT THIS ON. I'LL GET US A RIDE OUT OF HERE.

NERVOUS! NERVOUS AND EXCITED! WHERE IS PAMELA GOING? WHO'S THE CAT WITH BLUE HAIR? NOBODY KNOWS!

"YOU SEE, MR. ROY, I HAD VERY LITTLE TIME TO PLAN FOR ANY OF THIS. SO I NEEDED A BIGGER CREW THAN USUAL THIS TIME.

EL NIDO CATERING

"YOUR CATERERS? THEY NEVER MADE IT PAST EXIT 14.

"NOT THAT YOUR KIND WOULD NOTICE THE DIFFERENCE, BUT IT'S THE *ALLEYTOWN STRAYS* THAT'VE BEEN BRINGING YOU YOUR WINE TONIGHT."

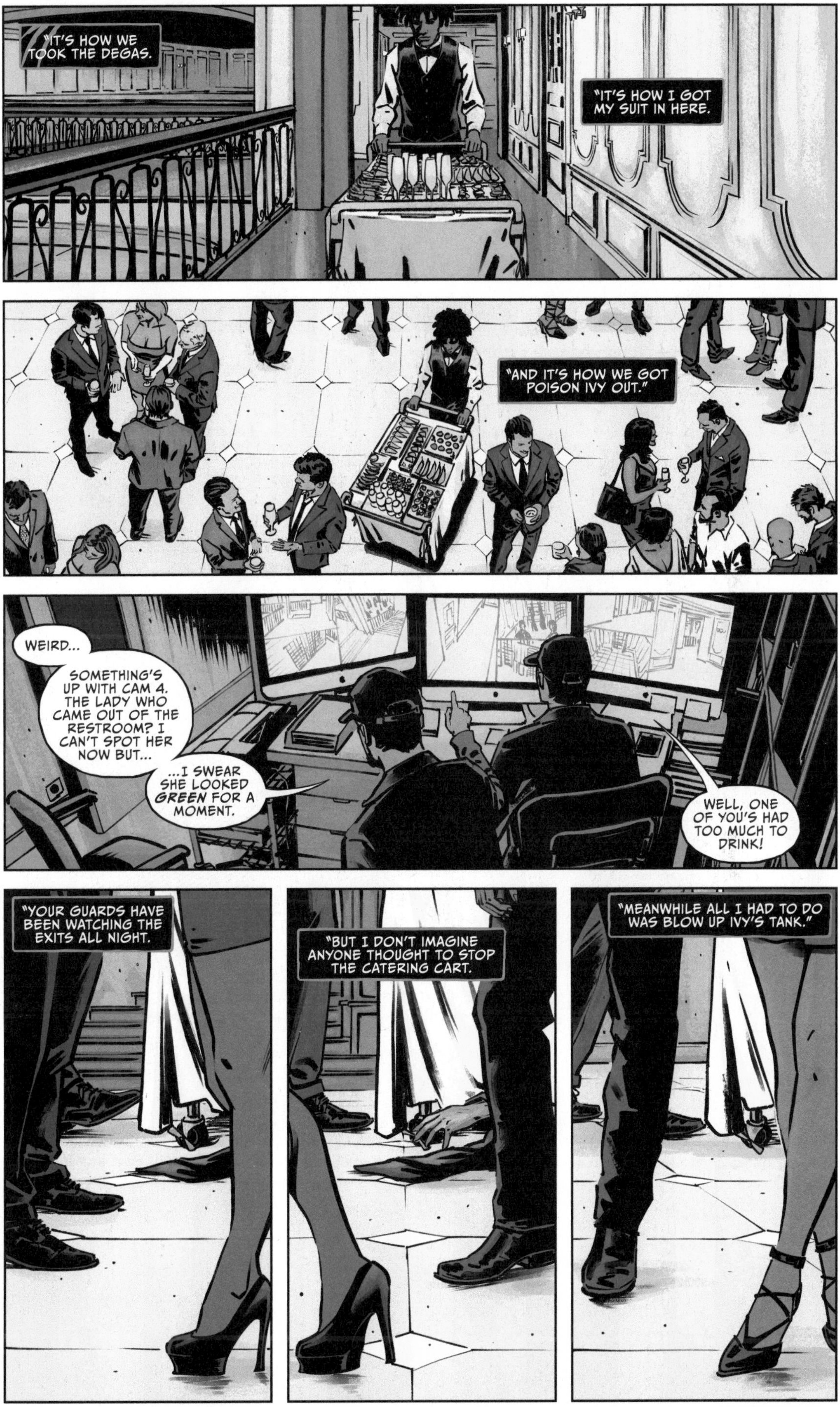
"IT'S HOW WE TOOK THE DEGAS.
"IT'S HOW I GOT MY SUIT IN HERE.
"AND IT'S HOW WE GOT POISON IVY OUT."
WEIRD...
SOMETHING'S UP WITH CAM 4. THE LADY WHO CAME OUT OF THE RESTROOM? I CAN'T SPOT HER NOW BUT...
...I SWEAR SHE LOOKED GREEN FOR A MOMENT.
WELL, ONE OF YOU'S HAD TOO MUCH TO DRINK!
"YOUR GUARDS HAVE BEEN WATCHING THE EXITS ALL NIGHT.
"BUT I DON'T IMAGINE ANYONE THOUGHT TO STOP THE CATERING CART.
"MEANWHILE ALL I HAD TO DO WAS BLOW UP IVY'S TANK."

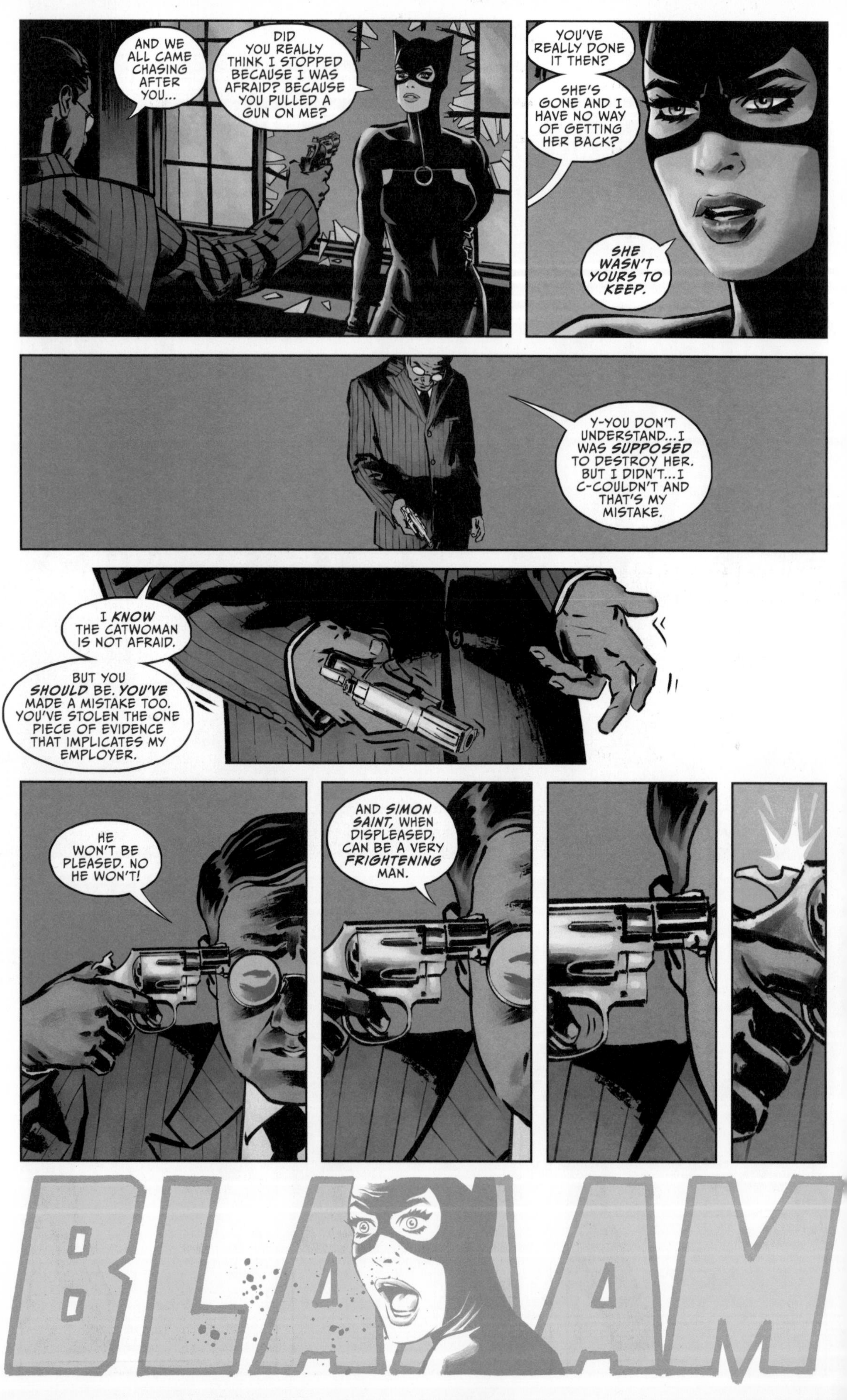

AND WE ALL CAME CHASING AFTER YOU...
DID YOU REALLY THINK I STOPPED BECAUSE I WAS AFRAID? BECAUSE YOU PULLED A GUN ON ME?
YOU'VE REALLY DONE IT THEN?
SHE'S GONE AND I HAVE NO WAY OF GETTING HER BACK?
SHE WASN'T YOURS TO KEEP.
Y-YOU DON'T UNDERSTAND...I WAS SUPPOSED TO DESTROY HER. BUT I DIDN'T...I C-COULDN'T AND THAT'S MY MISTAKE.
I KNOW THE CATWOMAN IS NOT AFRAID.
BUT YOU SHOULD BE. YOU'VE MADE A MISTAKE TOO. YOU'VE STOLEN THE ONE PIECE OF EVIDENCE THAT IMPLICATES MY EMPLOYER.
HE WON'T BE PLEASED. NO HE WON'T!
AND SIMON SAINT, WHEN DISPLEASED, CAN BE A VERY FRIGHTENING MAN.
BLAM

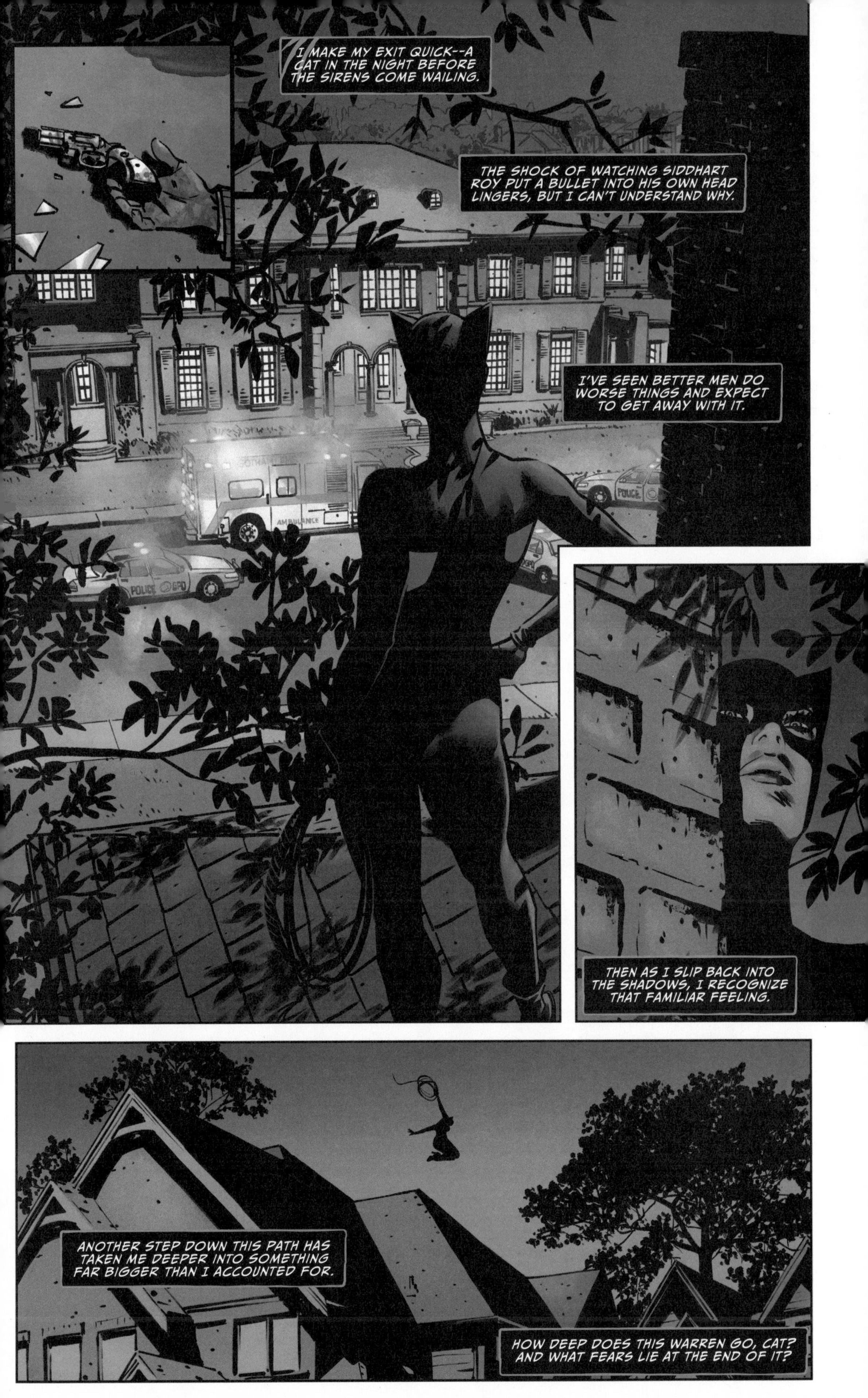
I MAKE MY EXIT QUICK--A CAT IN THE NIGHT BEFORE THE SIRENS COME WAILING.
THE SHOCK OF WATCHING SIDDHART ROY PUT A BULLET INTO HIS OWN HEAD LINGERS, BUT I CAN'T UNDERSTAND WHY.
I'VE SEEN BETTER MEN DO WORSE THINGS AND EXPECT TO GET AWAY WITH IT.
AMBULANCE
POLICE
POLICE GPD
THEN AS I SLIP BACK INTO THE SHADOWS, I RECOGNIZE THAT FAMILIAR FEELING.
ANOTHER STEP DOWN THIS PATH HAS TAKEN ME DEEPER INTO SOMETHING FAR BIGGER THAN I ACCOUNTED FOR.
HOW DEEP DOES THIS WARREN GO, CAT? AND WHAT FEARS LIE AT THE END OF IT?

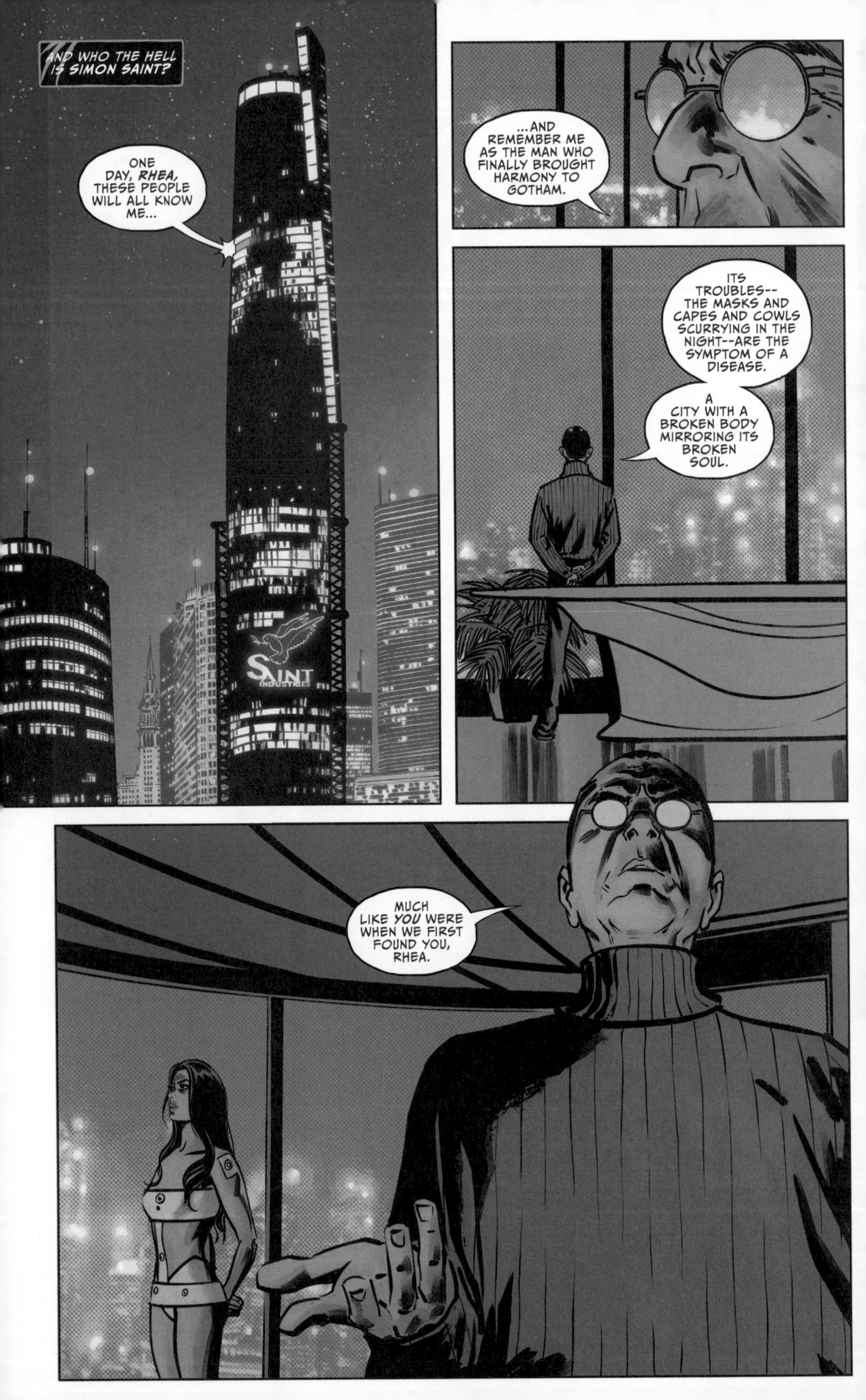
AND WHO THE HELL IS SIMON SAINT?
ONE DAY, RHEA, THESE PEOPLE WILL ALL KNOW ME...
SAINT INDUSTRIES
...AND REMEMBER ME AS THE MAN WHO FINALLY BROUGHT HARMONY TO GOTHAM.
ITS TROUBLES--THE MASKS AND CAPES AND COWLS SCURRYING IN THE NIGHT--ARE THE SYMPTOM OF A DISEASE.
A CITY WITH A BROKEN BODY MIRRORING ITS BROKEN SOUL.
MUCH LIKE YOU WERE WHEN WE FIRST FOUND YOU, RHEA.

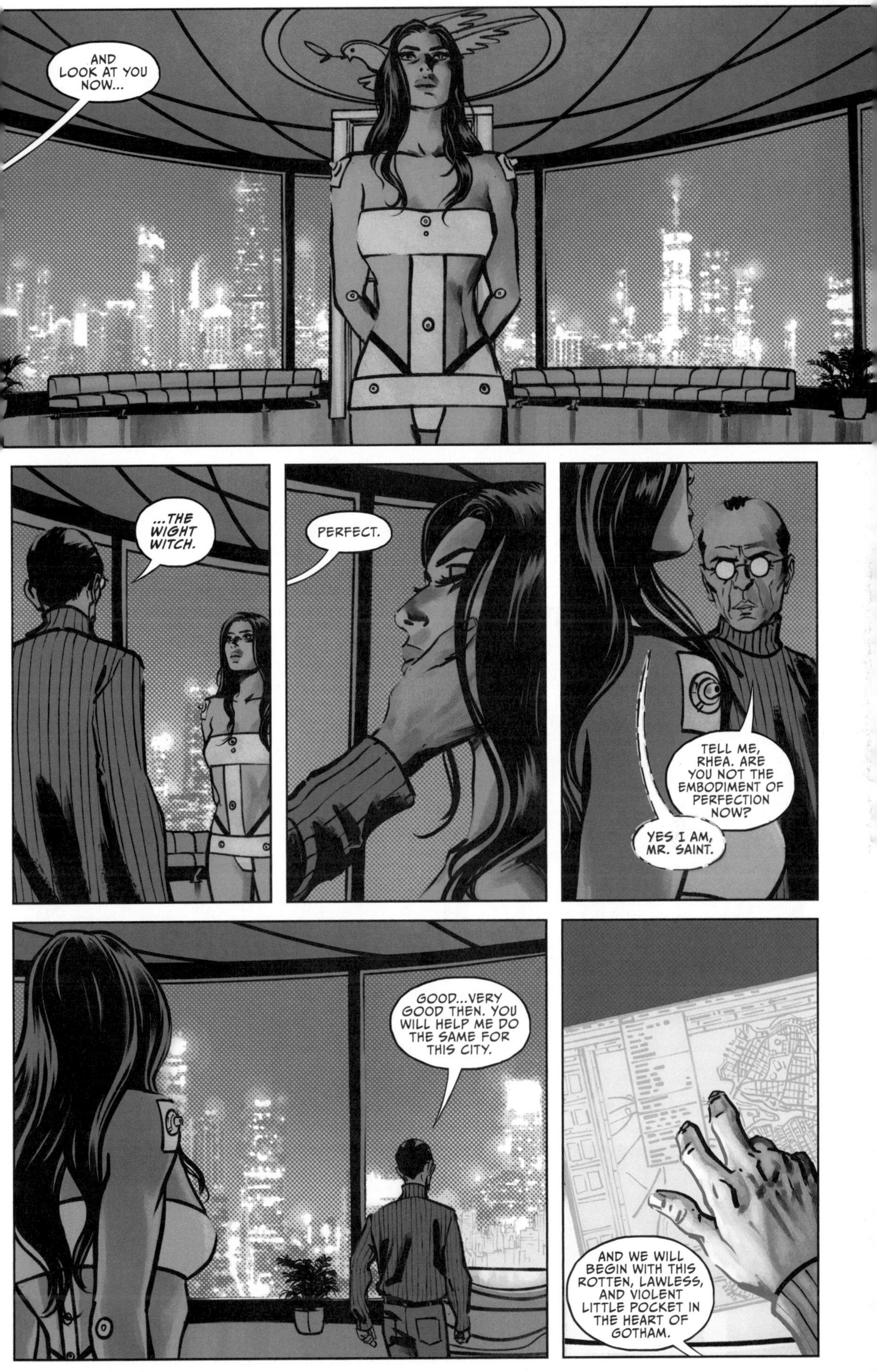
AND LOOK AT YOU NOW...
...THE WIGHT WITCH.
PERFECT.
TELL ME, RHEA. ARE YOU NOT THE EMBODIMENT OF PERFECTION NOW?
YES I AM, MR. SAINT.
GOOD...VERY GOOD THEN. YOU WILL HELP ME DO THE SAME FOR THIS CITY.
AND WE WILL BEGIN WITH THIS ROTTEN, LAWLESS, AND VIOLENT LITTLE POCKET IN THE HEART OF GOTHAM.

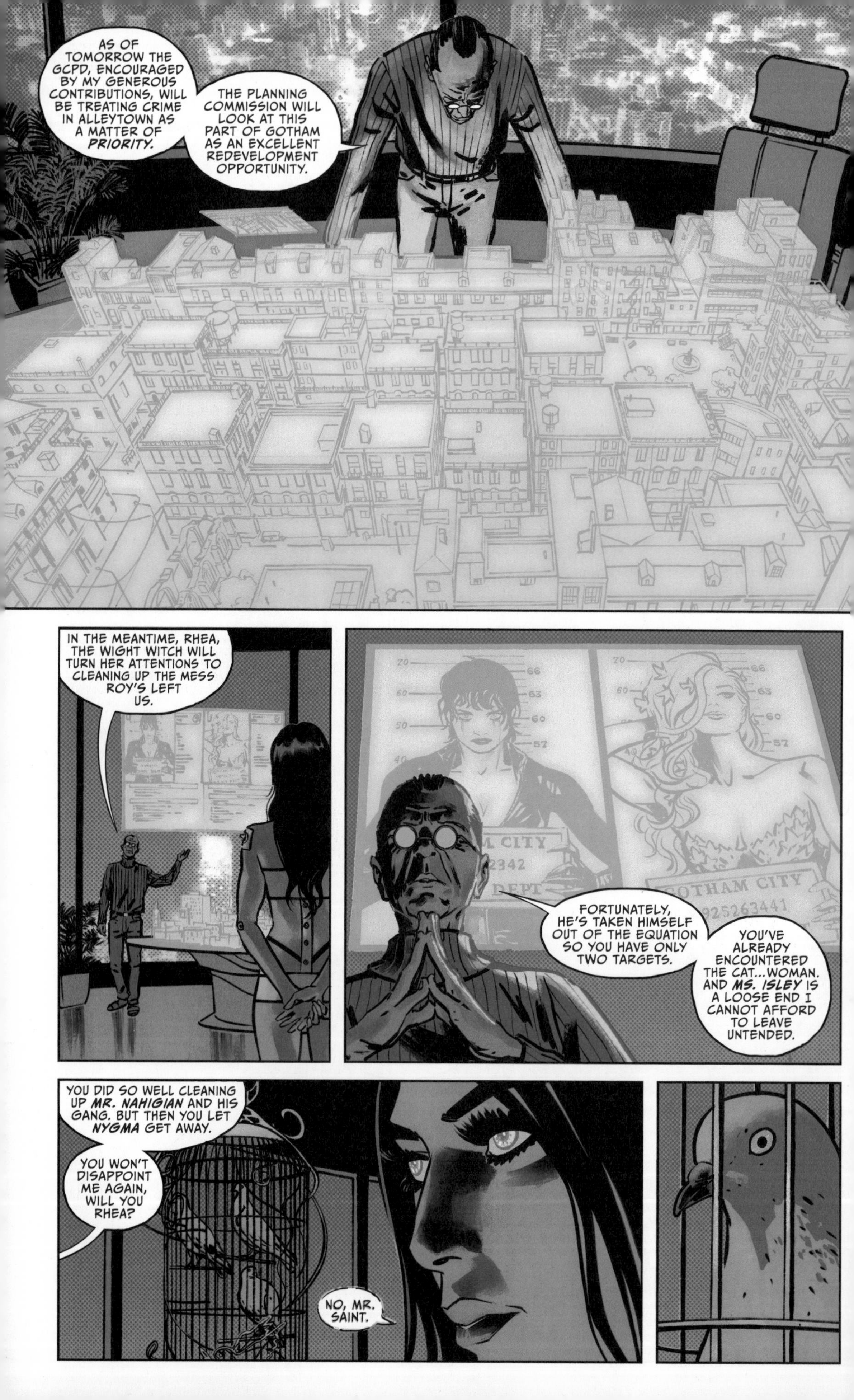
AS OF TOMORROW THE GCPD, ENCOURAGED BY MY GENEROUS CONTRIBUTIONS, WILL BE TREATING CRIME IN ALLEYTOWN AS A MATTER OF *PRIORITY.*
THE PLANNING COMMISSION WILL LOOK AT THIS PART OF GOTHAM AS AN EXCELLENT REDEVELOPMENT OPPORTUNITY.
IN THE MEANTIME, RHEA, THE WIGHT WITCH WILL TURN HER ATTENTIONS TO CLEANING UP THE MESS ROY'S LEFT US.
FORTUNATELY, HE'S TAKEN HIMSELF OUT OF THE EQUATION SO YOU HAVE ONLY TWO TARGETS.
YOU'VE ALREADY ENCOUNTERED THE CAT...WOMAN. AND *MS. ISLEY* IS A LOOSE END I CANNOT AFFORD TO LEAVE UNTENDED.
GOTHAM CITY
925263441
YOU DID SO WELL CLEANING UP *MR. NAHIGIAN* AND HIS GANG. BUT THEN YOU LET *NYGMA* GET AWAY.
YOU WON'T DISAPPOINT ME AGAIN, WILL YOU RHEA?
NO, MR. SAINT.

BECAUSE THAT WOULD BE A REAL TRAGEDY.

NO TELLING HOW IT MIGHT BREAK A MAN...

...TO BECOME DISAPPOINTED IN PERFECTION.

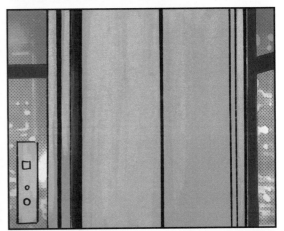

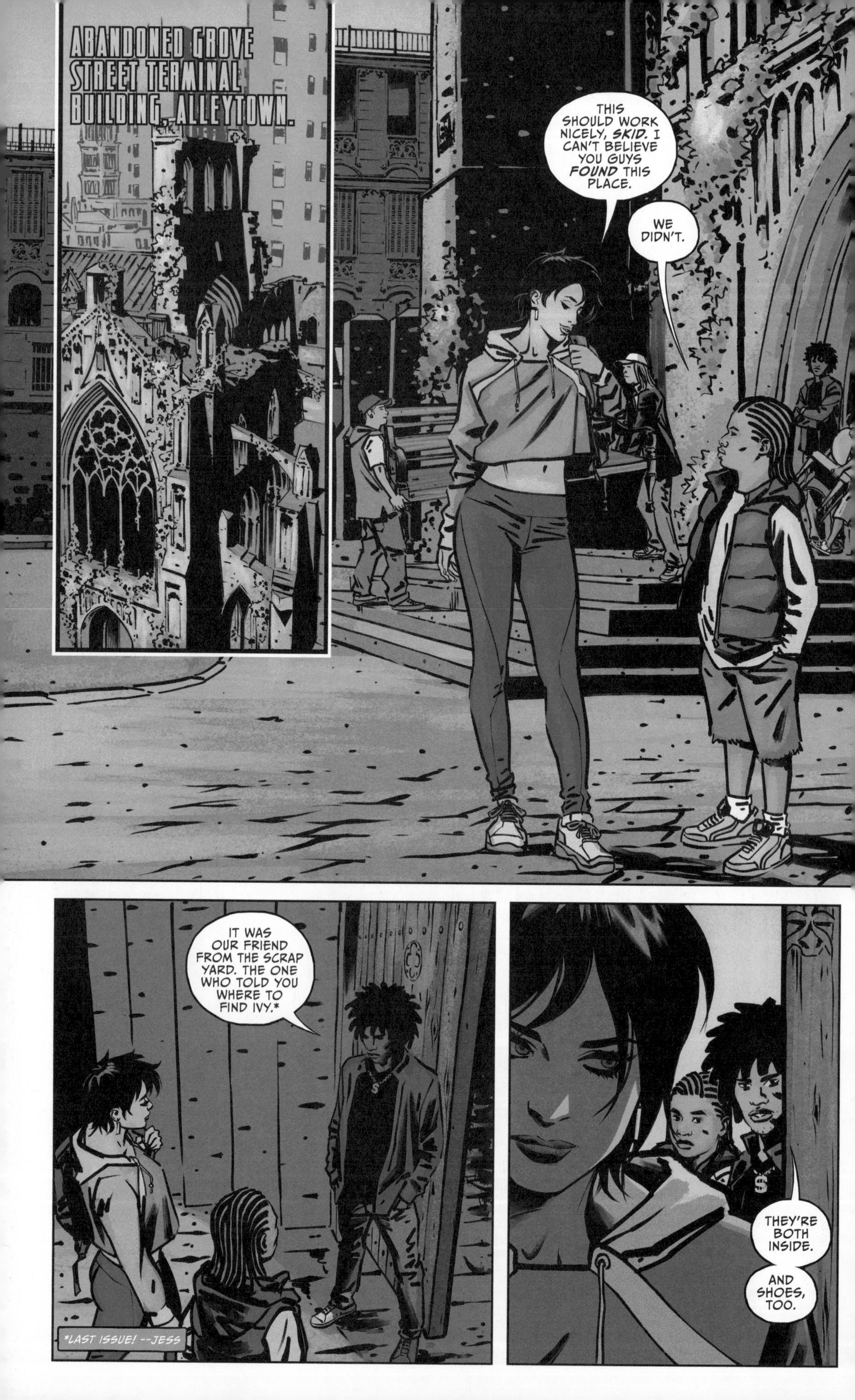
ABANDONED GROVE STREET TERMINAL BUILDING, ALLEYTOWN.
THIS SHOULD WORK NICELY, SKID. I CAN'T BELIEVE YOU GUYS FOUND THIS PLACE.
WE DIDN'T.
IT WAS OUR FRIEND FROM THE SCRAP YARD. THE ONE WHO TOLD YOU WHERE TO FIND IVY.*
*LAST ISSUE! --JESS
THEY'RE BOTH INSIDE.
AND SHOES, TOO.

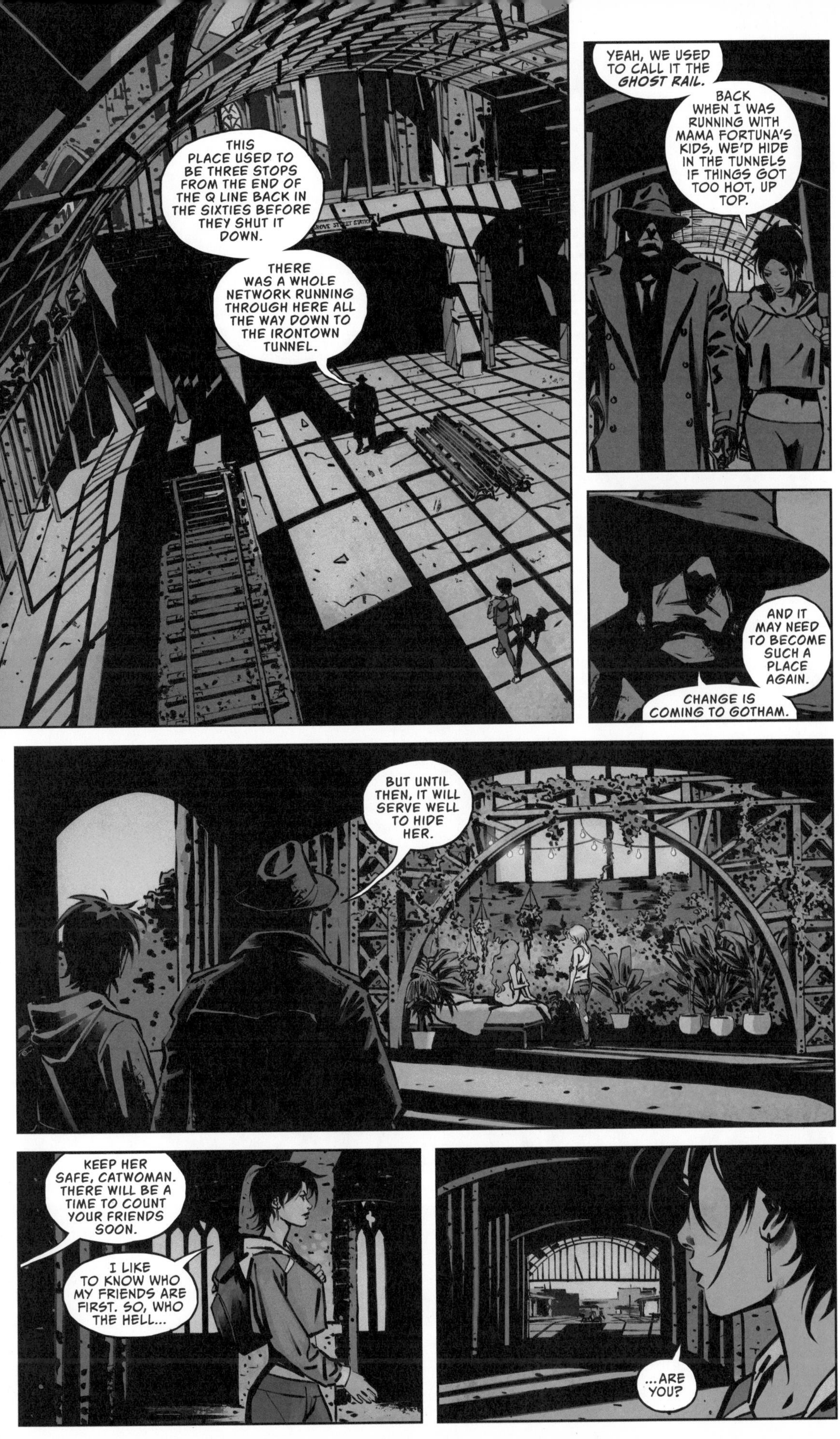
THIS PLACE USED TO BE THREE STOPS FROM THE END OF THE Q LINE BACK IN THE SIXTIES BEFORE THEY SHUT IT DOWN.
THERE WAS A WHOLE NETWORK RUNNING THROUGH HERE ALL THE WAY DOWN TO THE IRONTOWN TUNNEL.
YEAH, WE USED TO CALL IT THE *GHOST RAIL.*
BACK WHEN I WAS RUNNING WITH MAMA FORTUNA'S KIDS, WE'D HIDE IN THE TUNNELS IF THINGS GOT TOO HOT, UP TOP.
AND IT MAY NEED TO BECOME SUCH A PLACE AGAIN.
CHANGE IS COMING TO GOTHAM.
BUT UNTIL THEN, IT WILL SERVE WELL TO HIDE HER.
KEEP HER SAFE, CATWOMAN. THERE WILL BE A TIME TO COUNT YOUR FRIENDS SOON.
I LIKE TO KNOW WHO MY FRIENDS ARE FIRST. SO, WHO THE HELL...
...ARE YOU?

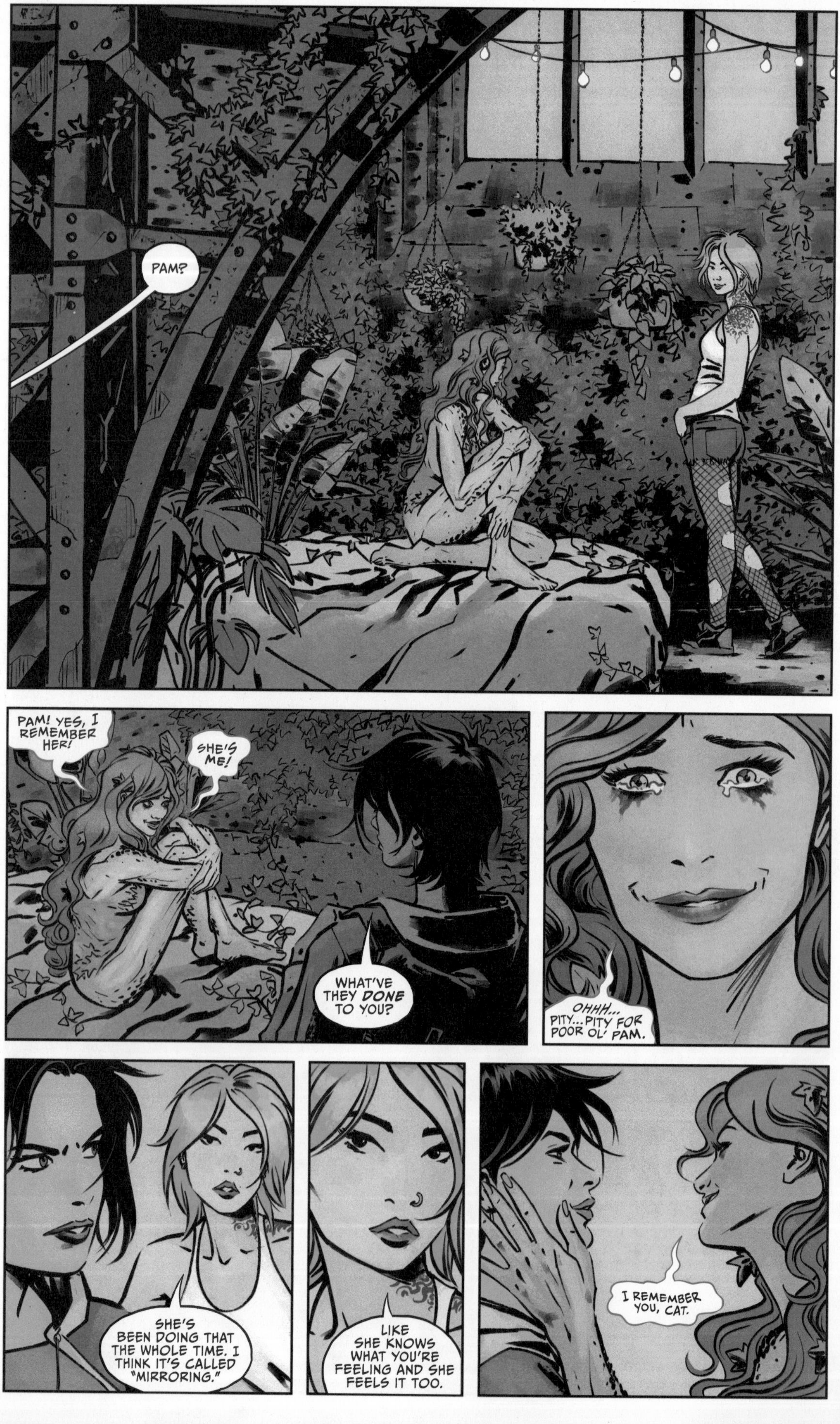
PAM?
PAM! YES, I REMEMBER HER!
SHE'S ME!
WHAT'VE THEY *DONE* TO YOU?
OHHH... PITY...PITY FOR POOR OL' PAM.
SHE'S BEEN DOING THAT THE WHOLE TIME. I THINK IT'S CALLED "MIRRORING."
LIKE SHE KNOWS WHAT YOU'RE FEELING AND SHE FEELS IT TOO.
I REMEMBER YOU, CAT.

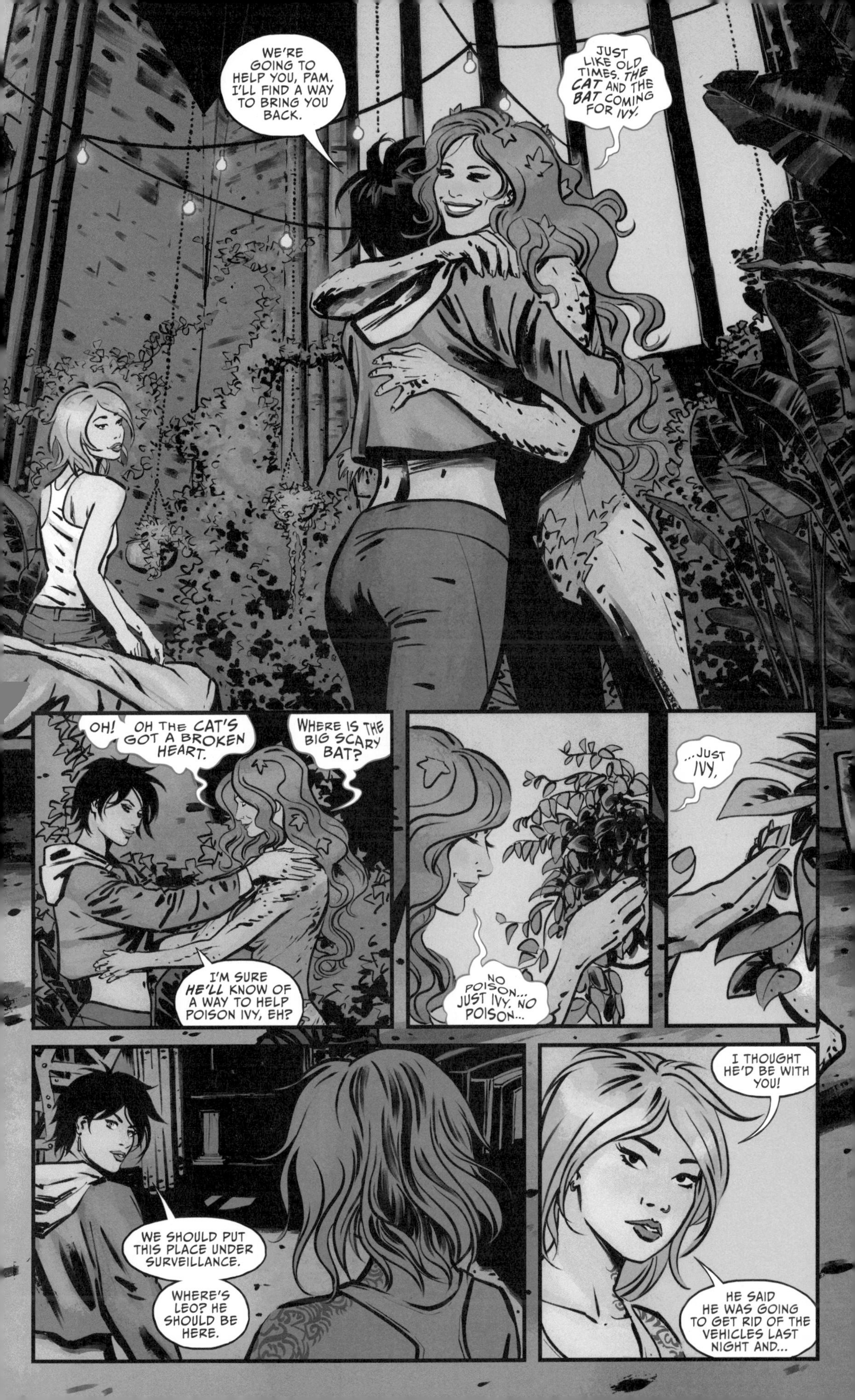
WE'RE GOING TO HELP YOU, PAM. I'LL FIND A WAY TO BRING YOU BACK.
JUST LIKE OLD TIMES. THE CAT AND THE BAT COMING FOR IVY.
OH!
OH THE CAT'S GOT A BROKEN HEART.
WHERE IS THE BIG SCARY BAT?
I'M SURE HE'LL KNOW OF A WAY TO HELP POISON IVY, EH?
NO POISON... JUST IVY. NO POISON...
...JUST IVY.
WE SHOULD PUT THIS PLACE UNDER SURVEILLANCE.
WHERE'S LEO? HE SHOULD BE HERE.
I THOUGHT HE'D BE WITH YOU!
HE SAID HE WAS GOING TO GET RID OF THE VEHICLES LAST NIGHT AND...

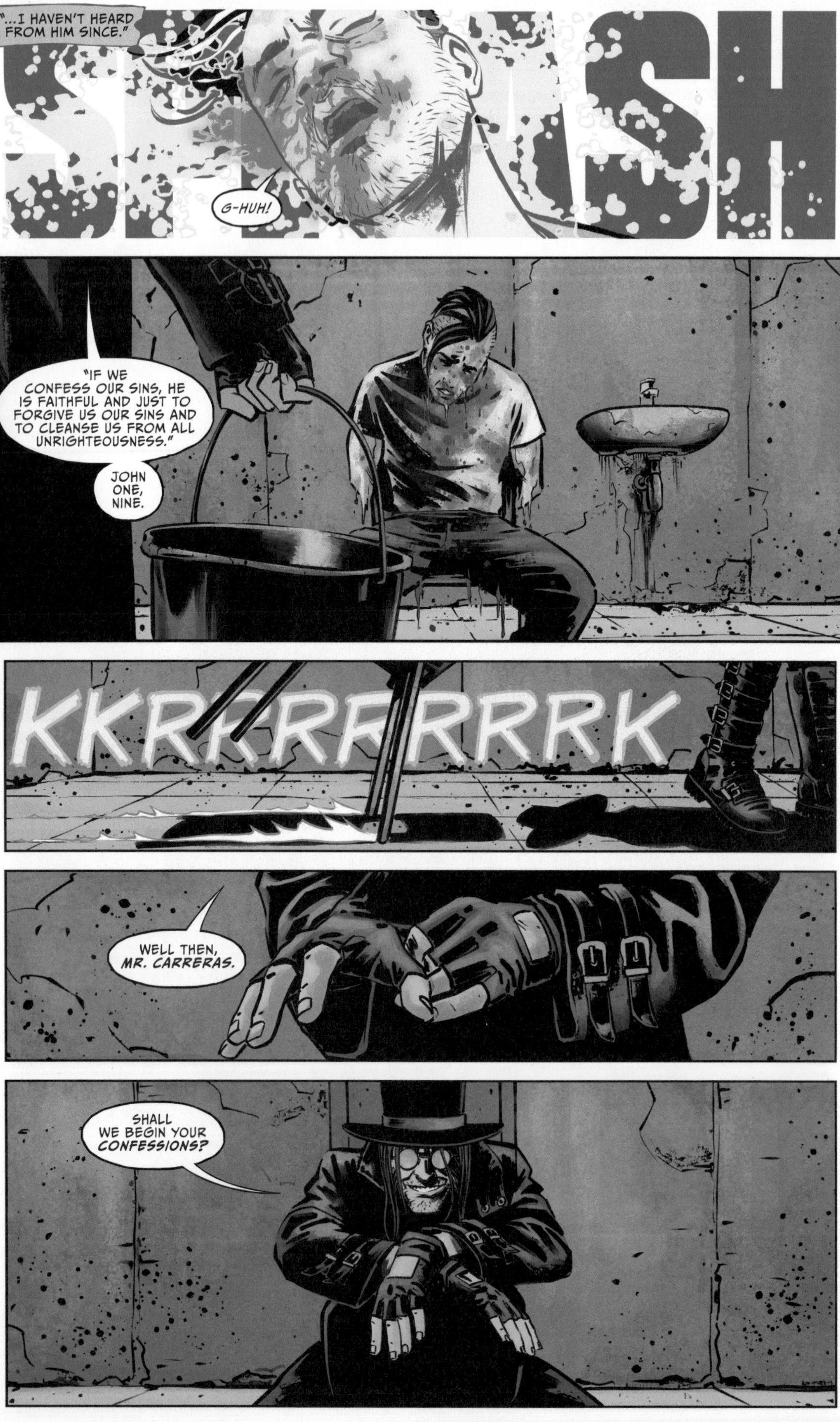
"...I HAVEN'T HEARD FROM HIM SINCE."
G-HUH!
"IF WE CONFESS OUR SINS, HE IS FAITHFUL AND JUST TO FORGIVE US OUR SINS AND TO CLEANSE US FROM ALL UNRIGHTEOUSNESS."
JOHN ONE, NINE.
KKRRRRRRRK
WELL THEN, *MR. CARRERAS.*
SHALL WE BEGIN YOUR *CONFESSIONS?*

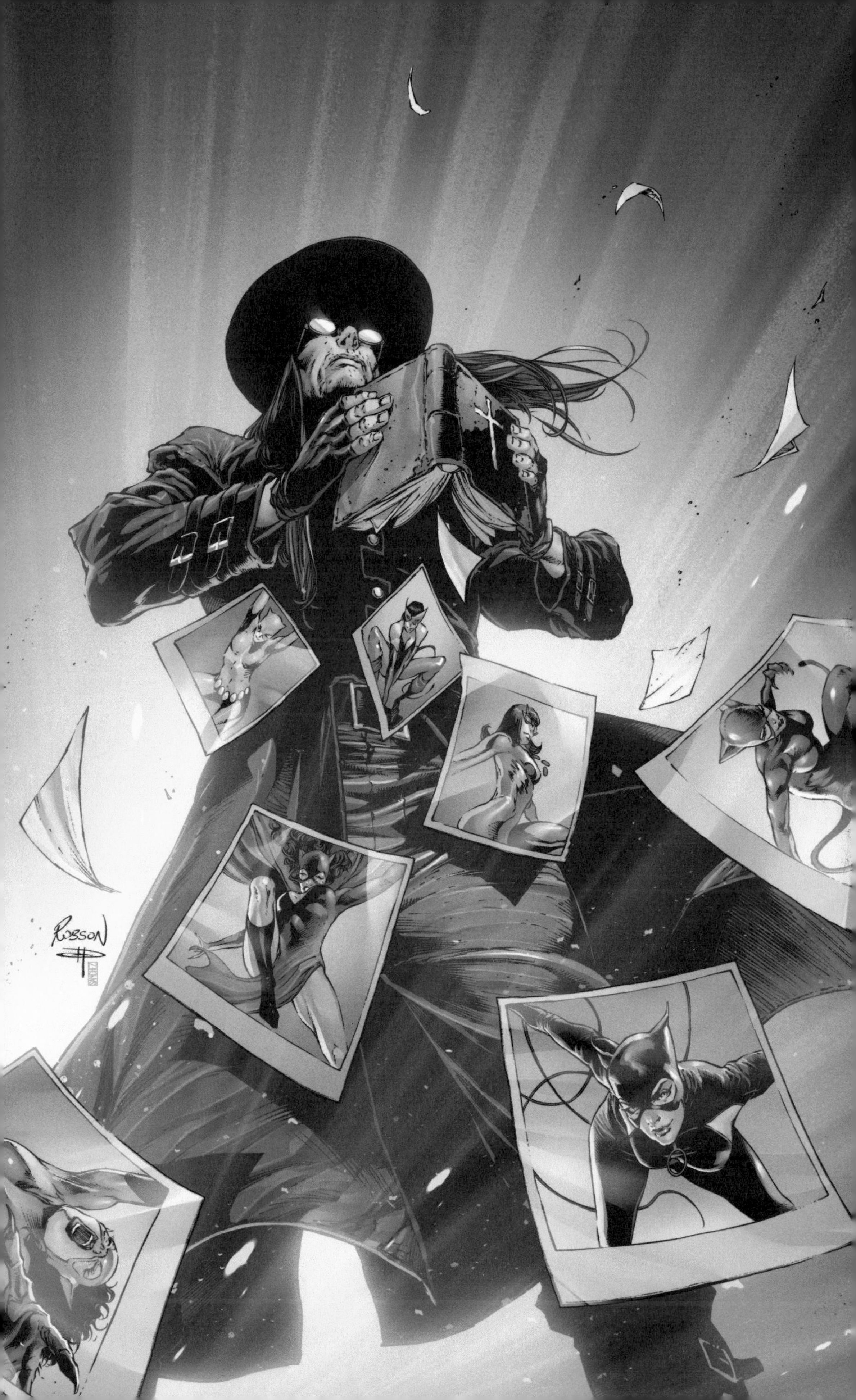
ROBSON

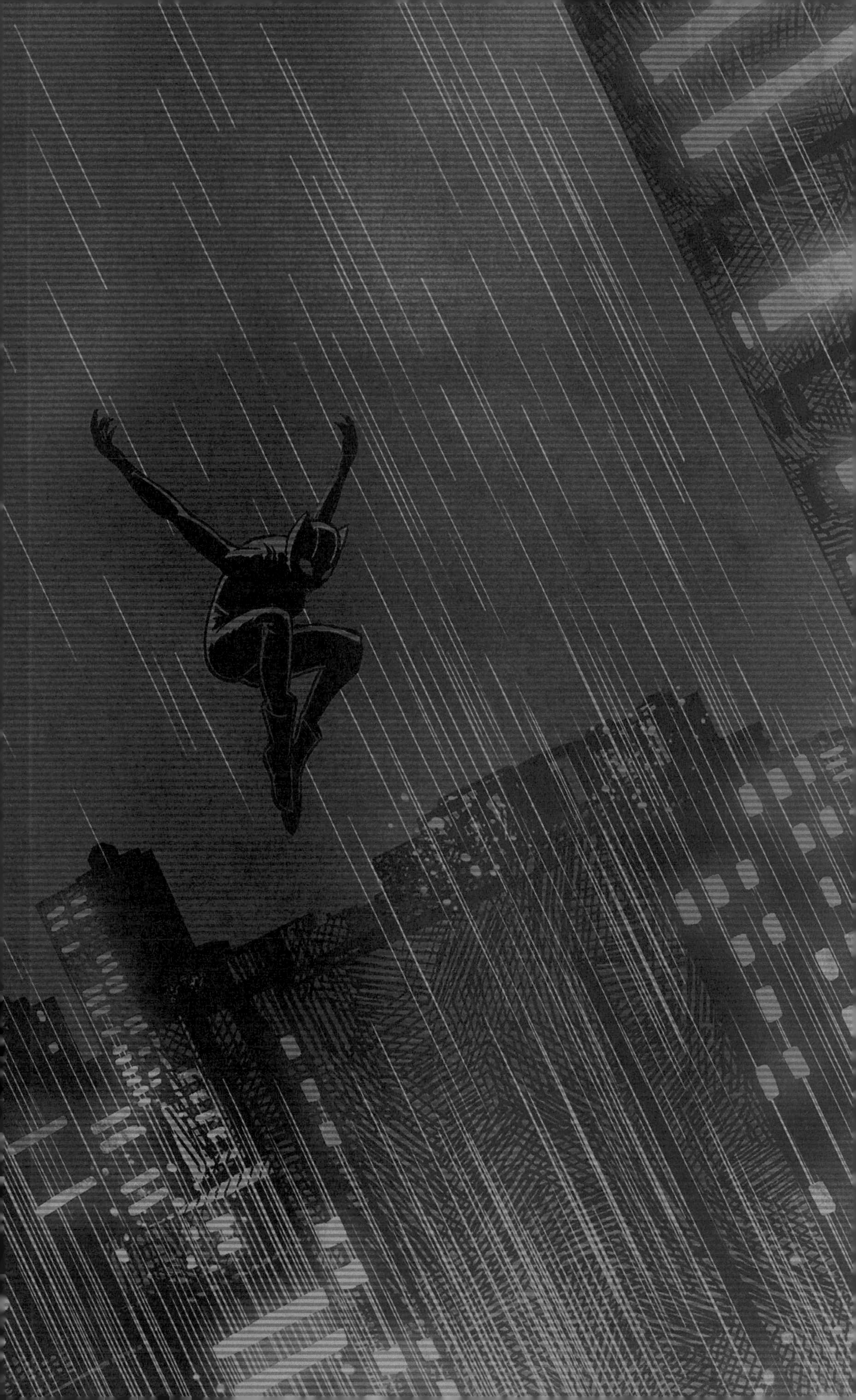

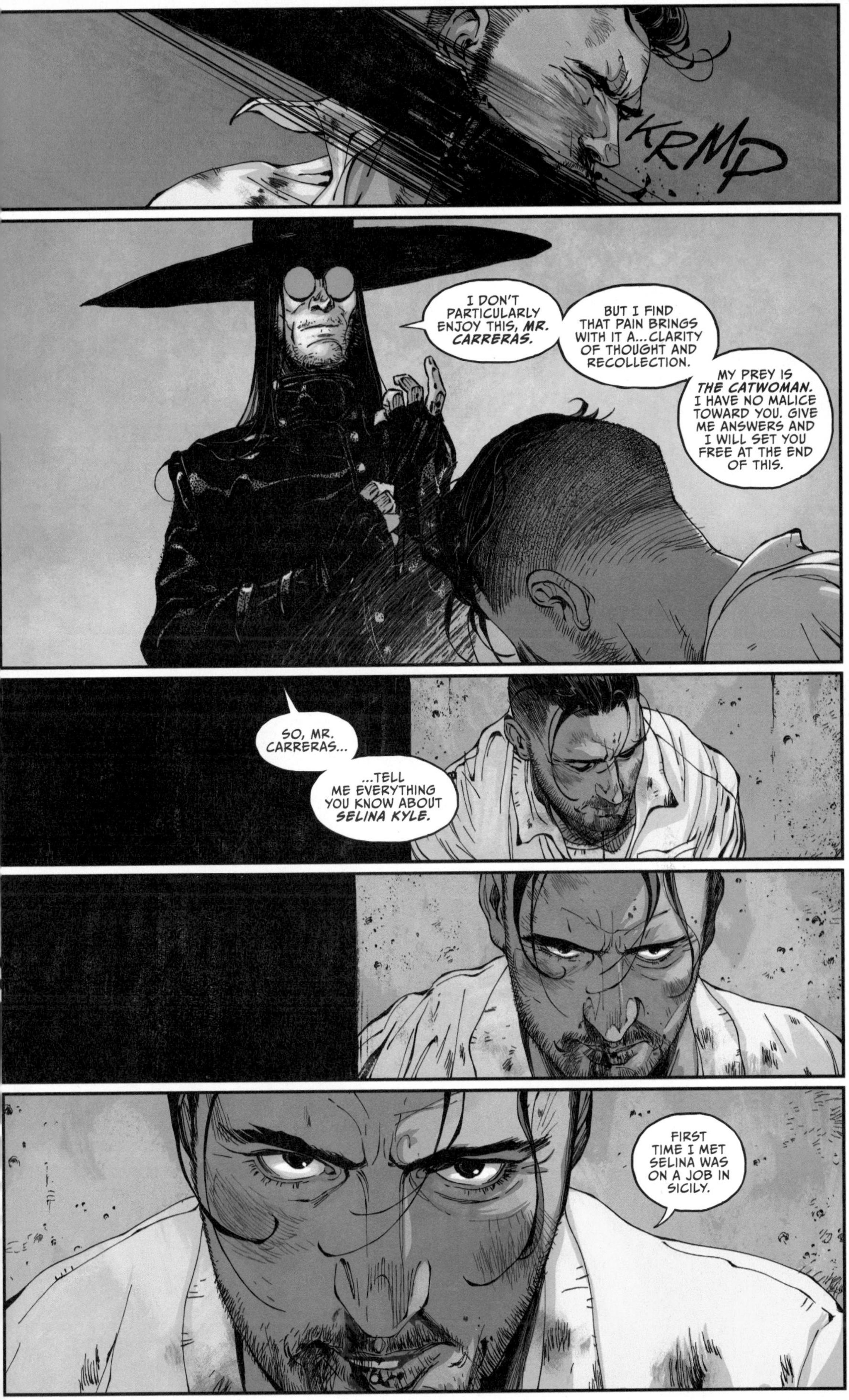
KRMP
I DON'T PARTICULARLY ENJOY THIS, MR. CARRERAS.
BUT I FIND THAT PAIN BRINGS WITH IT A...CLARITY OF THOUGHT AND RECOLLECTION.
MY PREY IS THE CATWOMAN. I HAVE NO MALICE TOWARD YOU. GIVE ME ANSWERS AND I WILL SET YOU FREE AT THE END OF THIS.
SO, MR. CARRERAS...
...TELL ME EVERYTHING YOU KNOW ABOUT SELINA KYLE.
FIRST TIME I MET SELINA WAS ON A JOB IN SICILY.

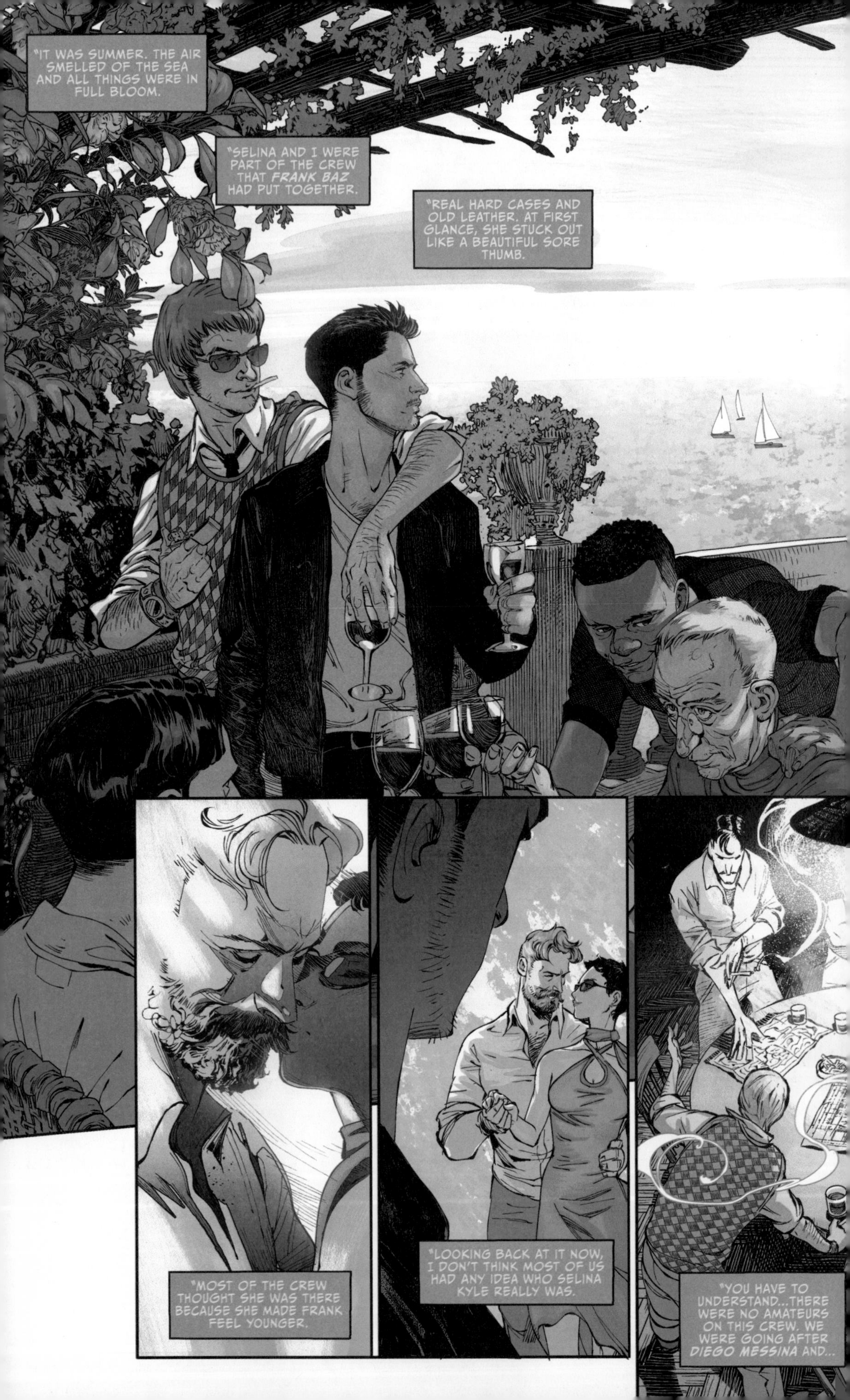
"IT WAS SUMMER. THE AIR SMELLED OF THE SEA AND ALL THINGS WERE IN FULL BLOOM.
"SELINA AND I WERE PART OF THE CREW THAT *FRANK BAZ* HAD PUT TOGETHER.
"REAL HARD CASES AND OLD LEATHER. AT FIRST GLANCE, SHE STUCK OUT LIKE A BEAUTIFUL SORE THUMB.
"MOST OF THE CREW THOUGHT SHE WAS THERE BECAUSE SHE MADE FRANK FEEL YOUNGER.
"LOOKING BACK AT IT NOW, I DON'T THINK MOST OF US HAD ANY IDEA WHO SELINA KYLE REALLY WAS.
"YOU HAVE TO UNDERSTAND...THERE WERE NO AMATEURS ON THIS CREW. WE WERE GOING AFTER *DIEGO MESSINA* AND...

EVERYTHING YOU KNOW ABOUT SELINA KYLE

RAM V WRITER **EVAN CAGLE** ARTIST
JORDIE BELLAIRE COLORIST **TOM NAPOLITANO** LETTERER
ROBSON ROCHA, DANIEL HENRIQUES + ALEJANDRO SÁNCHEZ COVER
JENNY FRISON VARIANT COVER **BEN MEARES** ASSISTANT EDITOR
JESSICA CHEN EDITOR **BEN ABERNATHY** GROUP EDITOR

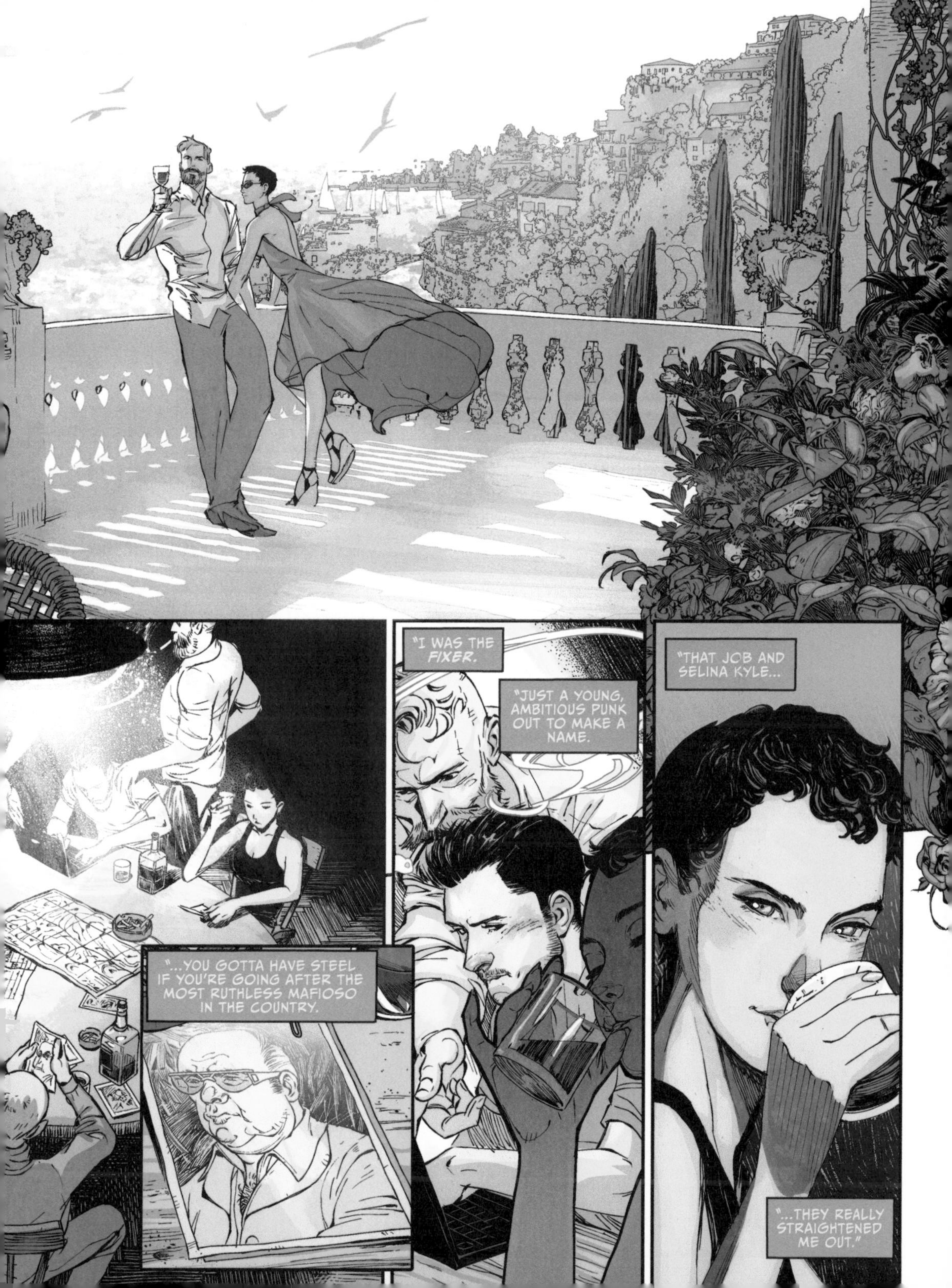
"...YOU GOTTA HAVE STEEL IF YOU'RE GOING AFTER THE MOST RUTHLESS MAFIOSO IN THE COUNTRY.
"I WAS THE *FIXER.*
"JUST A YOUNG, AMBITIOUS PUNK OUT TO MAKE A NAME.
"THAT JOB AND SELINA KYLE...
"...THEY REALLY STRAIGHTENED ME OUT."

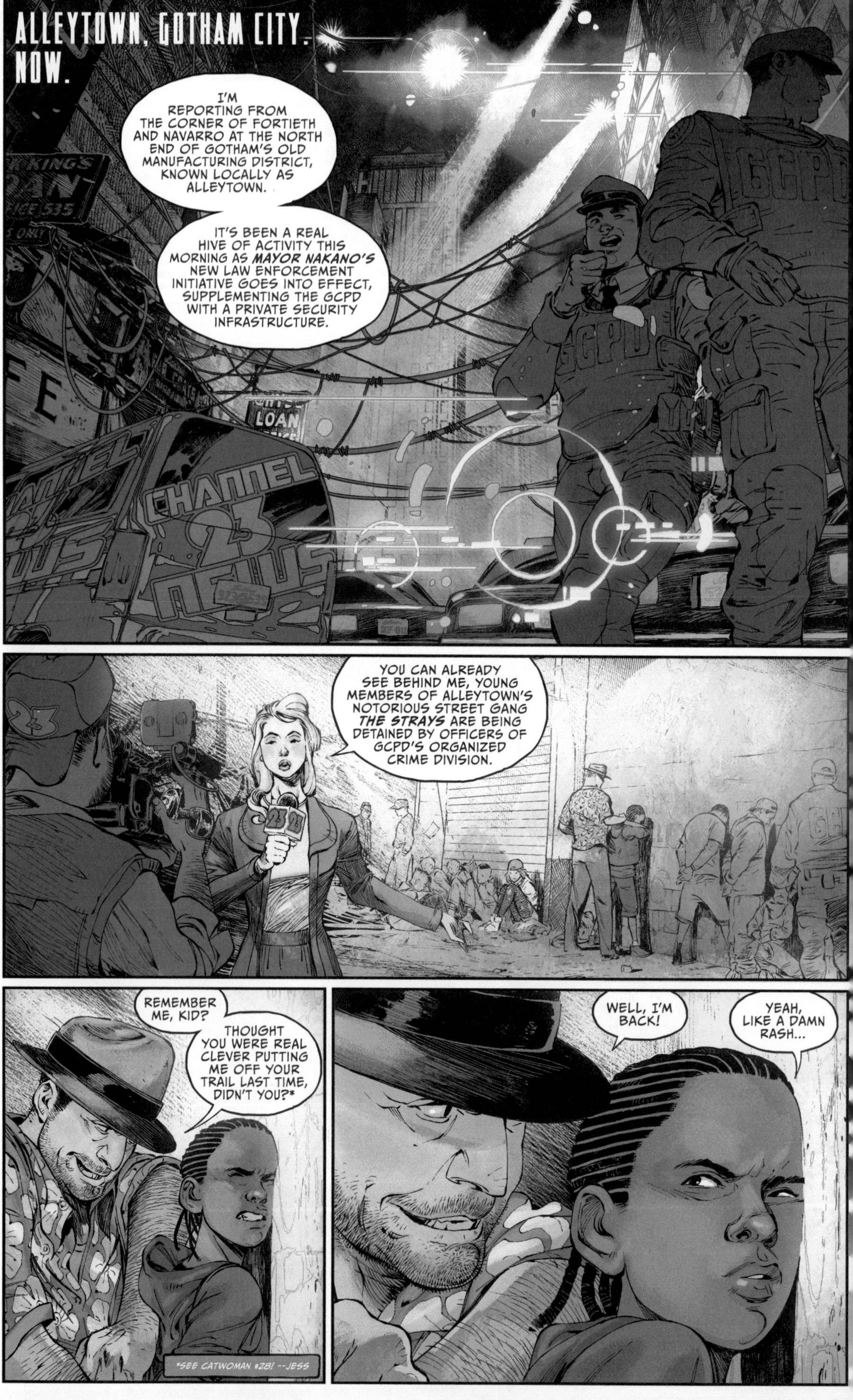
ALLEYTOWN, GOTHAM CITY. NOW.
I'M REPORTING FROM THE CORNER OF FORTIETH AND NAVARRO AT THE NORTH END OF GOTHAM'S OLD MANUFACTURING DISTRICT, KNOWN LOCALLY AS ALLEYTOWN.
IT'S BEEN A REAL HIVE OF ACTIVITY THIS MORNING AS MAYOR NAKANO'S NEW LAW ENFORCEMENT INITIATIVE GOES INTO EFFECT, SUPPLEMENTING THE GCPD WITH A PRIVATE SECURITY INFRASTRUCTURE.
GCPD
CHANNEL 23 NEWS
LOAN
YOU CAN ALREADY SEE BEHIND ME, YOUNG MEMBERS OF ALLEYTOWN'S NOTORIOUS STREET GANG THE STRAYS ARE BEING DETAINED BY OFFICERS OF GCPD'S ORGANIZED CRIME DIVISION.
REMEMBER ME, KID?
THOUGHT YOU WERE REAL CLEVER PUTTING ME OFF YOUR TRAIL LAST TIME, DIDN'T YOU?*
*SEE CATWOMAN #28! --JESS
WELL, I'M BACK!
YEAH, LIKE A DAMN RASH...

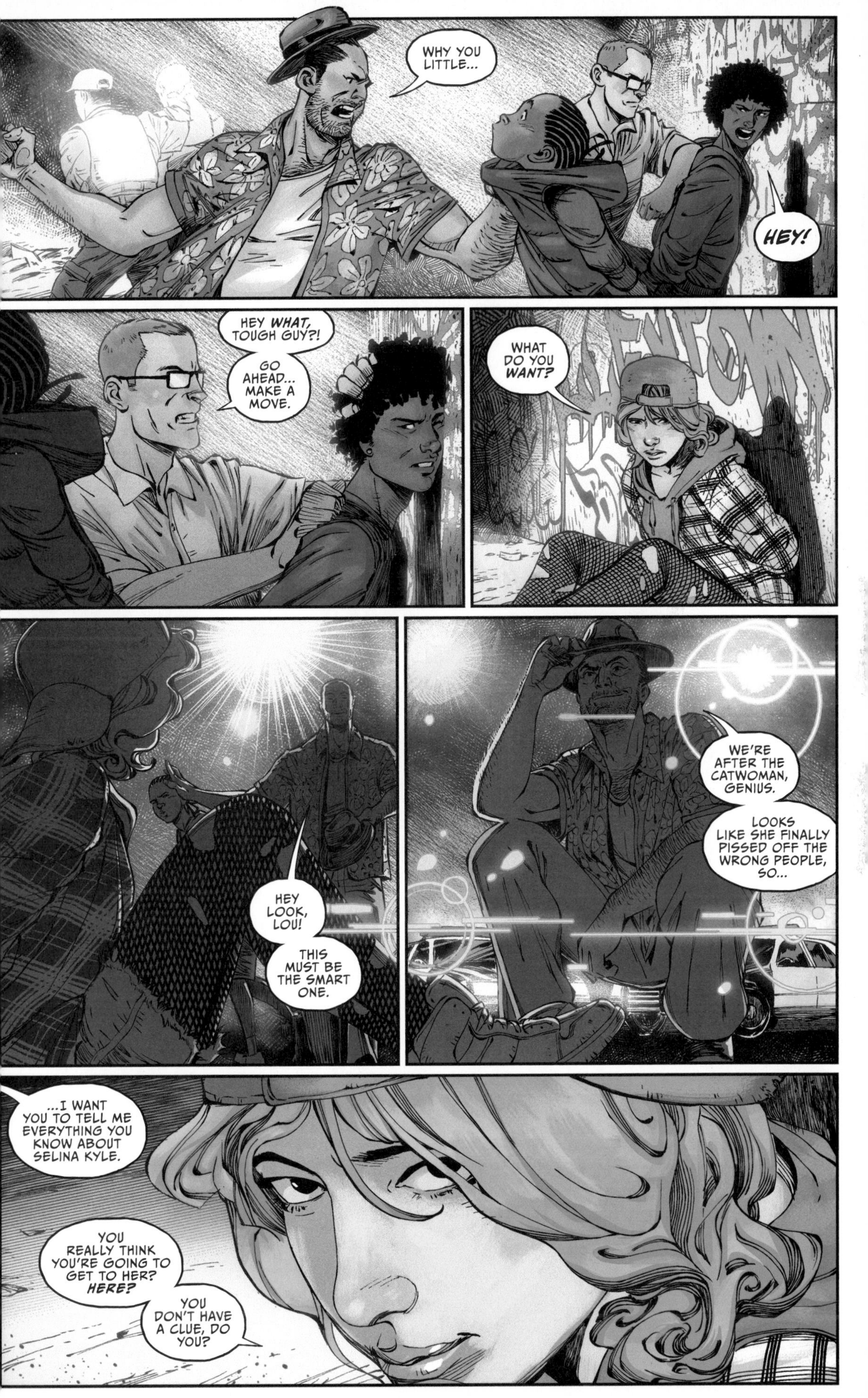
WHY YOU LITTLE...
HEY!
HEY *WHAT*, TOUGH GUY?!
GO AHEAD... MAKE A MOVE.
WHAT DO YOU *WANT?*
HEY LOOK, LOU!
THIS MUST BE THE SMART ONE.
WE'RE AFTER THE CATWOMAN, GENIUS.
LOOKS LIKE SHE FINALLY PISSED OFF THE WRONG PEOPLE, SO...
...I WANT YOU TO TELL ME EVERYTHING YOU KNOW ABOUT SELINA KYLE.
YOU REALLY THINK YOU'RE GOING TO GET TO HER? *HERE?*
YOU DON'T HAVE A CLUE, DO YOU?

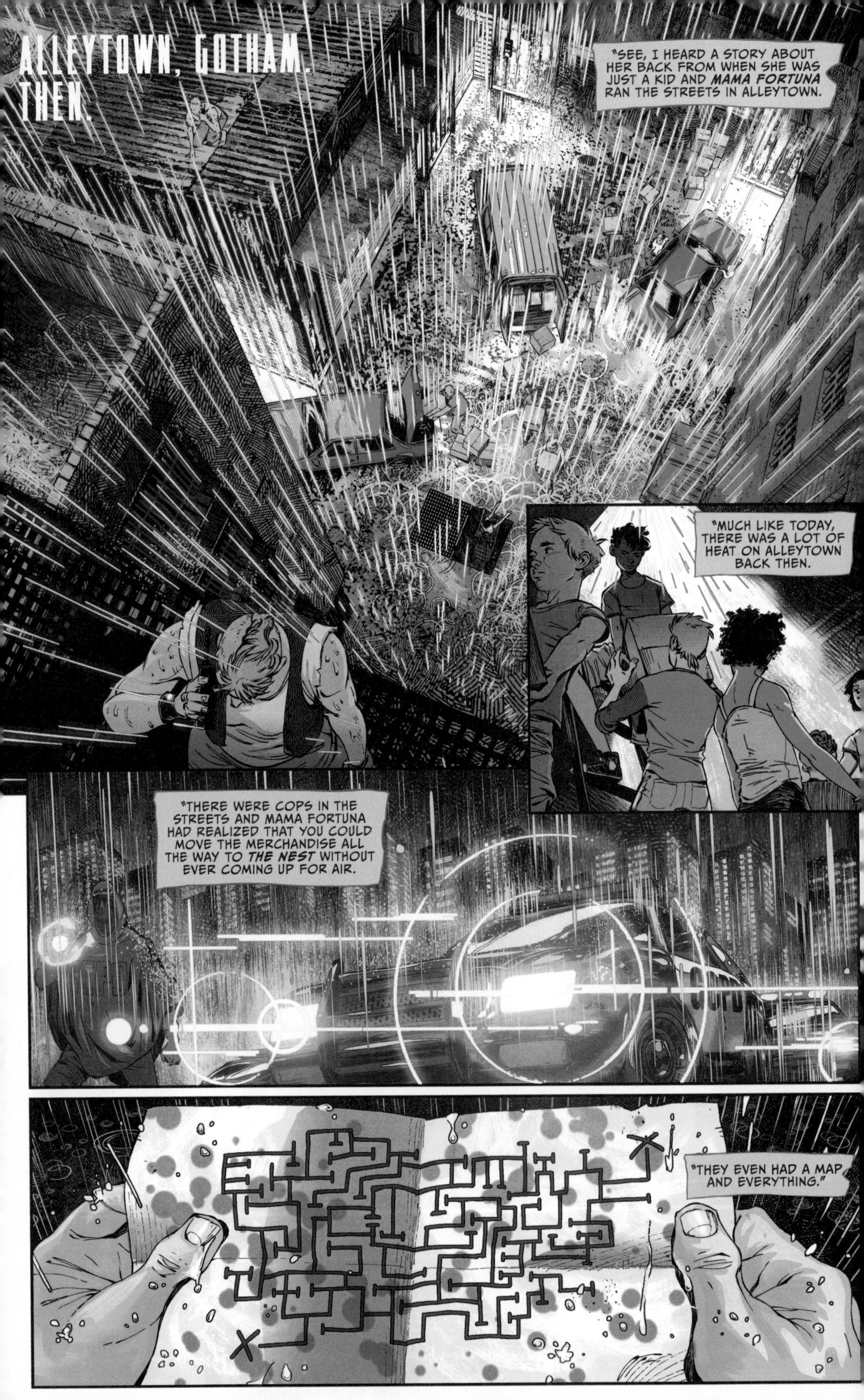
ALLEYTOWN, GOTHAM. THEN.
"SEE, I HEARD A STORY ABOUT HER BACK FROM WHEN SHE WAS JUST A KID AND MAMA FORTUNA RAN THE STREETS IN ALLEYTOWN.
"MUCH LIKE TODAY, THERE WAS A LOT OF HEAT ON ALLEYTOWN BACK THEN.
"THERE WERE COPS IN THE STREETS AND MAMA FORTUNA HAD REALIZED THAT YOU COULD MOVE THE MERCHANDISE ALL THE WAY TO THE NEST WITHOUT EVER COMING UP FOR AIR.
"THEY EVEN HAD A MAP AND EVERYTHING."

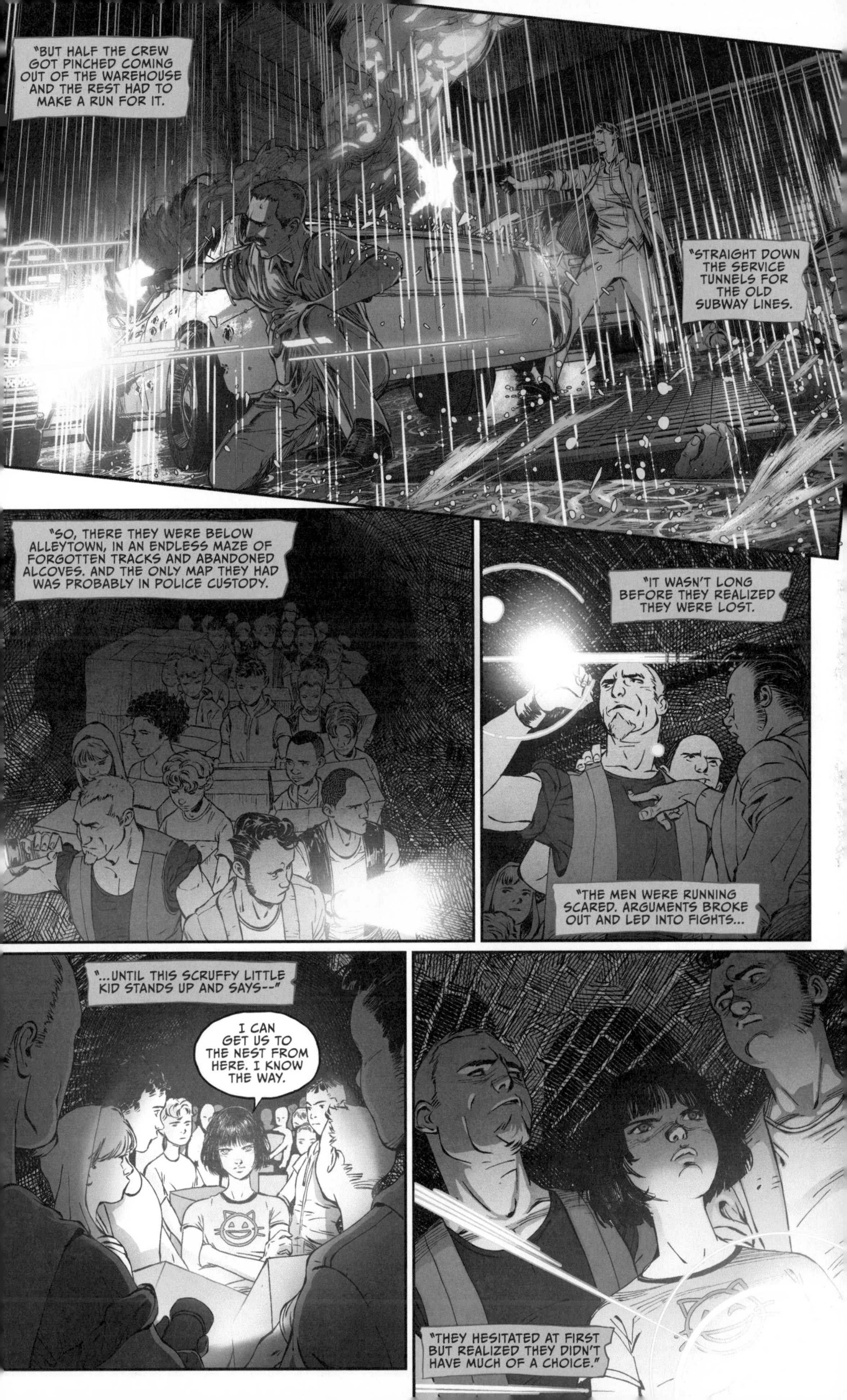
"BUT HALF THE CREW GOT PINCHED COMING OUT OF THE WAREHOUSE AND THE REST HAD TO MAKE A RUN FOR IT.
"STRAIGHT DOWN THE SERVICE TUNNELS FOR THE OLD SUBWAY LINES.
"SO, THERE THEY WERE BELOW ALLEYTOWN, IN AN ENDLESS MAZE OF FORGOTTEN TRACKS AND ABANDONED ALCOVES. AND THE ONLY MAP THEY HAD WAS PROBABLY IN POLICE CUSTODY.
"IT WASN'T LONG BEFORE THEY REALIZED THEY WERE LOST.
"THE MEN WERE RUNNING SCARED. ARGUMENTS BROKE OUT AND LED INTO FIGHTS...
"...UNTIL THIS SCRUFFY LITTLE KID STANDS UP AND SAYS--"
I CAN GET US TO THE NEST FROM HERE. I KNOW THE WAY.
"THEY HESITATED AT FIRST BUT REALIZED THEY DIDN'T HAVE MUCH OF A CHOICE."

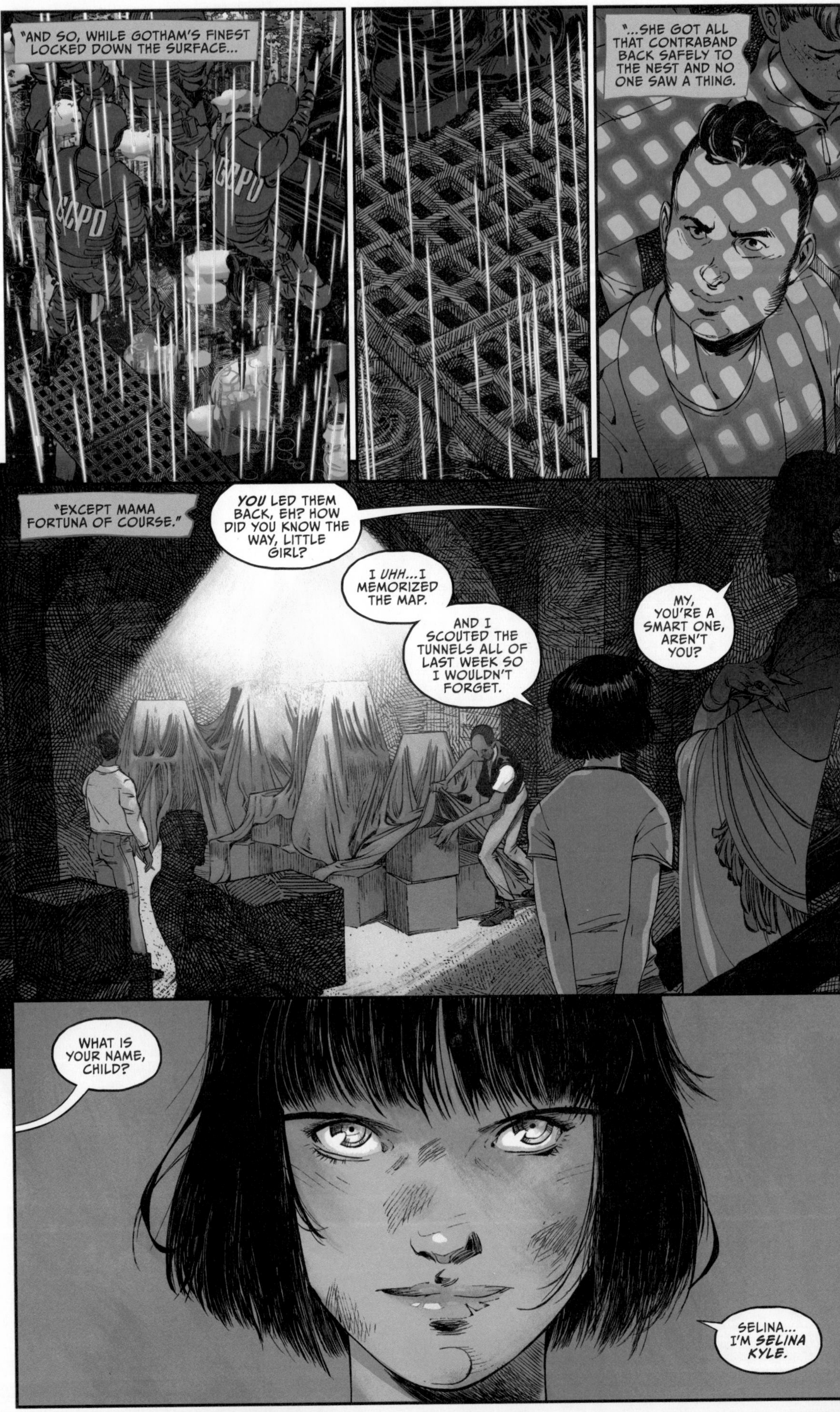
"AND SO, WHILE GOTHAM'S FINEST LOCKED DOWN THE SURFACE...
GCPD
GCPD
"...SHE GOT ALL THAT CONTRABAND BACK SAFELY TO THE NEST AND NO ONE SAW A THING.
"EXCEPT MAMA FORTUNA OF COURSE."
YOU LED THEM BACK, EH? HOW DID YOU KNOW THE WAY, LITTLE GIRL?
I UHH...I MEMORIZED THE MAP.
AND I SCOUTED THE TUNNELS ALL OF LAST WEEK SO I WOULDN'T FORGET.
MY, YOU'RE A SMART ONE, AREN'T YOU?
WHAT IS YOUR NAME, CHILD?
SELINA... I'M SELINA KYLE.

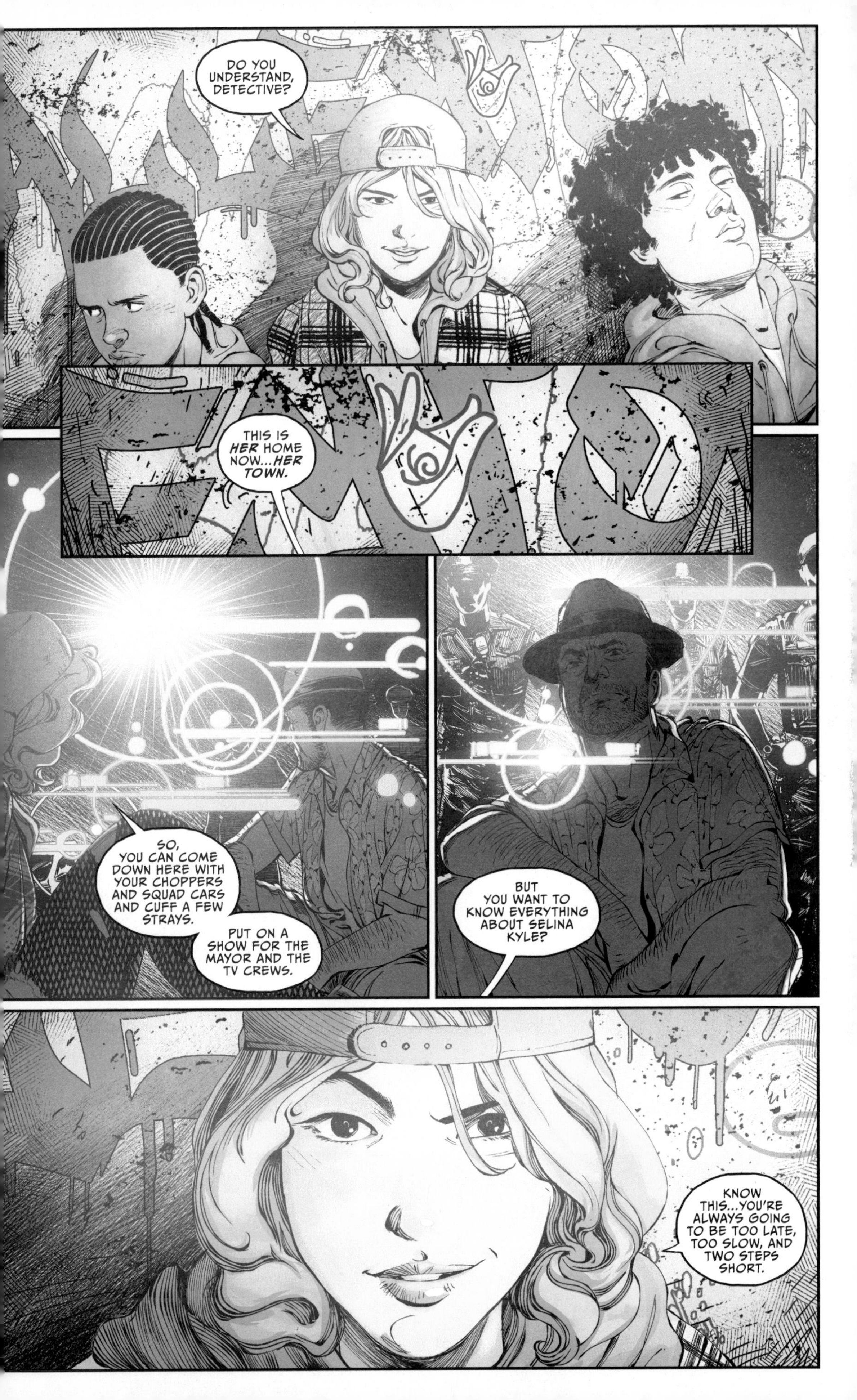
DO YOU UNDERSTAND, DETECTIVE?
THIS IS *HER* HOME NOW...*HER TOWN.*
SO, YOU CAN COME DOWN HERE WITH YOUR CHOPPERS AND SQUAD CARS AND CUFF A FEW STRAYS.
PUT ON A SHOW FOR THE MAYOR AND THE TV CREWS.
BUT YOU WANT TO KNOW EVERYTHING ABOUT SELINA KYLE?
KNOW THIS...YOU'RE ALWAYS GOING TO BE TOO LATE, TOO SLOW, AND TWO STEPS SHORT.

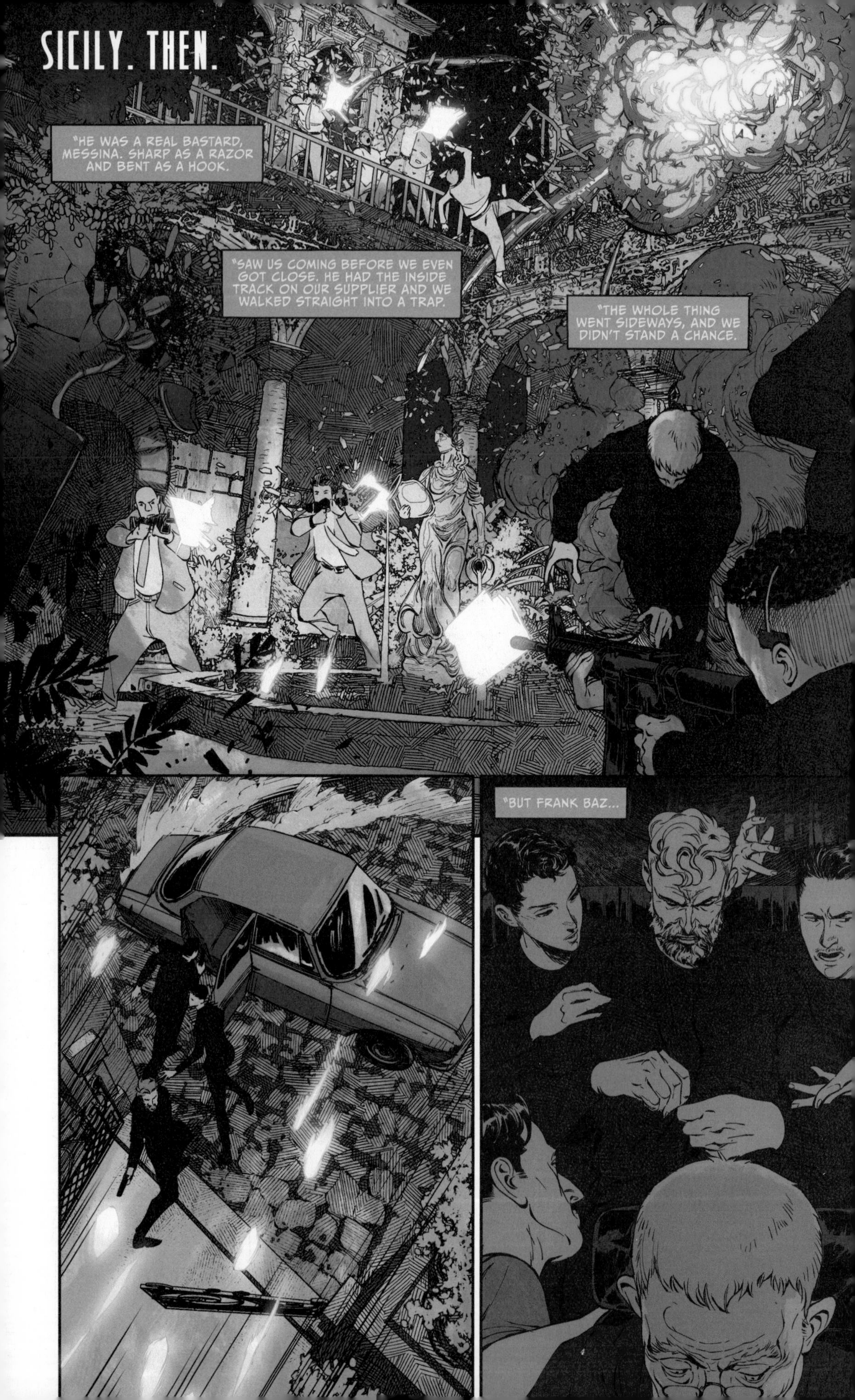
SICILY. THEN.
"HE WAS A REAL BASTARD, MESSINA. SHARP AS A RAZOR AND BENT AS A HOOK.
"SAW US COMING BEFORE WE EVEN GOT CLOSE. HE HAD THE INSIDE TRACK ON OUR SUPPLIER AND WE WALKED STRAIGHT INTO A TRAP.
"THE WHOLE THING WENT SIDEWAYS, AND WE DIDN'T STAND A CHANCE.
"BUT FRANK BAZ...

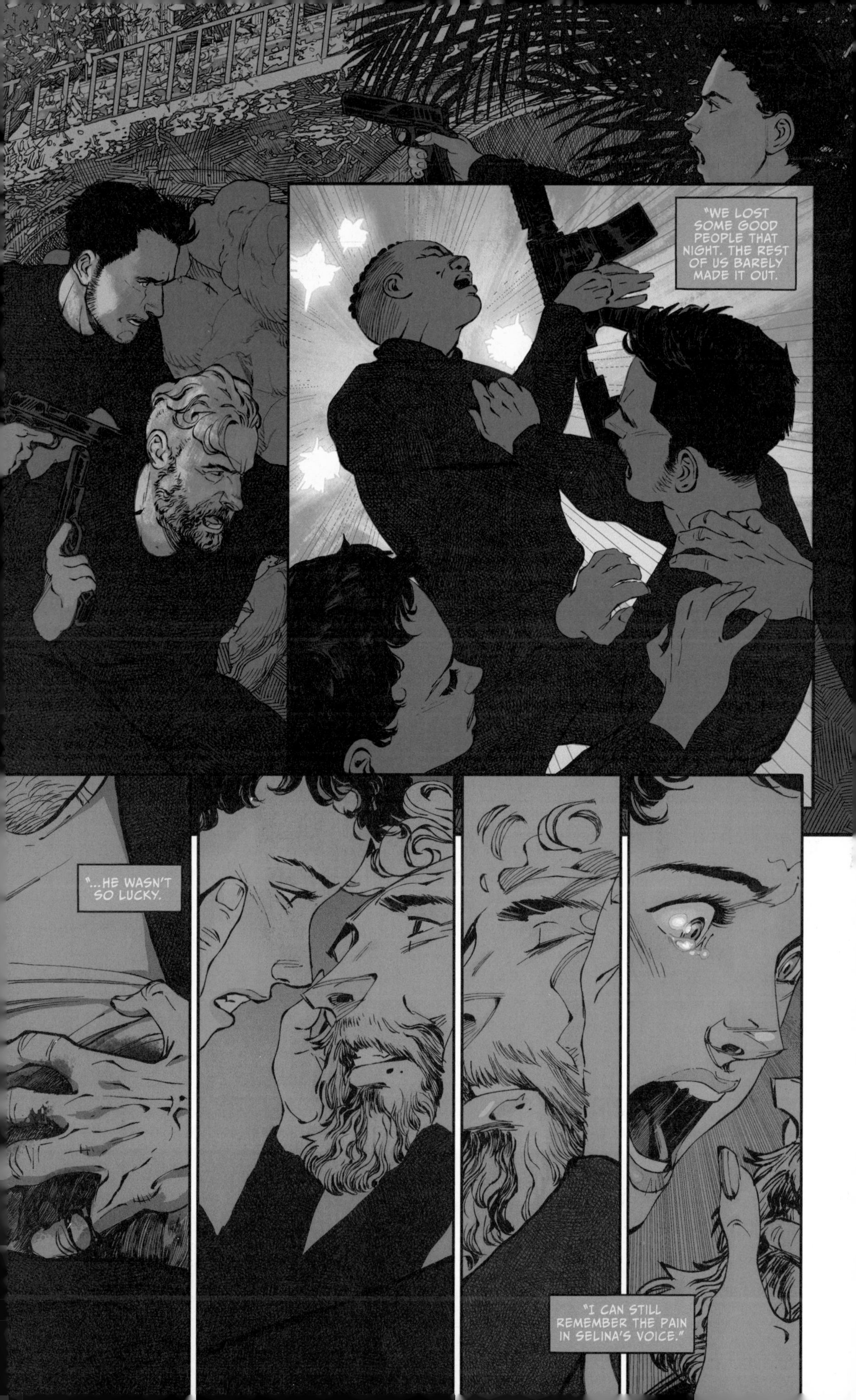
"WE LOST SOME GOOD PEOPLE THAT NIGHT. THE REST OF US BARELY MADE IT OUT.
"...HE WASN'T SO LUCKY.
"I CAN STILL REMEMBER THE PAIN IN SELINA'S VOICE."

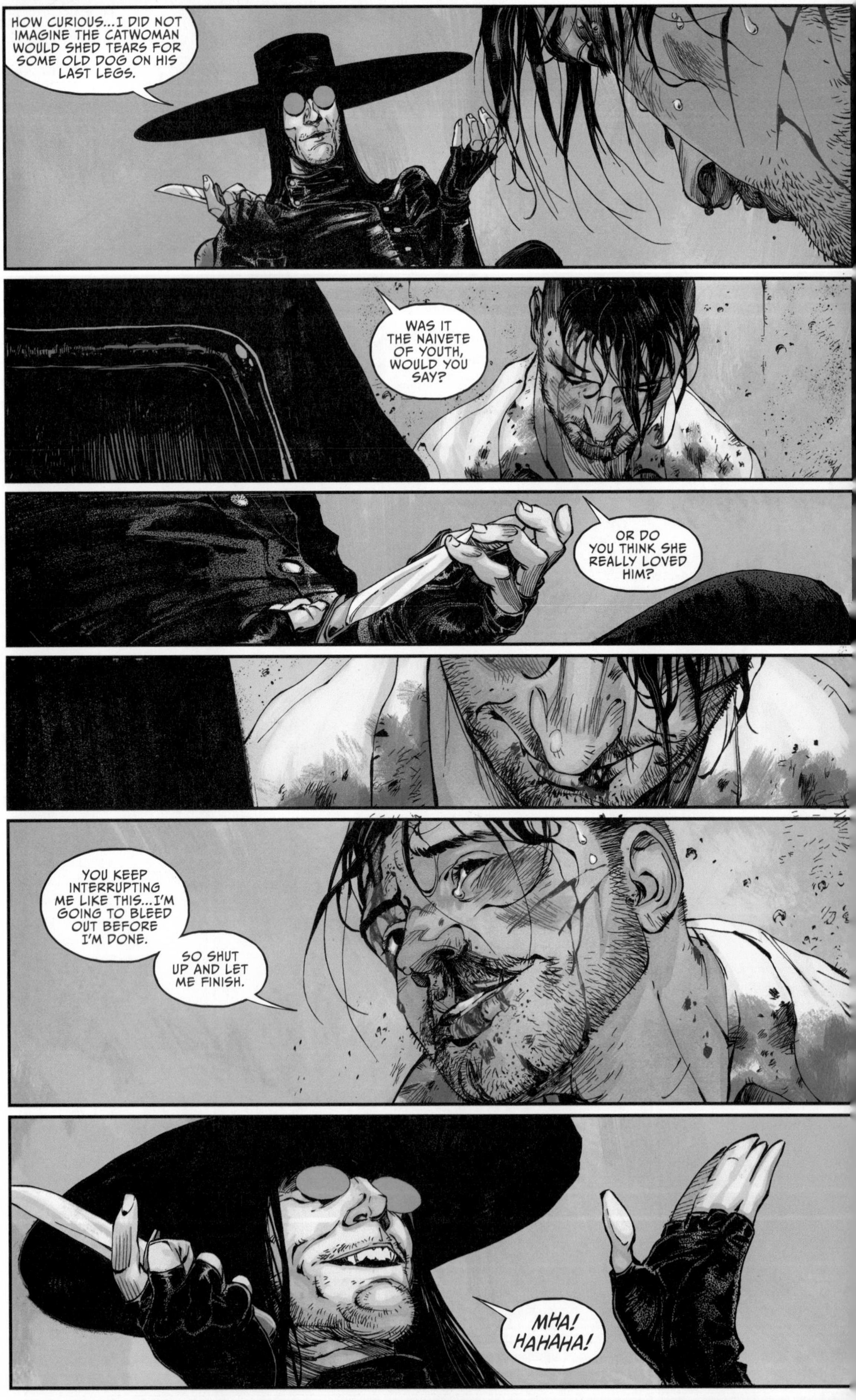

HOW CURIOUS...I DID NOT IMAGINE THE CATWOMAN WOULD SHED TEARS FOR SOME OLD DOG ON HIS LAST LEGS.
WAS IT THE NAIVETE OF YOUTH, WOULD YOU SAY?
OR DO YOU THINK SHE REALLY LOVED HIM?
YOU KEEP INTERRUPTING ME LIKE THIS...I'M GOING TO BLEED OUT BEFORE I'M DONE.
SO SHUT UP AND LET ME FINISH.
MHA! HAHAHA!

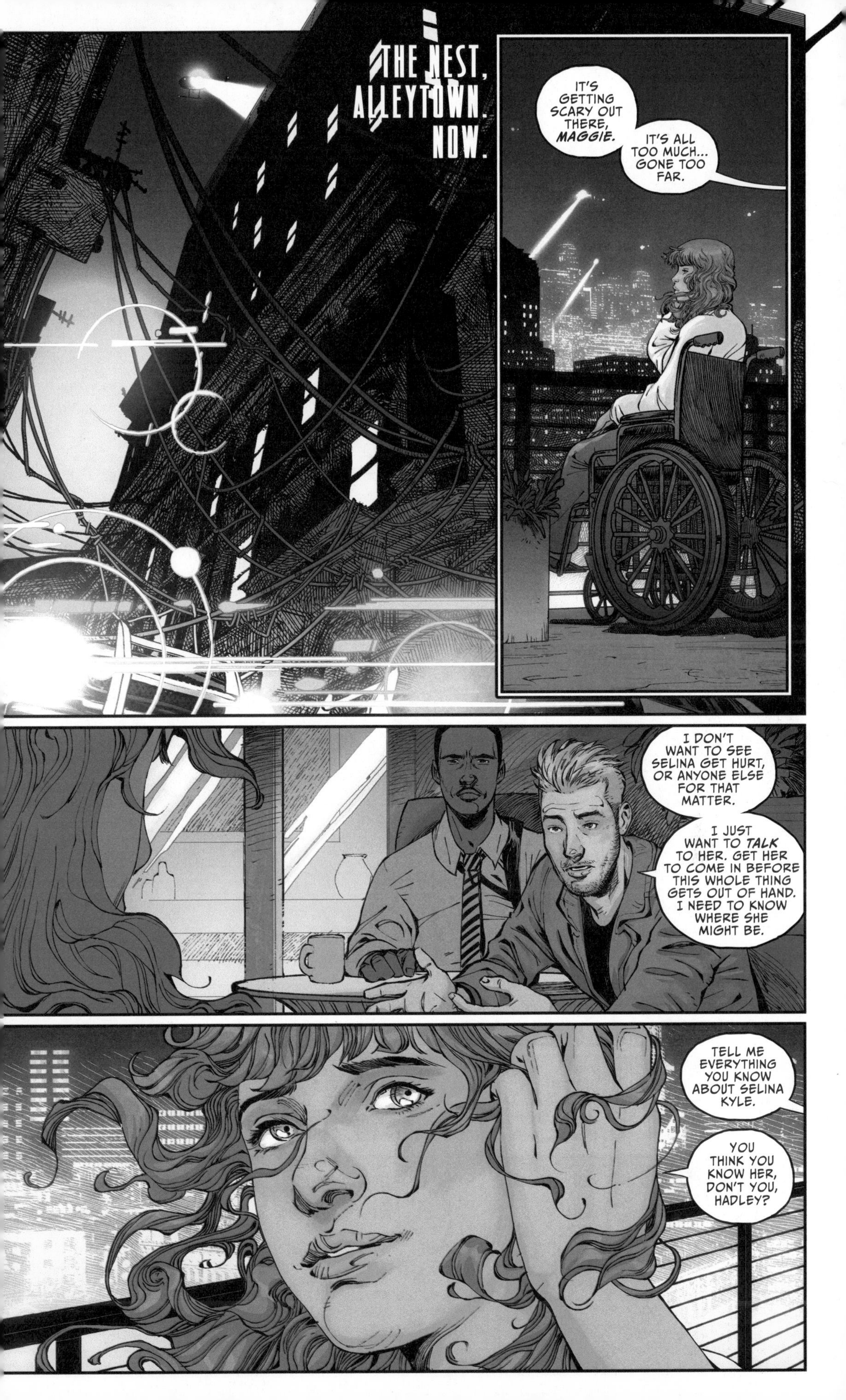
THE NEST, ALLEYTOWN. NOW.
IT'S GETTING SCARY OUT THERE, MAGGIE.
IT'S ALL TOO MUCH... GONE TOO FAR.
I DON'T WANT TO SEE SELINA GET HURT, OR ANYONE ELSE FOR THAT MATTER.
I JUST WANT TO TALK TO HER. GET HER TO COME IN BEFORE THIS WHOLE THING GETS OUT OF HAND. I NEED TO KNOW WHERE SHE MIGHT BE.
TELL ME EVERYTHING YOU KNOW ABOUT SELINA KYLE.
YOU THINK YOU KNOW HER, DON'T YOU, HADLEY?

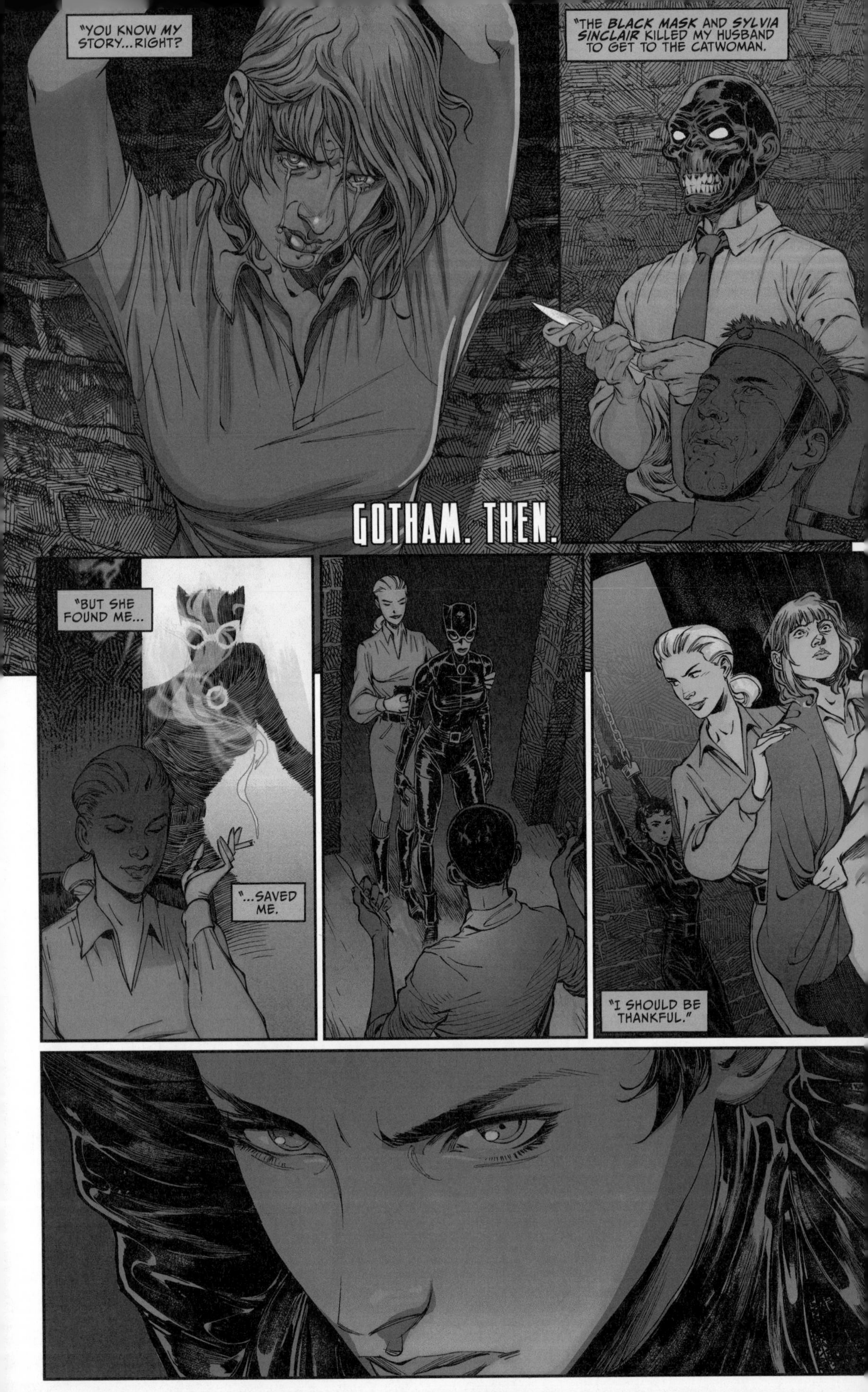
"YOU KNOW MY STORY...RIGHT?
"THE BLACK MASK AND SYLVIA SINCLAIR KILLED MY HUSBAND TO GET TO THE CATWOMAN.
GOTHAM. THEN.
"BUT SHE FOUND ME...
"...SAVED ME.
"I SHOULD BE THANKFUL."

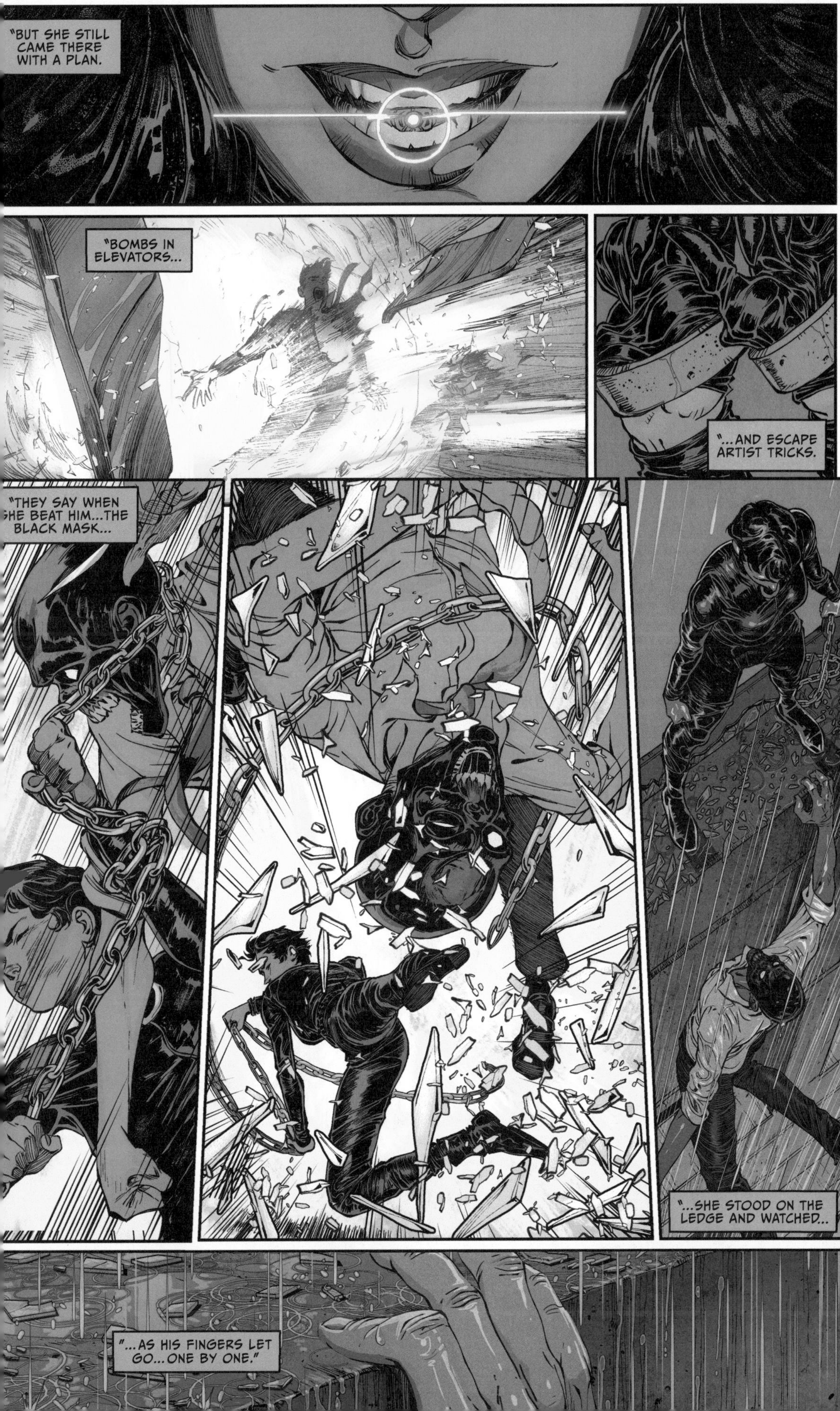
"BUT SHE STILL CAME THERE WITH A PLAN.
"BOMBS IN ELEVATORS...
"...AND ESCAPE ARTIST TRICKS.
"THEY SAY WHEN SHE BEAT HIM...THE BLACK MASK...
"...SHE STOOD ON THE LEDGE AND WATCHED...
"...AS HIS FINGERS LET GO...ONE BY ONE."

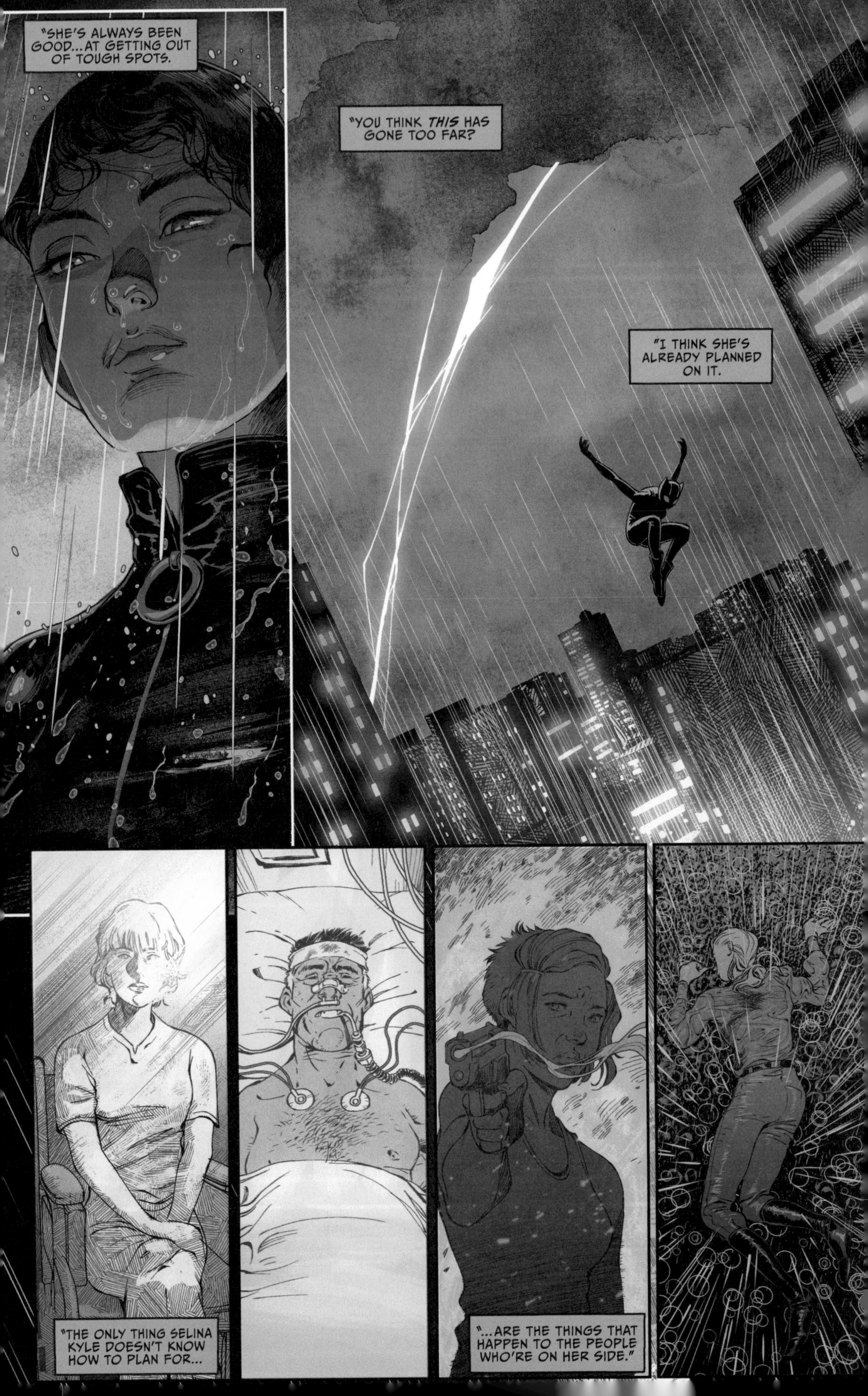
"SHE'S ALWAYS BEEN GOOD...AT GETTING OUT OF TOUGH SPOTS.
"YOU THINK THIS HAS GONE TOO FAR?
"I THINK SHE'S ALREADY PLANNED ON IT.
"THE ONLY THING SELINA KYLE DOESN'T KNOW HOW TO PLAN FOR...
"...ARE THE THINGS THAT HAPPEN TO THE PEOPLE WHO'RE ON HER SIDE."

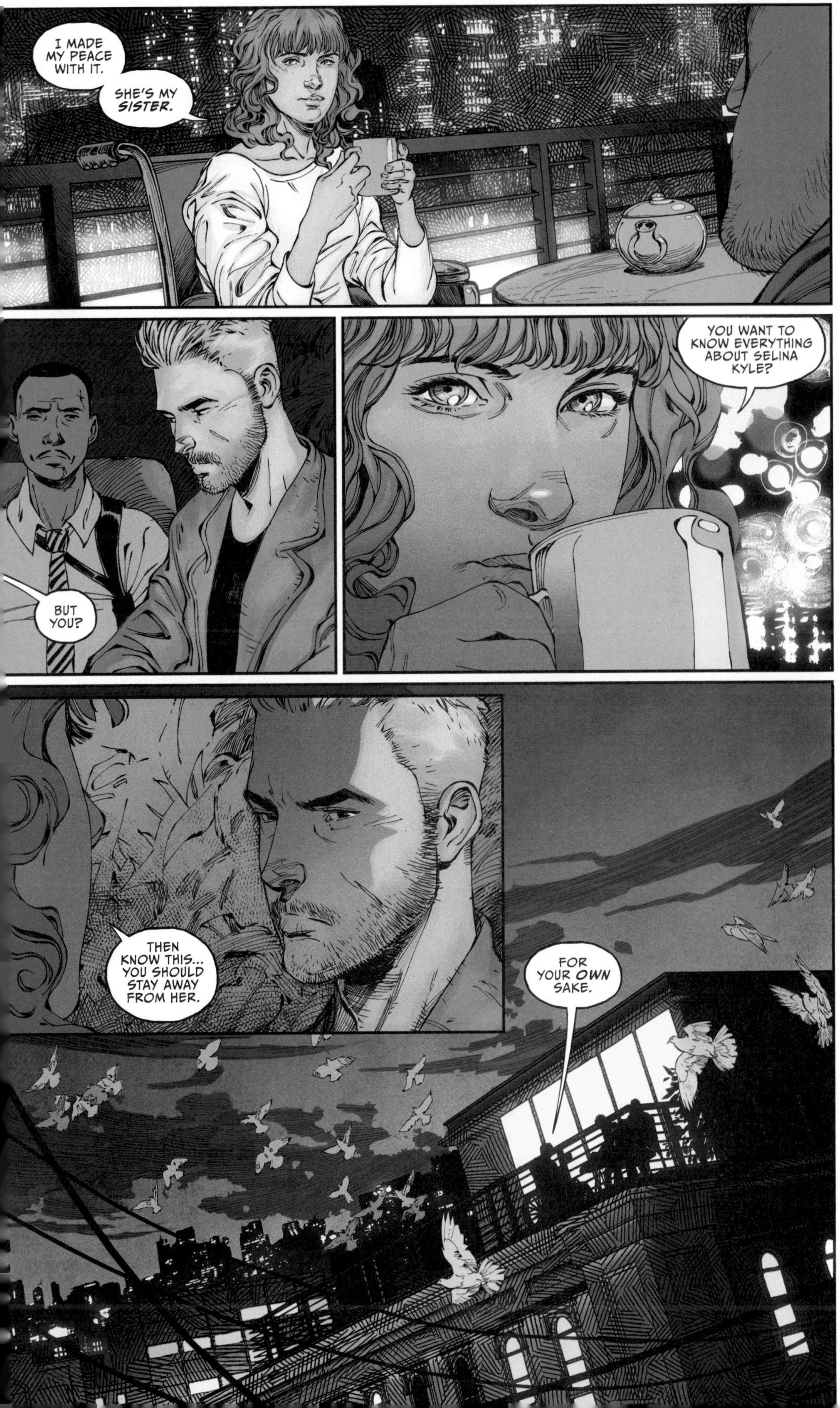
I MADE MY PEACE WITH IT.
SHE'S MY *SISTER.*
YOU WANT TO KNOW EVERYTHING ABOUT SELINA KYLE?
BUT YOU?
THEN KNOW THIS... YOU SHOULD STAY AWAY FROM HER.
FOR YOUR *OWN* SAKE.

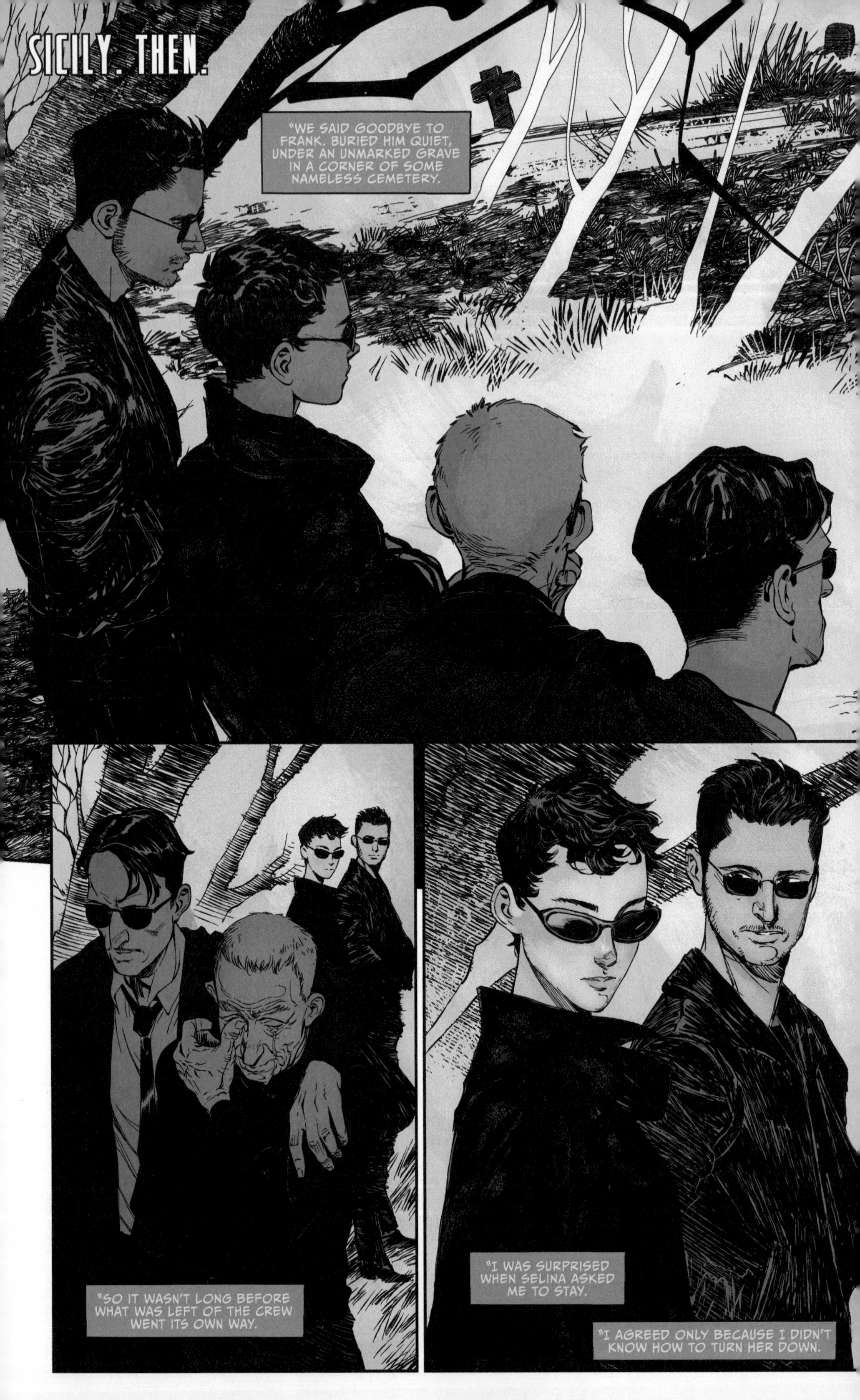
SICILY. THEN.
"WE SAID GOODBYE TO FRANK. BURIED HIM QUIET, UNDER AN UNMARKED GRAVE IN A CORNER OF SOME NAMELESS CEMETERY.
"SO IT WASN'T LONG BEFORE WHAT WAS LEFT OF THE CREW WENT ITS OWN WAY.
"I WAS SURPRISED WHEN SELINA ASKED ME TO STAY.
"I AGREED ONLY BECAUSE I DIDN'T KNOW HOW TO TURN HER DOWN.

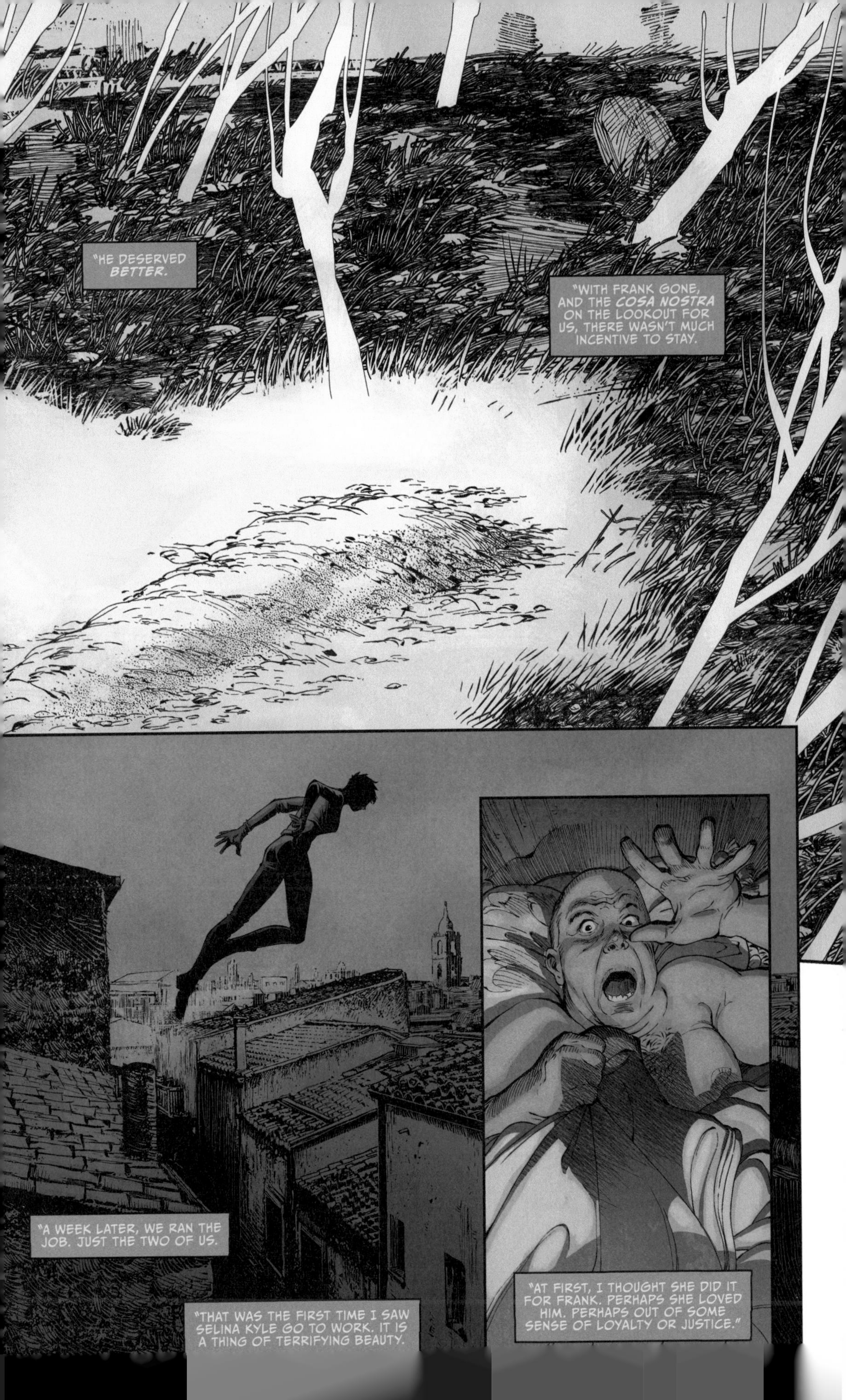
"HE DESERVED BETTER.
"WITH FRANK GONE, AND THE COSA NOSTRA ON THE LOOKOUT FOR US, THERE WASN'T MUCH INCENTIVE TO STAY.
"A WEEK LATER, WE RAN THE JOB. JUST THE TWO OF US.
"THAT WAS THE FIRST TIME I SAW SELINA KYLE GO TO WORK. IT IS A THING OF TERRIFYING BEAUTY.
"AT FIRST, I THOUGHT SHE DID IT FOR FRANK. PERHAPS SHE LOVED HIM. PERHAPS OUT OF SOME SENSE OF LOYALTY OR JUSTICE."

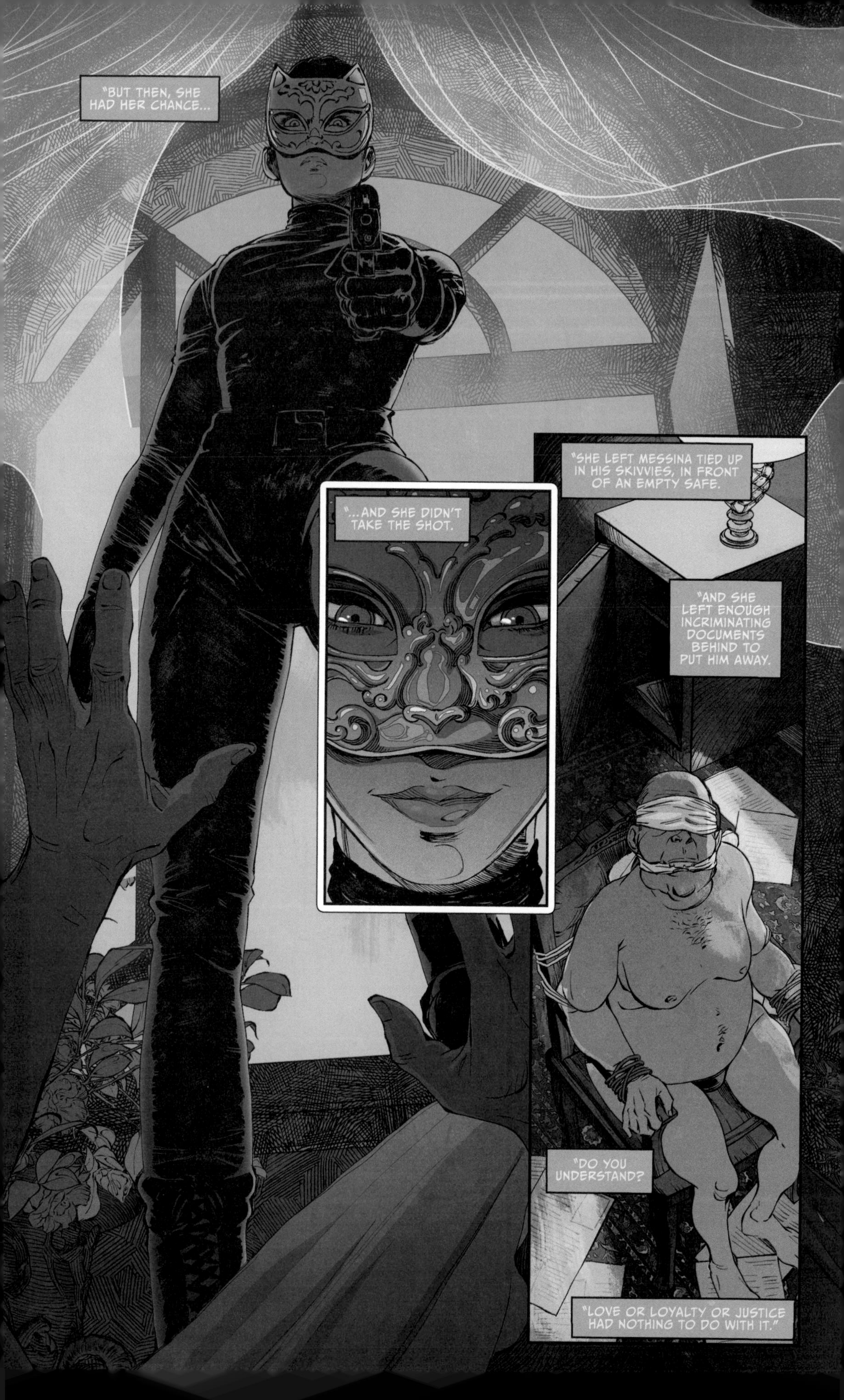
"BUT THEN, SHE HAD HER CHANCE...
"...AND SHE DIDN'T TAKE THE SHOT.
"SHE LEFT MESSINA TIED UP IN HIS SKIVVIES, IN FRONT OF AN EMPTY SAFE.
"AND SHE LEFT ENOUGH INCRIMINATING DOCUMENTS BEHIND TO PUT HIM AWAY.
"DO YOU UNDERSTAND?
"LOVE OR LOYALTY OR JUSTICE HAD NOTHING TO DO WITH IT."

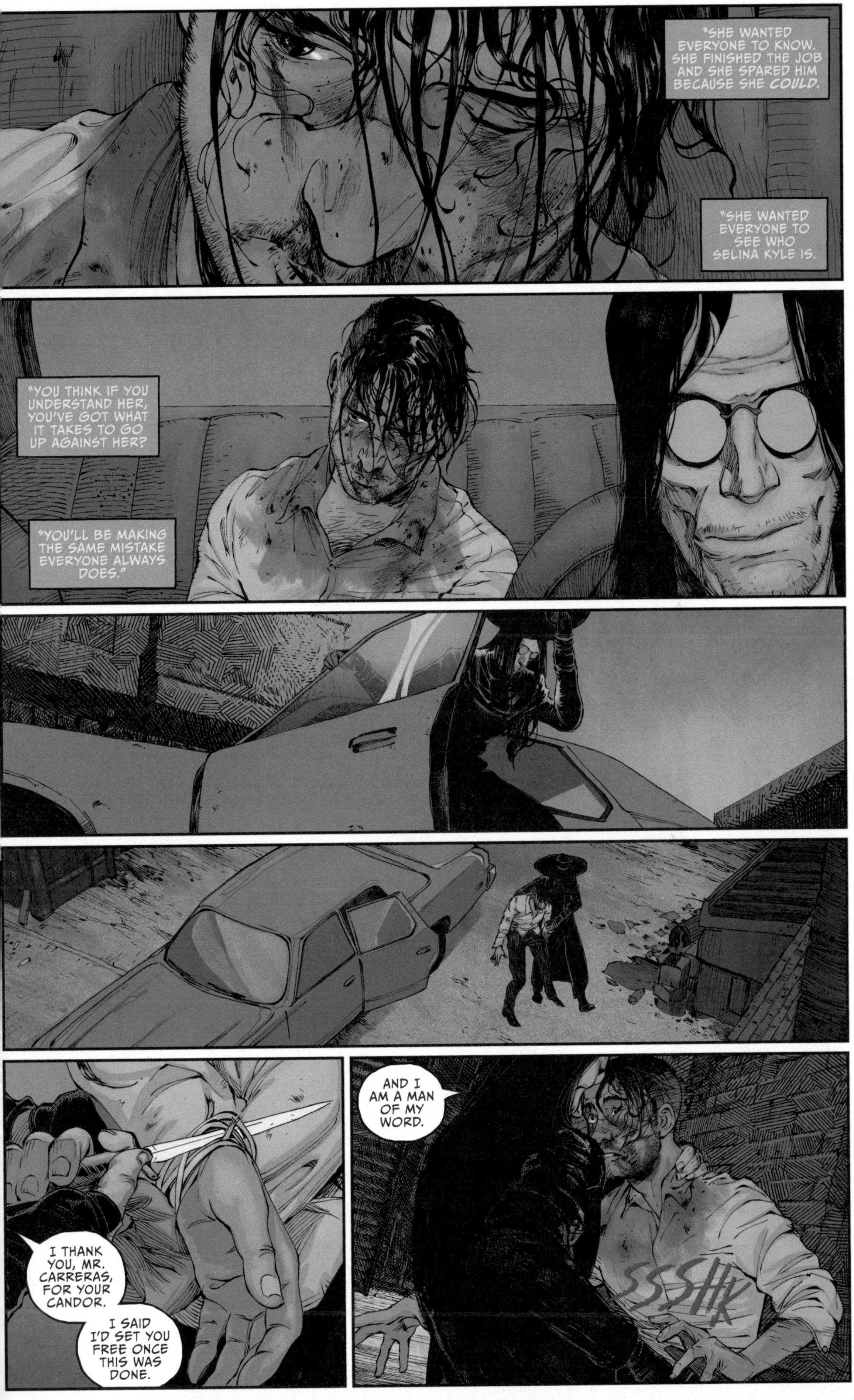
"SHE WANTED EVERYONE TO KNOW. SHE FINISHED THE JOB AND SHE SPARED HIM BECAUSE SHE *COULD*.
"SHE WANTED EVERYONE TO SEE WHO SELINA KYLE IS.
"YOU THINK IF YOU UNDERSTAND HER, YOU'VE GOT WHAT IT TAKES TO GO UP AGAINST HER?
"YOU'LL BE MAKING THE SAME MISTAKE EVERYONE ALWAYS DOES."
I THANK YOU, MR. CARRERAS, FOR YOUR CANDOR.
I SAID I'D SET YOU FREE ONCE THIS WAS DONE.
AND I AM A MAN OF MY WORD.
SSSHK

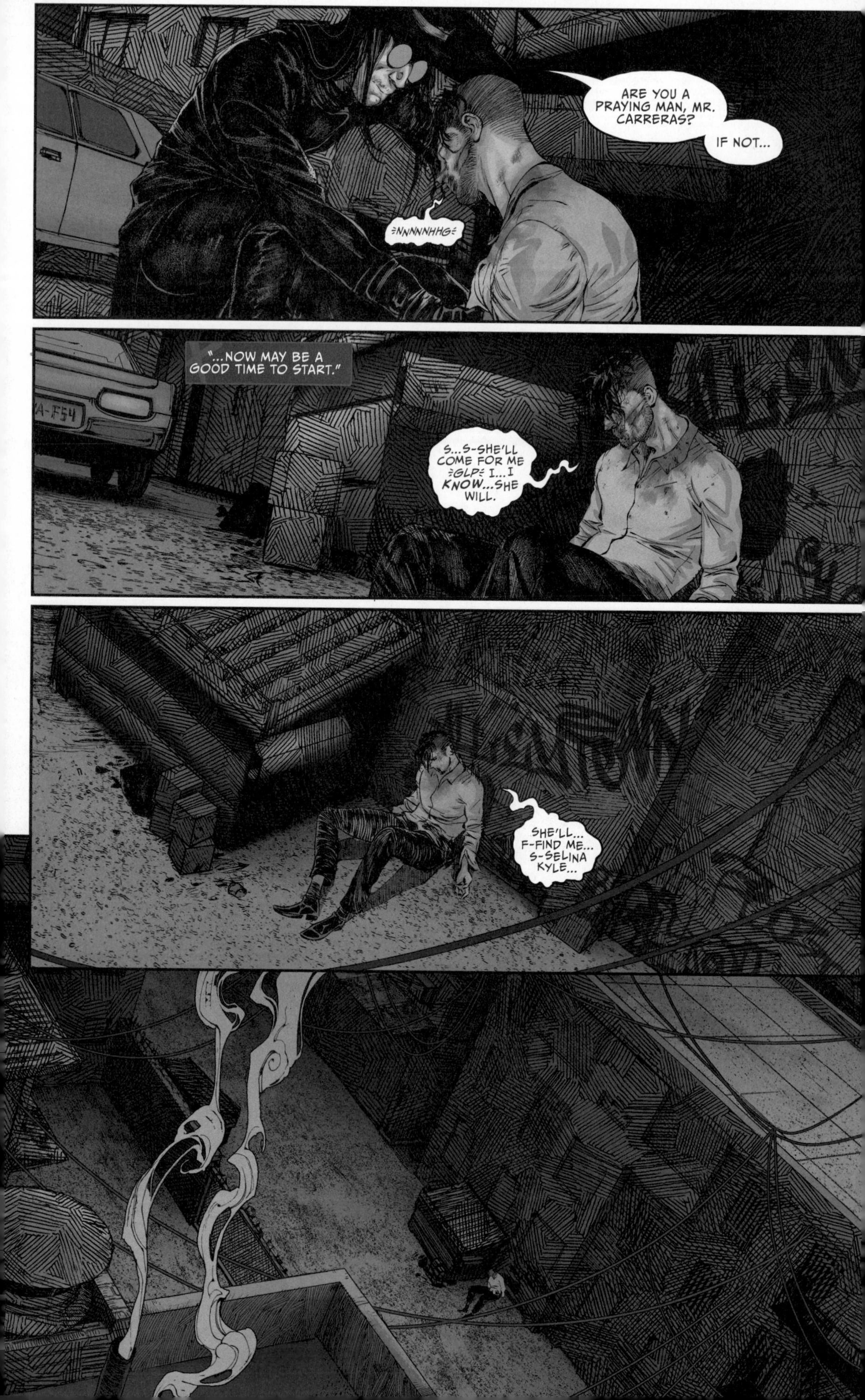
ARE YOU A PRAYING MAN, MR. CARRERAS?
IF NOT...
NNNNNHHG
"...NOW MAY BE A GOOD TIME TO START."
S...S-SHE'LL COME FOR ME GLP I...I KNOW...SHE WILL.
SHE'LL... F-FIND ME... S-SELINA KYLE...

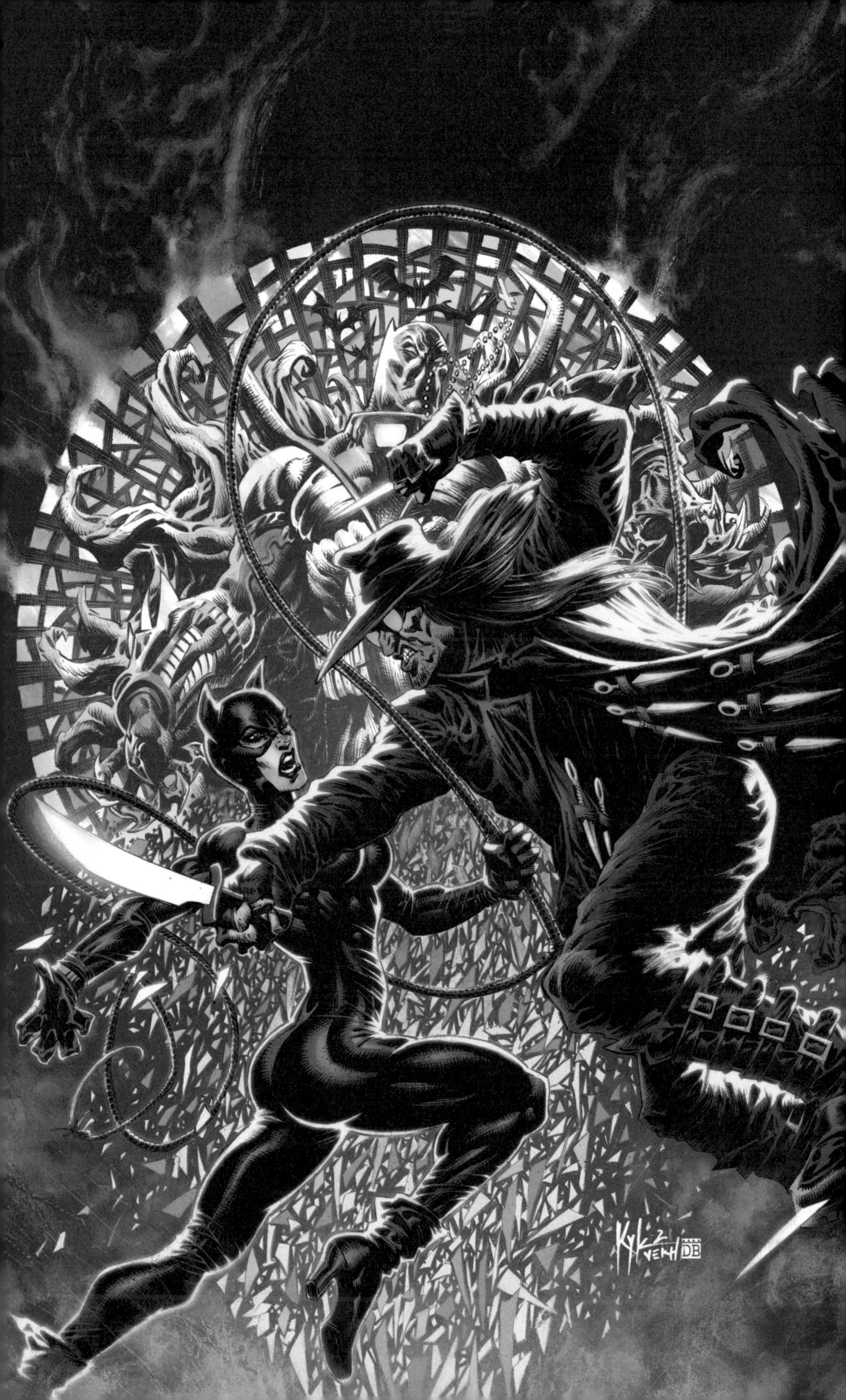

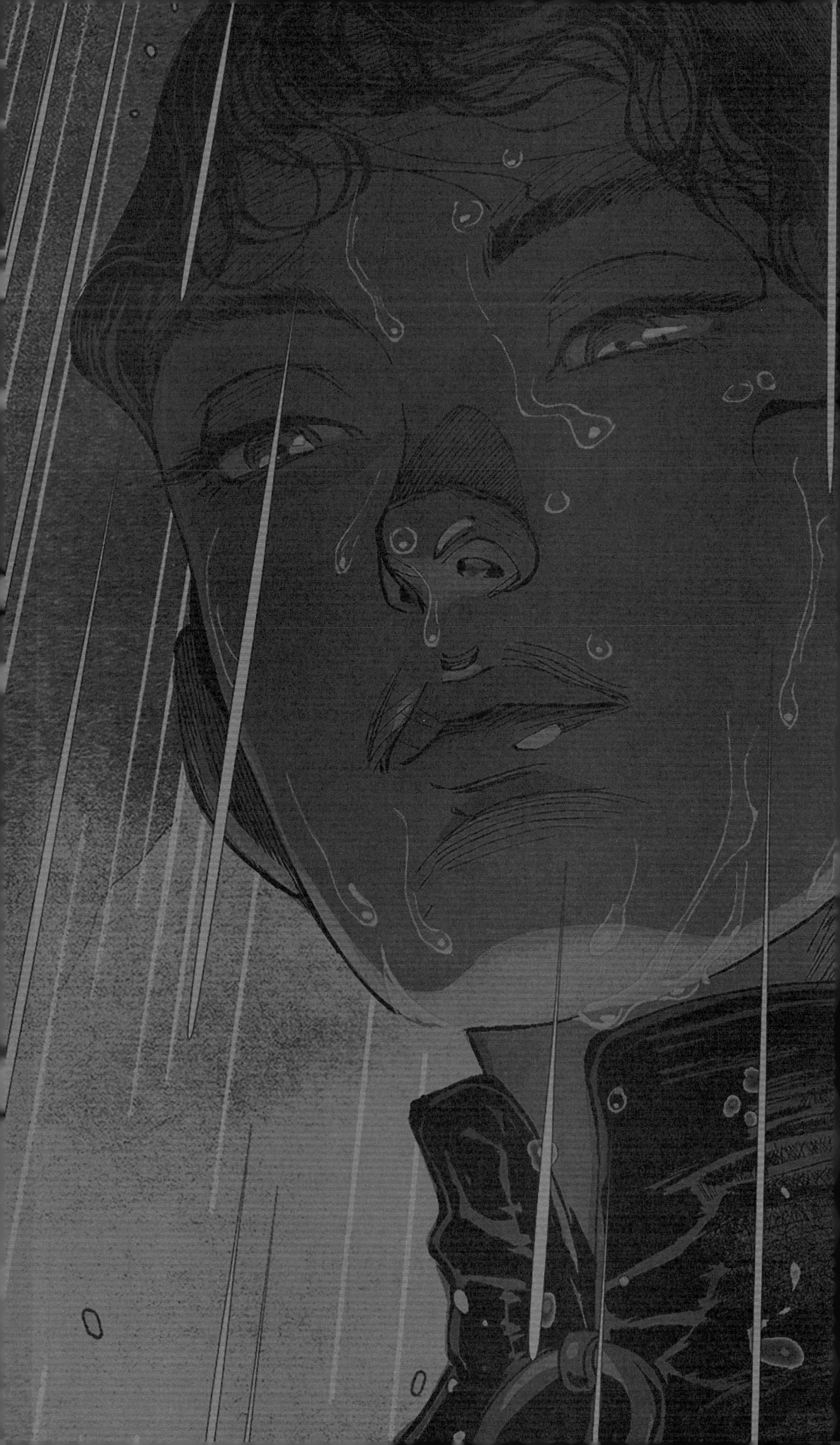

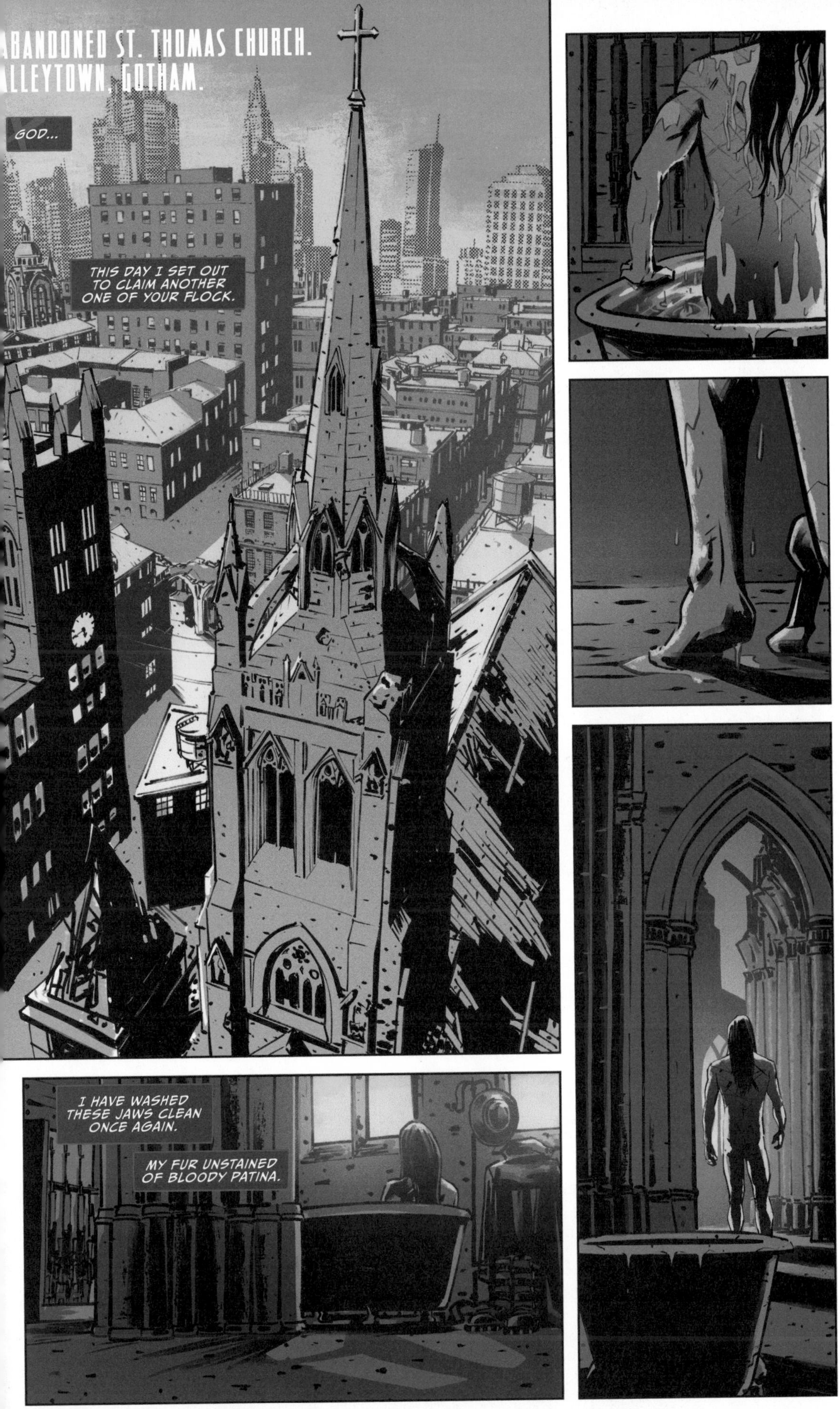
BANDONED ST. THOMAS CHURCH.
LLEYTOWN, GOTHAM.
GOD...
THIS DAY I SET OUT TO CLAIM ANOTHER ONE OF YOUR FLOCK.
I HAVE WASHED THESE JAWS CLEAN ONCE AGAIN.
MY FUR UNSTAINED OF BLOODY PATINA.

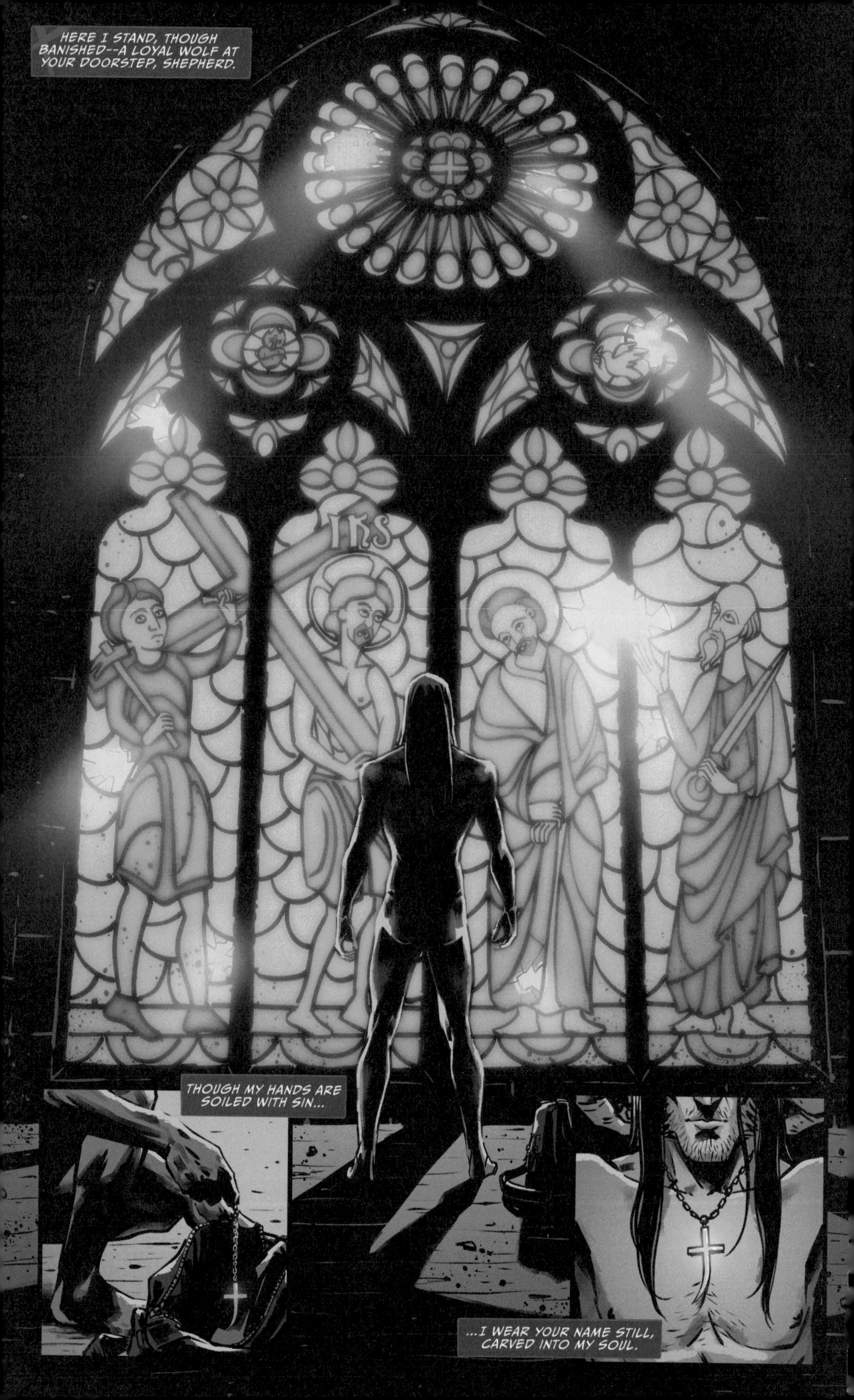
HERE I STAND, THOUGH BANISHED--A LOYAL WOLF AT YOUR DOORSTEP, SHEPHERD.
IHS
THOUGH MY HANDS ARE SOILED WITH SIN...
...I WEAR YOUR NAME STILL, CARVED INTO MY SOUL.

I HAVE LET THE BLOOD OF THE LAMB, IN YOUR NAME.*

*FATHER VALLEY LEFT LEO FOR DEAD IN *CATWOMAN* #32. --JESS

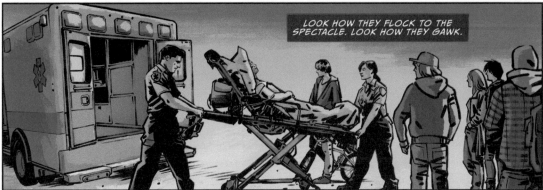

LOOK HOW THEY FLOCK TO THE SPECTACLE. LOOK HOW THEY GAWK.

THIS IS MY ENDEAVOR, LORD.

IN THEIR ABHORRENCE, THEY WILL CALL YOUR NAME AS I ONCE DID.

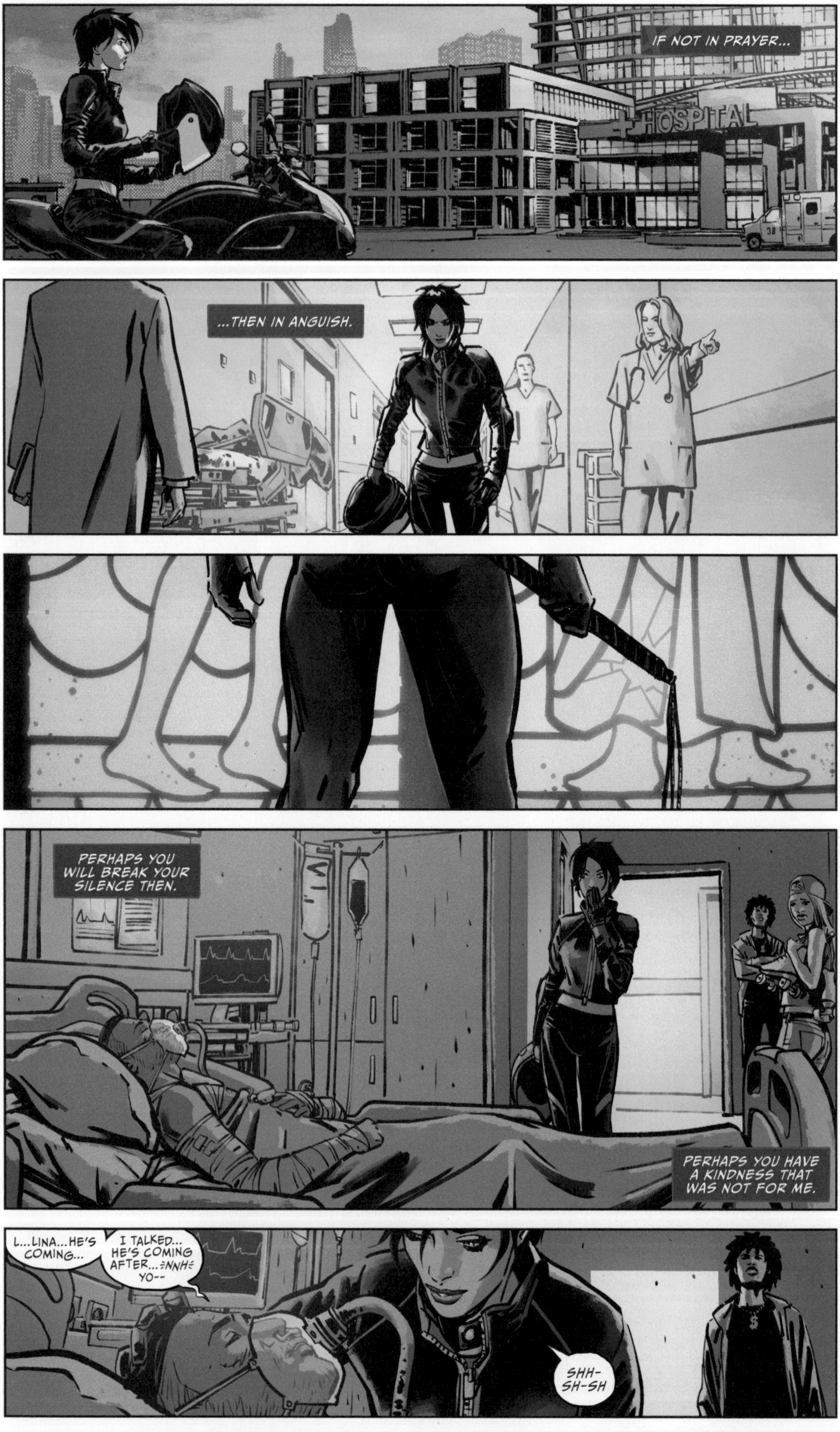
IF NOT IN PRAYER...
HOSPITAL
...THEN IN ANGUISH.
PERHAPS YOU WILL BREAK YOUR SILENCE THEN.
PERHAPS YOU HAVE A KINDNESS THAT WAS NOT FOR ME.
L...LINA...HE'S COMING...
I TALKED... HE'S COMING AFTER...ƐNNHƐ YO--
SHH-SH-SH

YOU NEED TO REST, *LEO.* FOCUS ON GETTING BETTER AND BACK ON YOUR FEET.

YOU LEAVE *HIM* TO ME... OKAY?

DON'T WORRY ABOUT A THING.

NOW ALL THAT REMAINS IS TO WASH THE MIND CLEAN...

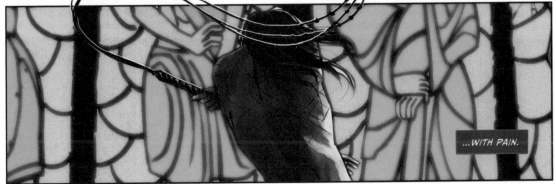

...WITH PAIN.

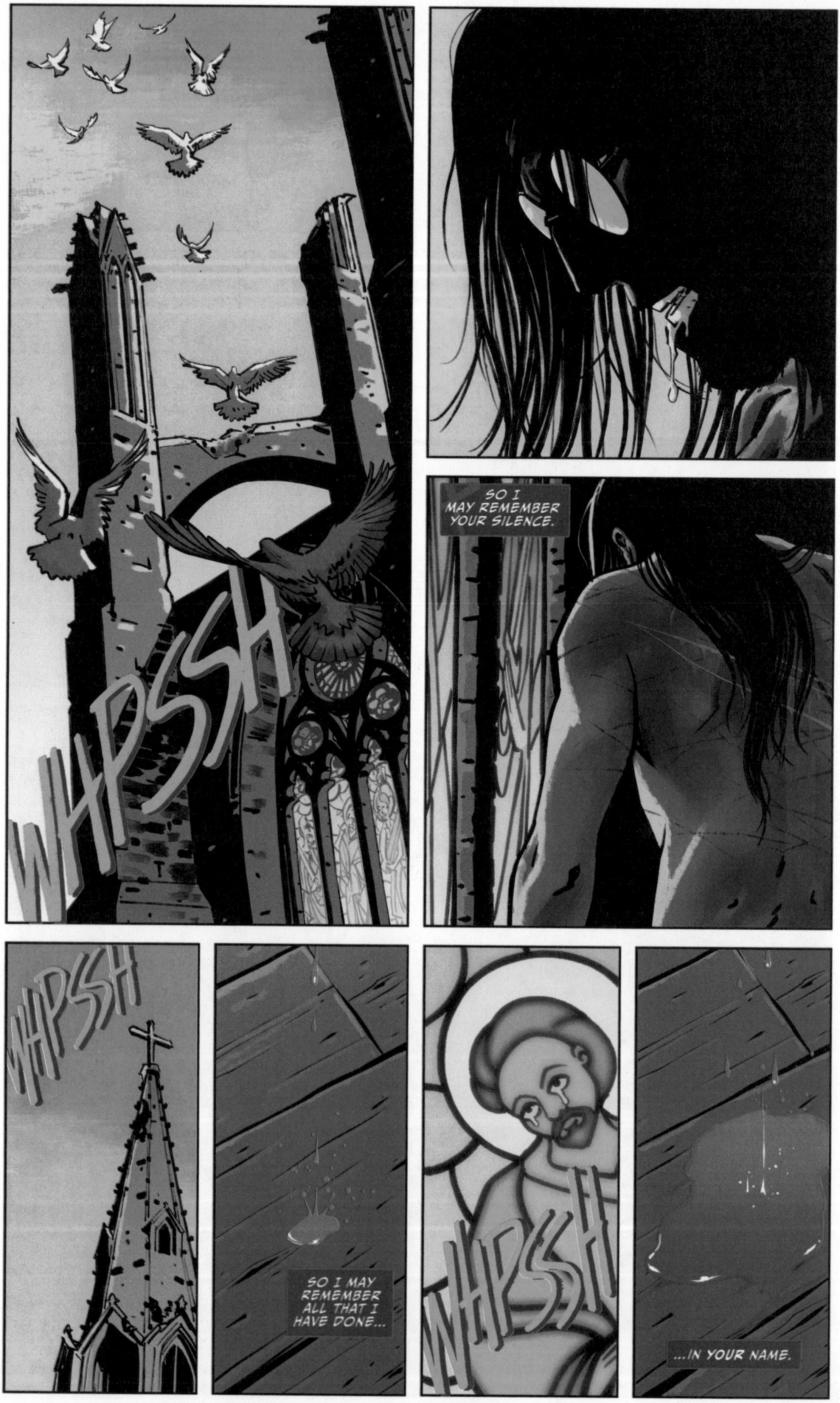
WHPSH
SO I MAY REMEMBER YOUR SILENCE.
WHPSH
SO I MAY REMEMBER ALL THAT I HAVE DONE...
WHPSH
...IN YOUR NAME.

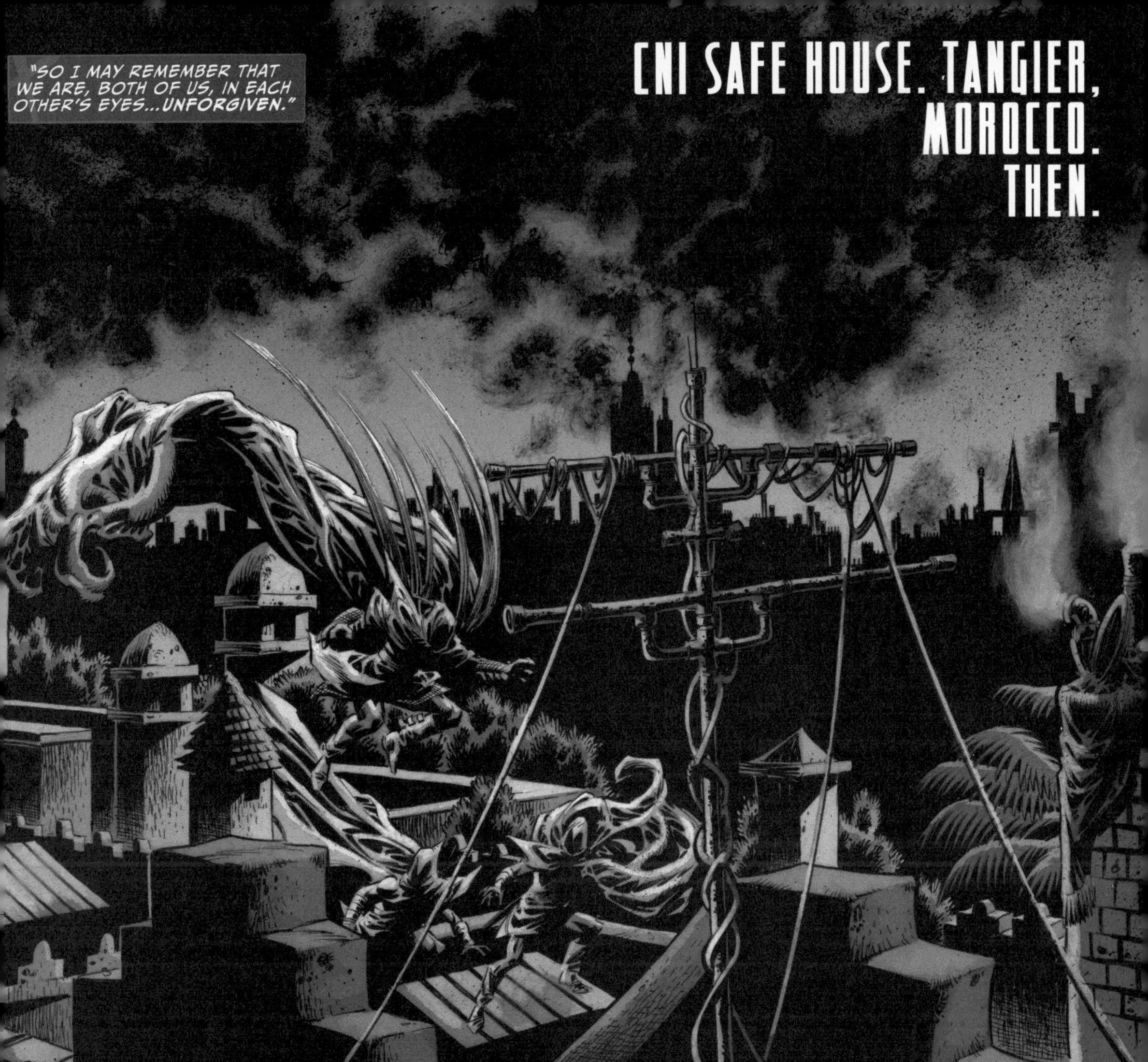
"SO I MAY REMEMBER THAT WE ARE, BOTH OF US, IN EACH OTHER'S EYES...UNFORGIVEN."
CNI SAFE HOUSE. TANGIER, MOROCCO. THEN.

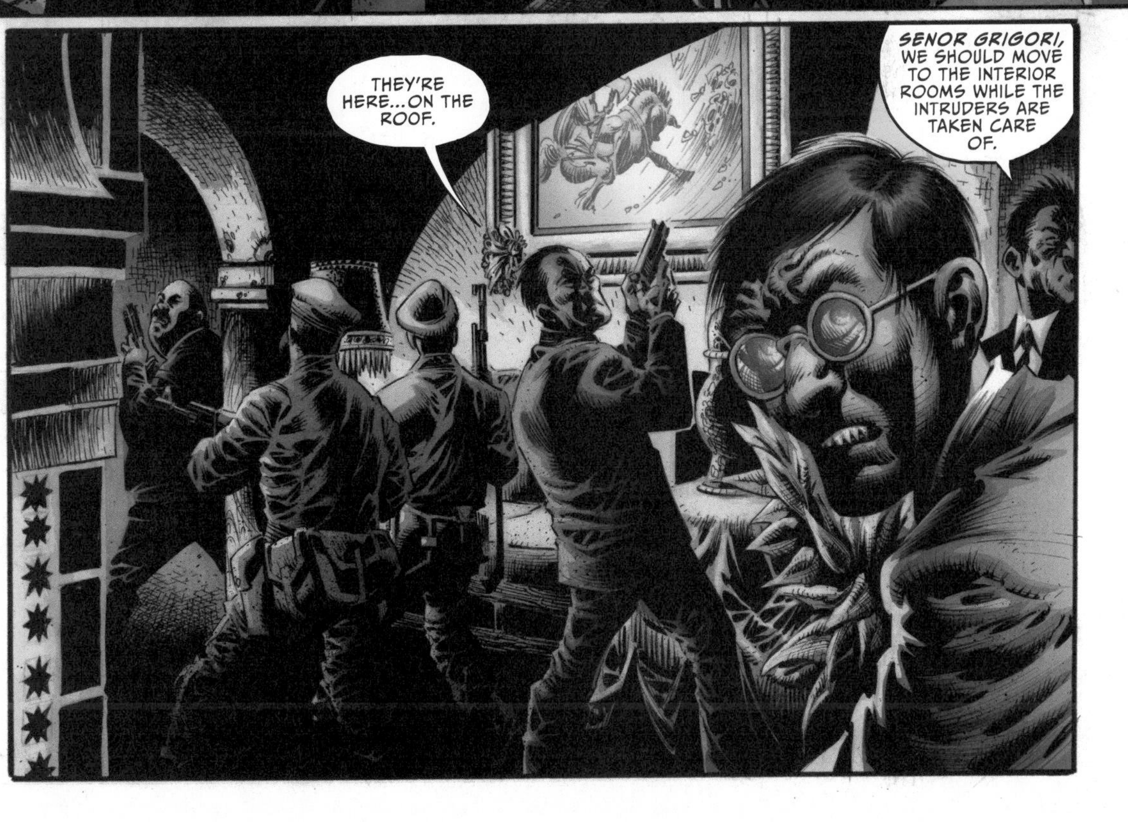
THEY'RE HERE...ON THE ROOF.
SENOR GRIGORI, WE SHOULD MOVE TO THE INTERIOR ROOMS WHILE THE INTRUDERS ARE TAKEN CARE OF.

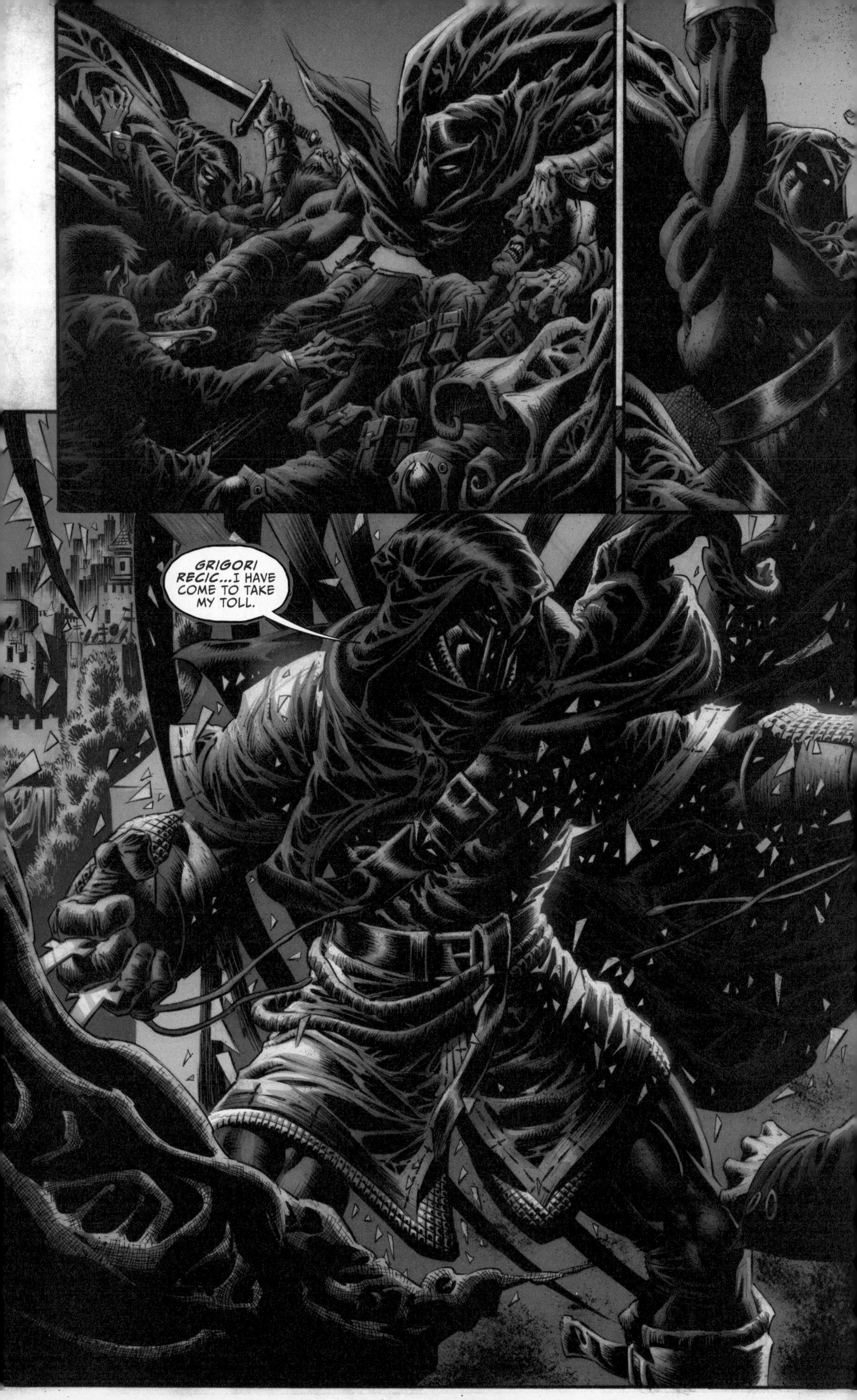
GRIGORI RECIC...I HAVE COME TO TAKE MY TOLL.

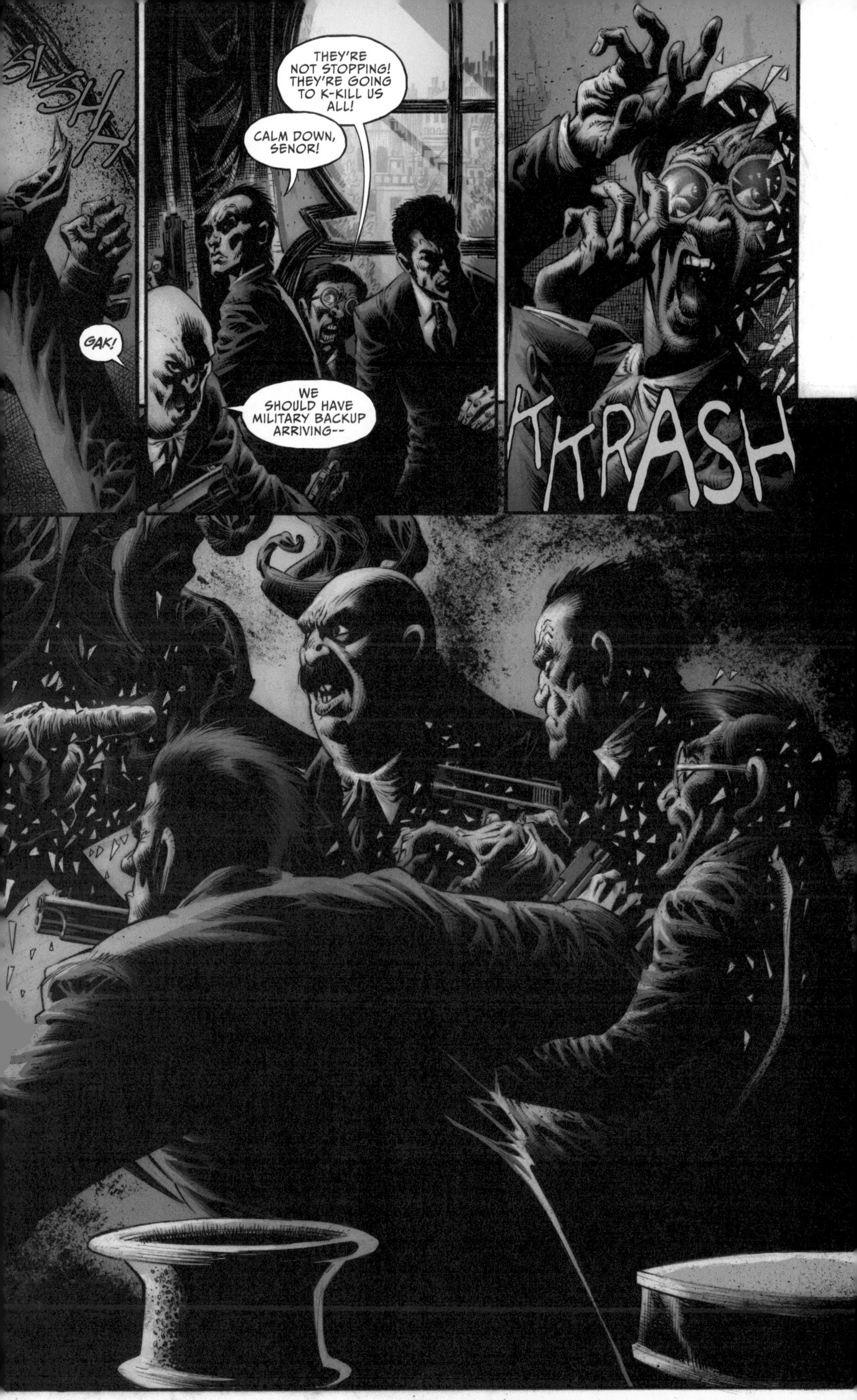
SLISH
GAK!
THEY'RE NOT STOPPING! THEY'RE GOING TO K-KILL US ALL!
CALM DOWN, SENOR!
WE SHOULD HAVE MILITARY BACKUP ARRIVING--
KKRASH

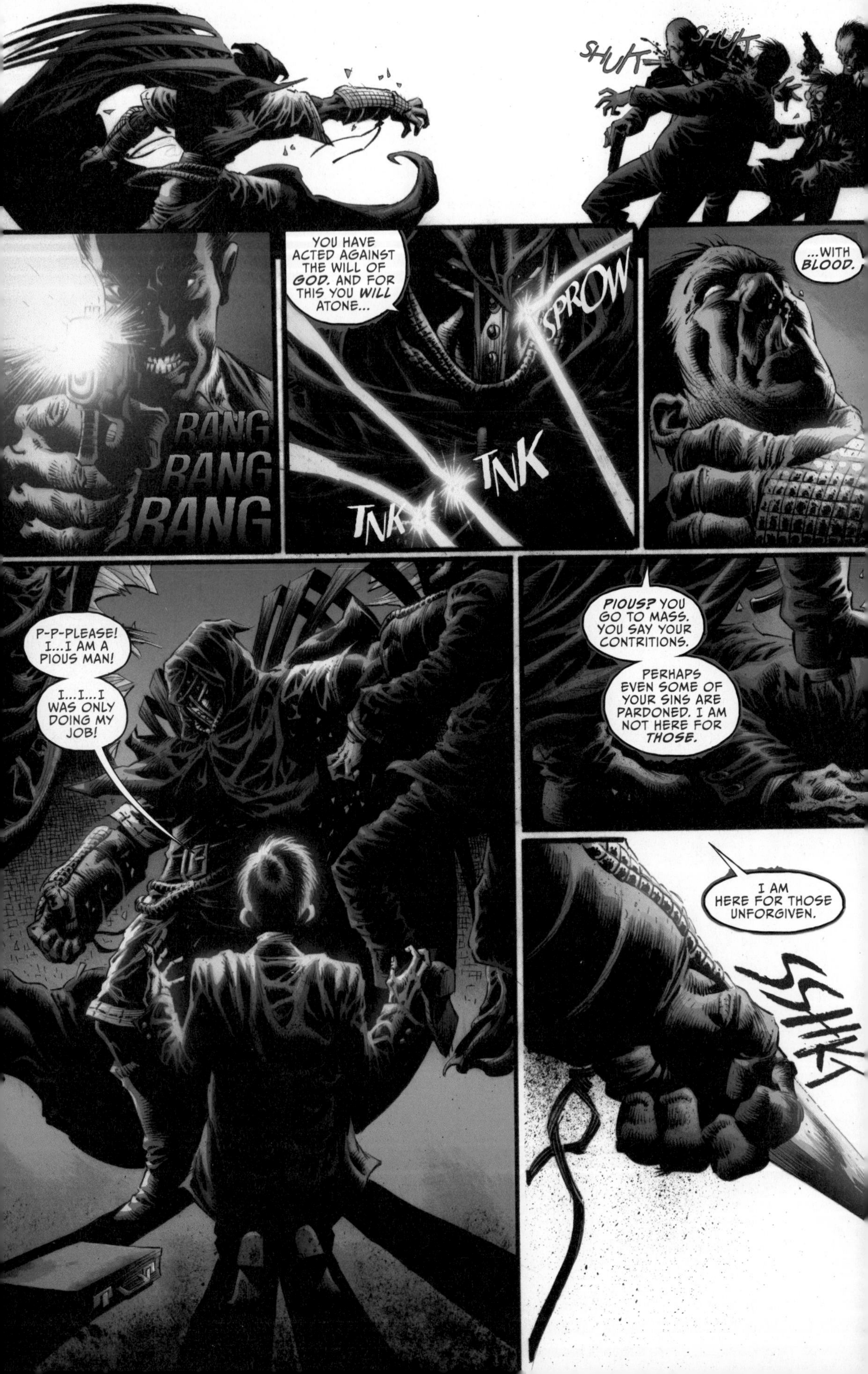
SHUK
SHUK
RANG
RANG
RANG
YOU HAVE ACTED AGAINST THE WILL OF GOD. AND FOR THIS YOU WILL ATONE...
SPROW
TNK
TNK
...WITH BLOOD.
P-P-PLEASE! I...I AM A PIOUS MAN!
I...I...I WAS ONLY DOING MY JOB!
PIOUS? YOU GO TO MASS. YOU SAY YOUR CONTRITIONS.
PERHAPS EVEN SOME OF YOUR SINS ARE PARDONED. I AM NOT HERE FOR THOSE.
I AM HERE FOR THOSE UNFORGIVEN.
SSHKT

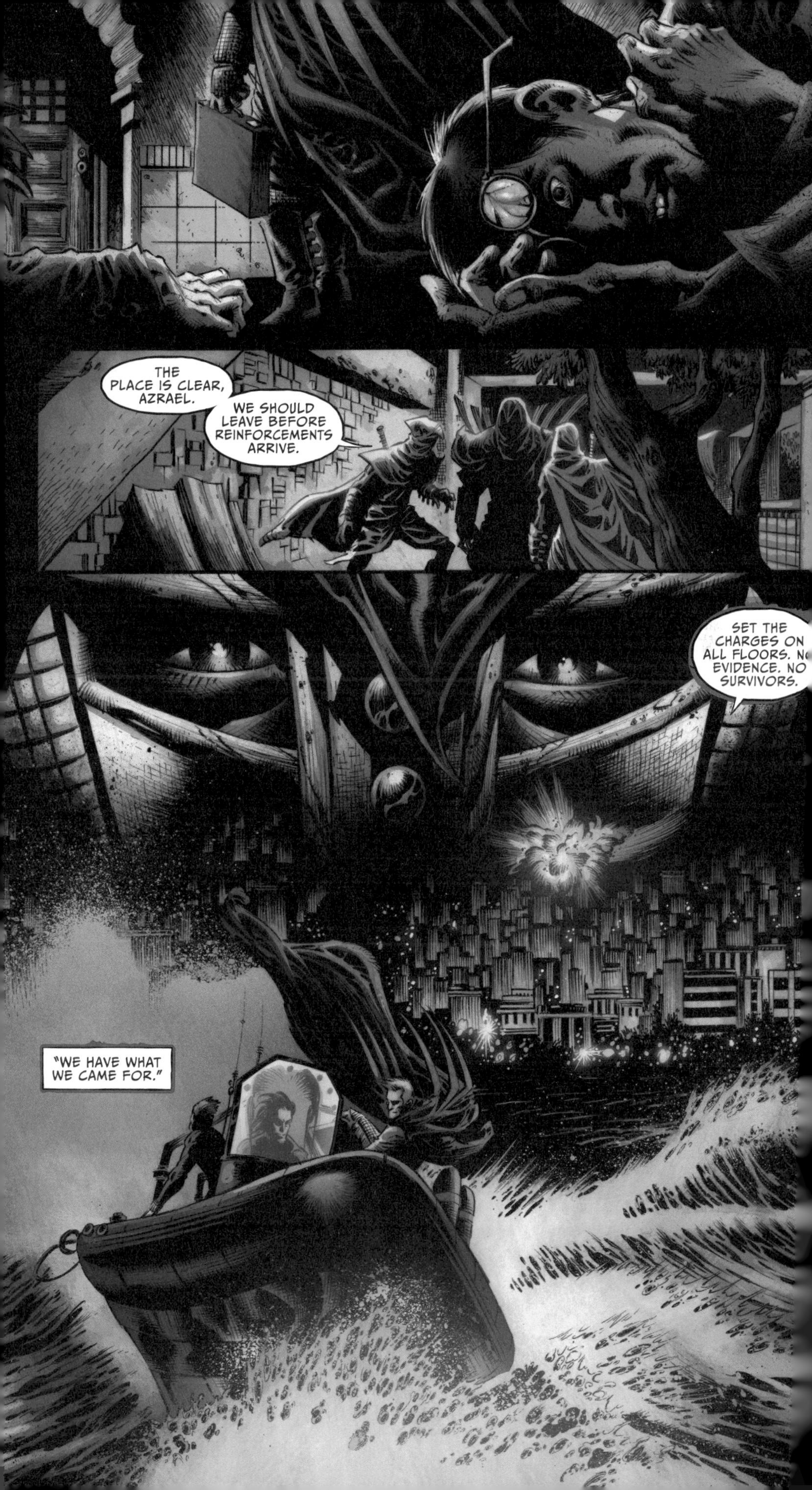
THE PLACE IS CLEAR, AZRAEL.
WE SHOULD LEAVE BEFORE REINFORCEMENTS ARRIVE.
SET THE CHARGES ON ALL FLOORS. NO EVIDENCE. NO SURVIVORS.
"WE HAVE WHAT WE CAME FOR."

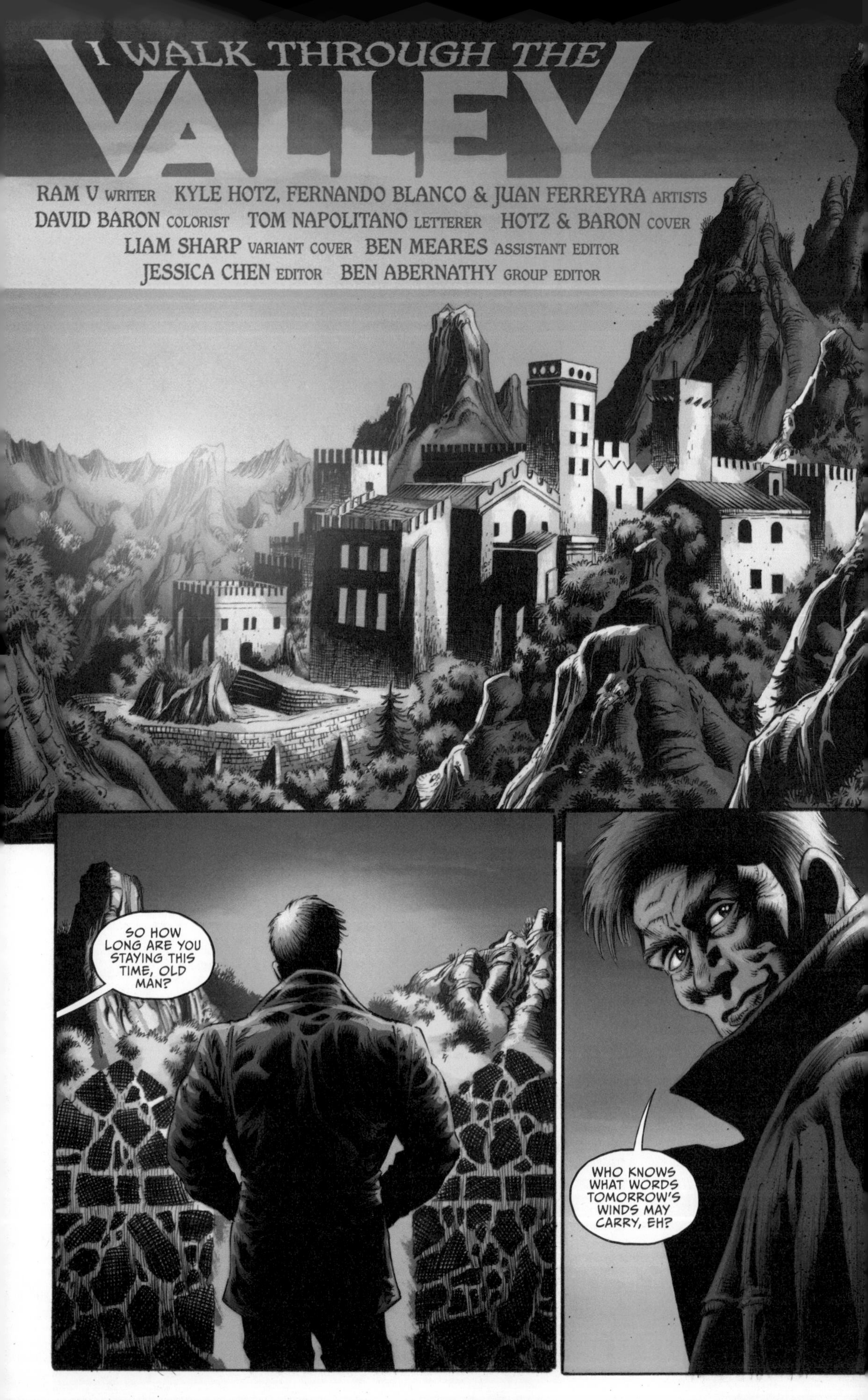
I WALK THROUGH THE
VALLEY
RAM V WRITER KYLE HOTZ, FERNANDO BLANCO & JUAN FERREYRA ARTISTS
DAVID BARON COLORIST TOM NAPOLITANO LETTERER HOTZ & BARON COVER
LIAM SHARP VARIANT COVER BEN MEARES ASSISTANT EDITOR
JESSICA CHEN EDITOR BEN ABERNATHY GROUP EDITOR
SO HOW LONG ARE YOU STAYING THIS TIME, OLD MAN?
WHO KNOWS WHAT WORDS TOMORROW'S WINDS MAY CARRY, EH?

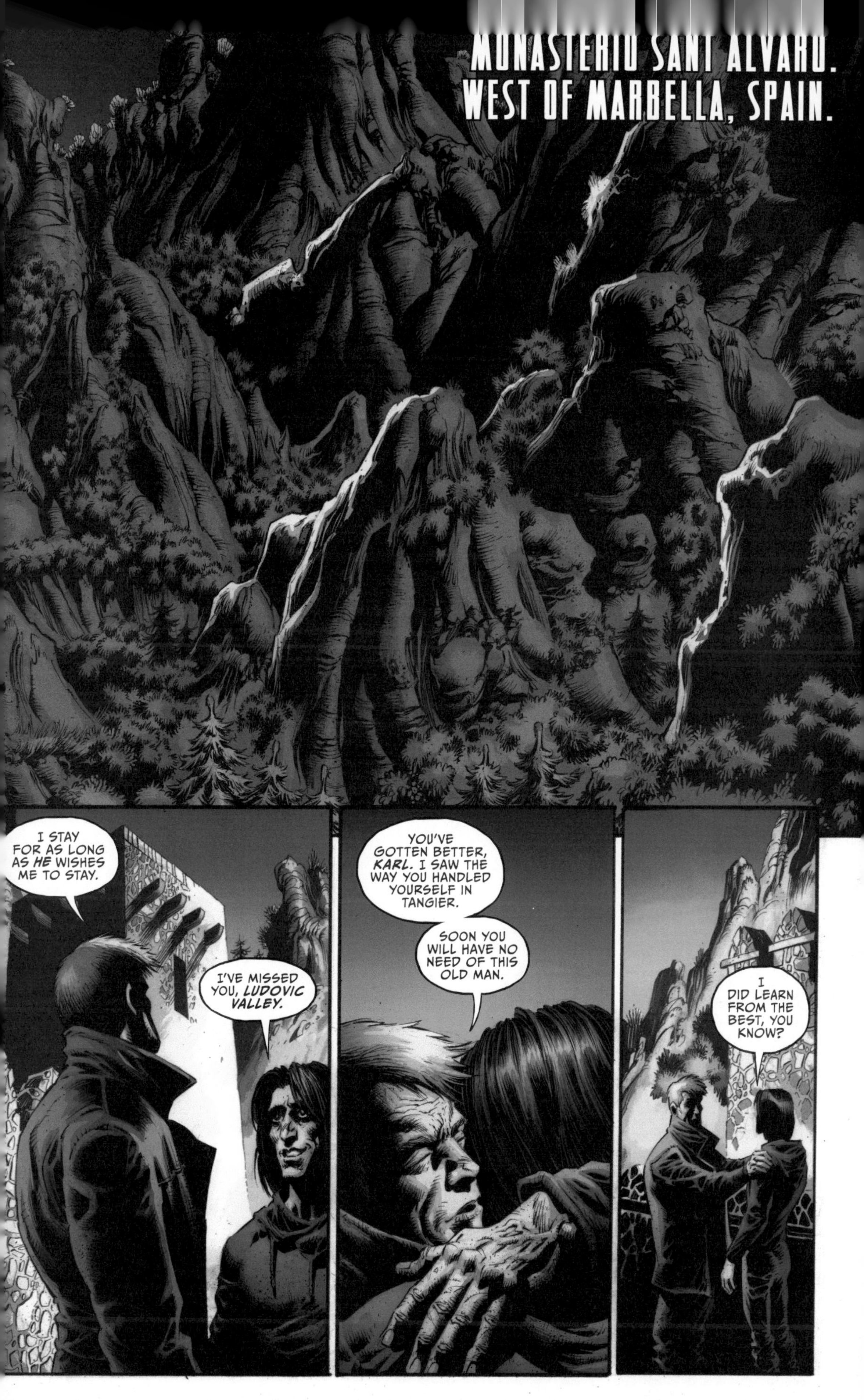
MONASTERIO SANT ALVARO.
WEST OF MARBELLA, SPAIN.
I STAY FOR AS LONG AS HE WISHES ME TO STAY.
I'VE MISSED YOU, LUDOVIC VALLEY.
YOU'VE GOTTEN BETTER, KARL. I SAW THE WAY YOU HANDLED YOURSELF IN TANGIER.
SOON YOU WILL HAVE NO NEED OF THIS OLD MAN.
I DID LEARN FROM THE BEST, YOU KNOW?

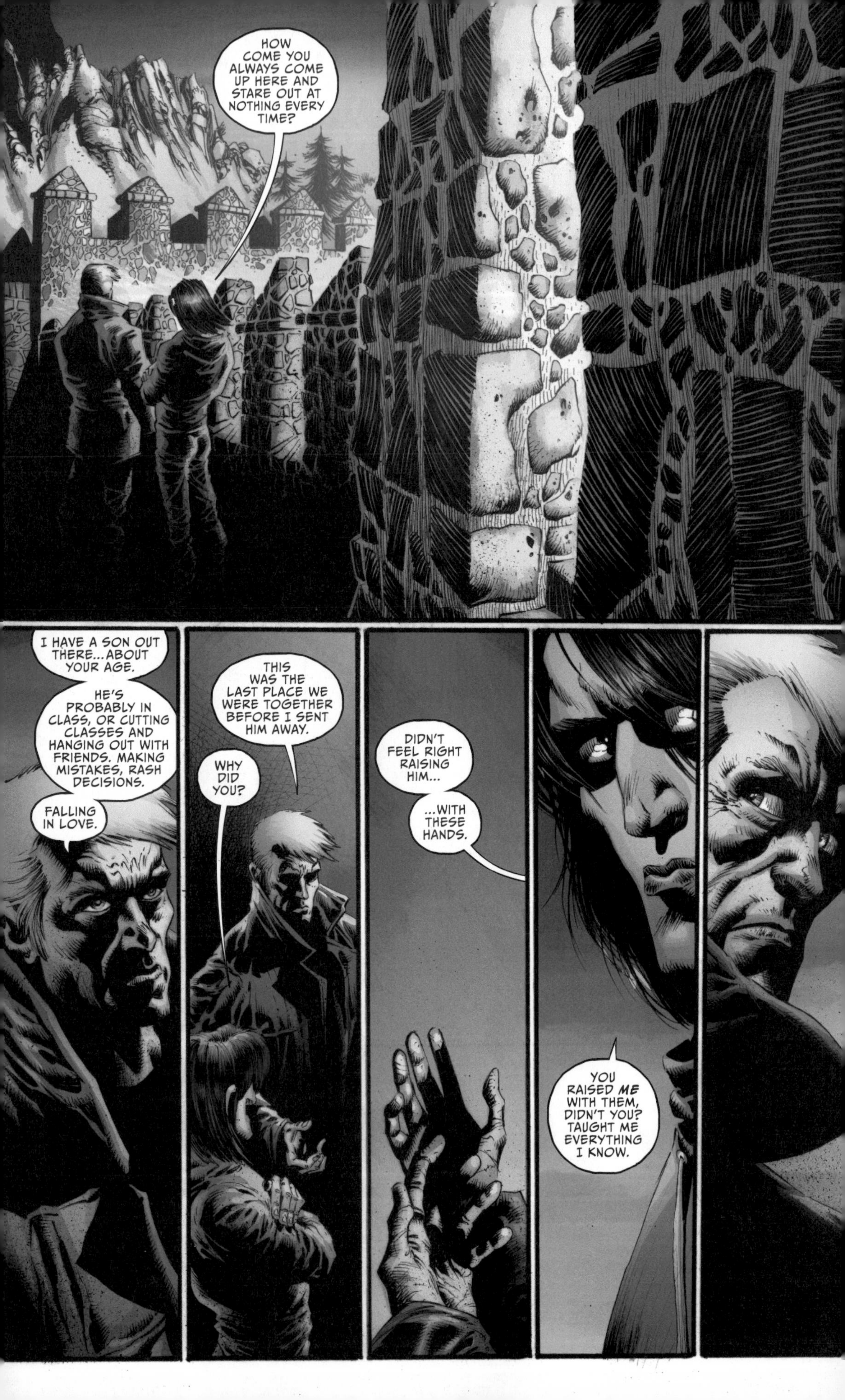
HOW COME YOU ALWAYS COME UP HERE AND STARE OUT AT NOTHING EVERY TIME?
I HAVE A SON OUT THERE...ABOUT YOUR AGE.
HE'S PROBABLY IN CLASS, OR CUTTING CLASSES AND HANGING OUT WITH FRIENDS. MAKING MISTAKES, RASH DECISIONS.
FALLING IN LOVE.
THIS WAS THE LAST PLACE WE WERE TOGETHER BEFORE I SENT HIM AWAY.
WHY DID YOU?
DIDN'T FEEL RIGHT RAISING HIM...
...WITH THESE HANDS.
YOU RAISED *ME* WITH THEM, DIDN'T YOU? TAUGHT ME EVERYTHING I KNOW.

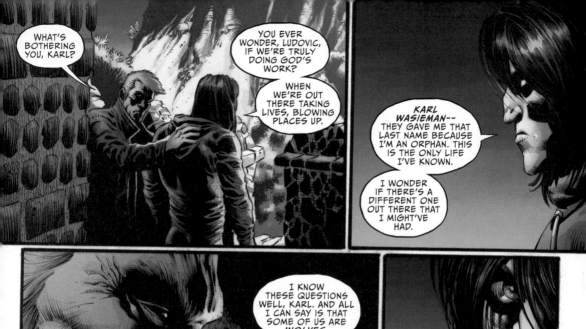

WHAT'S BOTHERING YOU, KARL?

YOU EVER WONDER, LUDOVIC, IF WE'RE TRULY DOING GOD'S WORK?

WHEN WE'RE OUT THERE TAKING LIVES, BLOWING PLACES UP.

KARL WASIEMAN-- THEY GAVE ME THAT LAST NAME BECAUSE I'M AN ORPHAN. THIS IS THE ONLY LIFE I'VE KNOWN.

I WONDER IF THERE'S A DIFFERENT ONE OUT THERE THAT I MIGHT'VE HAD.

I KNOW THESE QUESTIONS WELL, KARL. AND ALL I CAN SAY IS THAT SOME OF US ARE *WOLVES.*

WE WEAR SKIN AND WALK ON TWO FEET AND SPEAK OF WISE AND GENTLE THINGS. BUT WE ARE TRULY WOLVES.

BETTER BLOODY OUR JAWS IN SERVICE OF A WRATHFUL GOD THAN BLOODY THEM FOR SOMETHING LESS.

AND YOU SHOULD BE CAREFUL WITH SUCH QUESTIONS IN THIS PLACE...LEST THEY FALL UPON UNKIND EARS.

LUDOVIC VALLEY, *PADRE SPERANZA* WOULD LIKE TO SPEAK WITH YOU.

NOW.

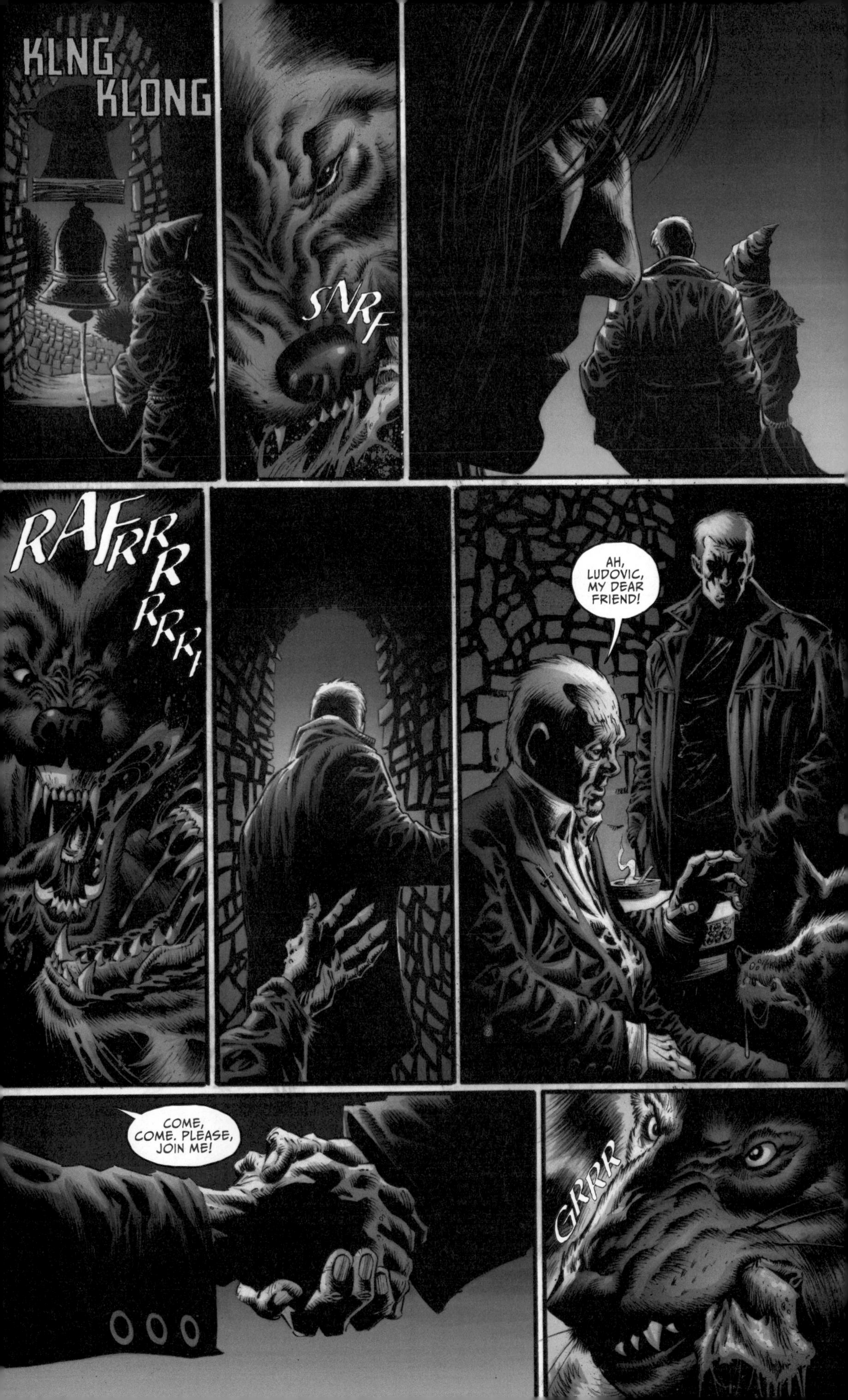
KLNG
KLONG
SNRF
RAFRRRRRRRI
AH, LUDOVIC, MY DEAR FRIEND!
COME, COME. PLEASE, JOIN ME!
GRRR

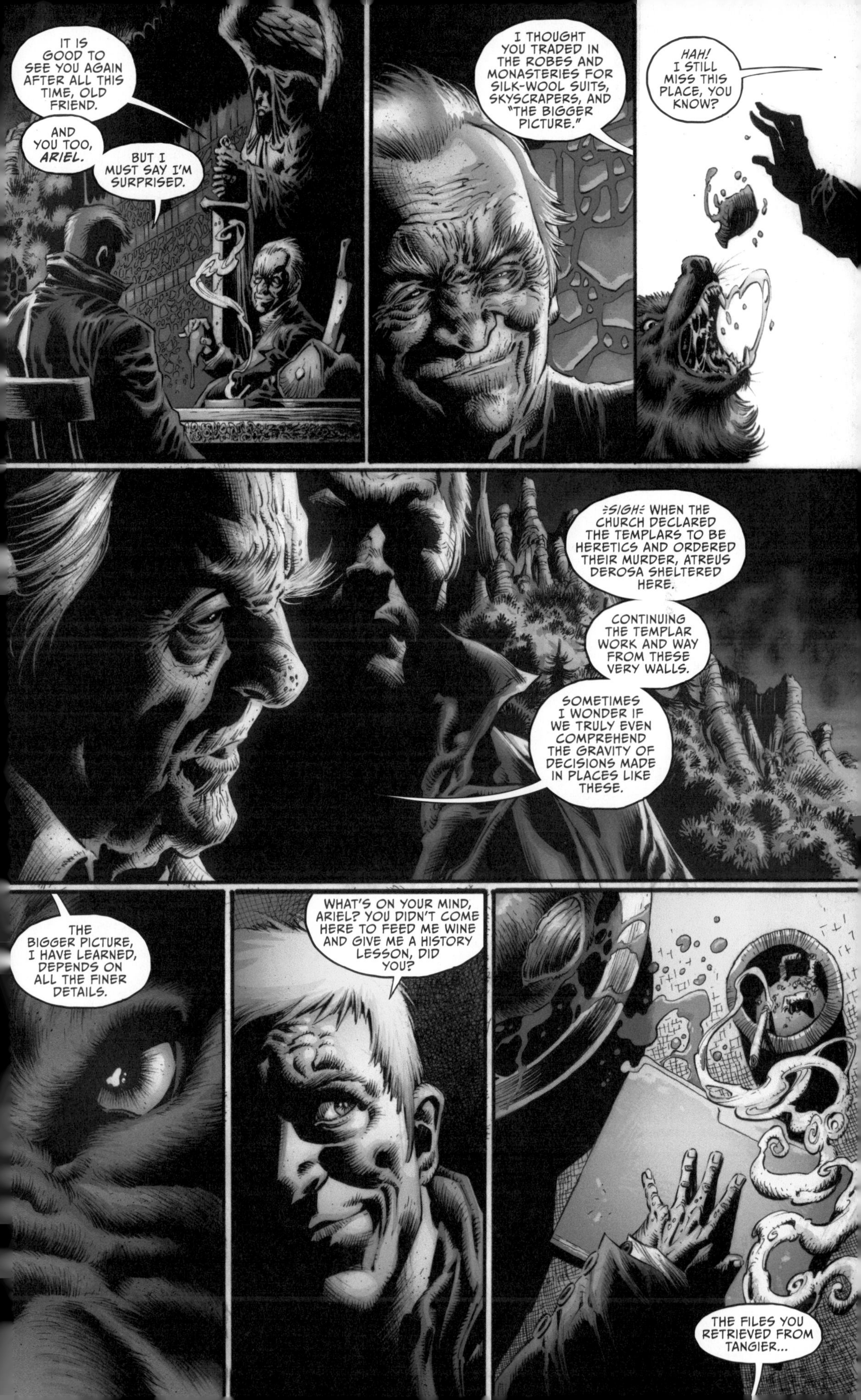
IT IS GOOD TO SEE YOU AGAIN AFTER ALL THIS TIME, OLD FRIEND.
AND YOU TOO, *ARIEL.*
BUT I MUST SAY I'M SURPRISED.
I THOUGHT YOU TRADED IN THE ROBES AND MONASTERIES FOR SILK-WOOL SUITS, SKYSCRAPERS, AND "THE BIGGER PICTURE."
HAH! I STILL MISS THIS PLACE, YOU KNOW?
=SIGH= WHEN THE CHURCH DECLARED THE TEMPLARS TO BE HERETICS AND ORDERED THEIR MURDER, ATREUS DEROSA SHELTERED HERE.
CONTINUING THE TEMPLAR WORK AND WAY FROM THESE VERY WALLS.
SOMETIMES I WONDER IF WE TRULY EVEN COMPREHEND THE GRAVITY OF DECISIONS MADE IN PLACES LIKE THESE.
THE BIGGER PICTURE, I HAVE LEARNED, DEPENDS ON ALL THE FINER DETAILS.
WHAT'S ON YOUR MIND, ARIEL? YOU DIDN'T COME HERE TO FEED ME WINE AND GIVE ME A HISTORY LESSON, DID YOU?
THE FILES YOU RETRIEVED FROM TANGIER...

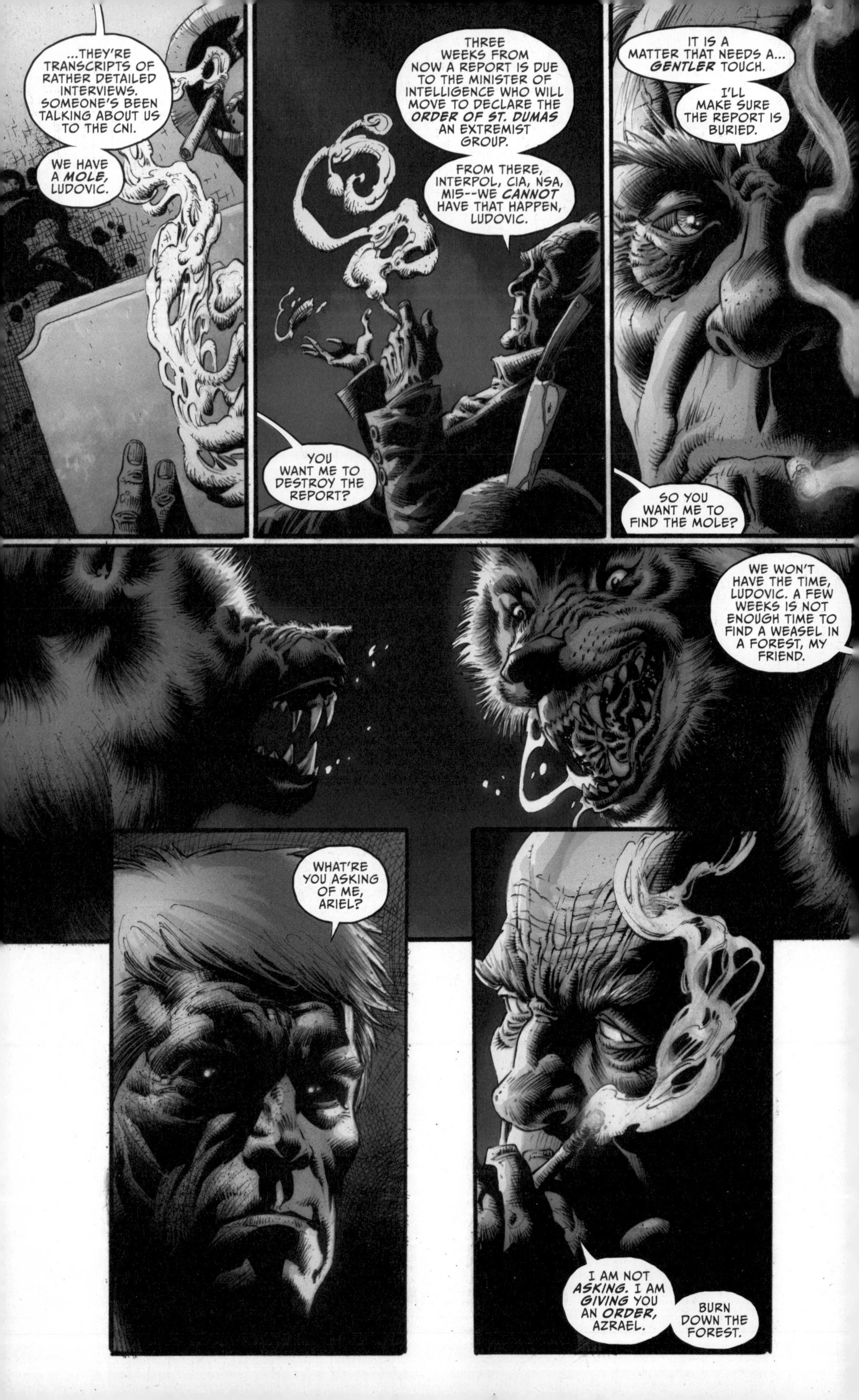
...THEY'RE TRANSCRIPTS OF RATHER DETAILED INTERVIEWS. SOMEONE'S BEEN TALKING ABOUT US TO THE CNI.
WE HAVE A MOLE, LUDOVIC.
THREE WEEKS FROM NOW A REPORT IS DUE TO THE MINISTER OF INTELLIGENCE WHO WILL MOVE TO DECLARE THE ORDER OF ST. DUMAS AN EXTREMIST GROUP.
FROM THERE, INTERPOL, CIA, NSA, MI5--WE CANNOT HAVE THAT HAPPEN, LUDOVIC.
YOU WANT ME TO DESTROY THE REPORT?
IT IS A MATTER THAT NEEDS A... GENTLER TOUCH.
I'LL MAKE SURE THE REPORT IS BURIED.
SO YOU WANT ME TO FIND THE MOLE?
WE WON'T HAVE THE TIME, LUDOVIC. A FEW WEEKS IS NOT ENOUGH TIME TO FIND A WEASEL IN A FOREST, MY FRIEND.
WHAT'RE YOU ASKING OF ME, ARIEL?
I AM NOT ASKING. I AM GIVING YOU AN ORDER, AZRAEL.
BURN DOWN THE FOREST.

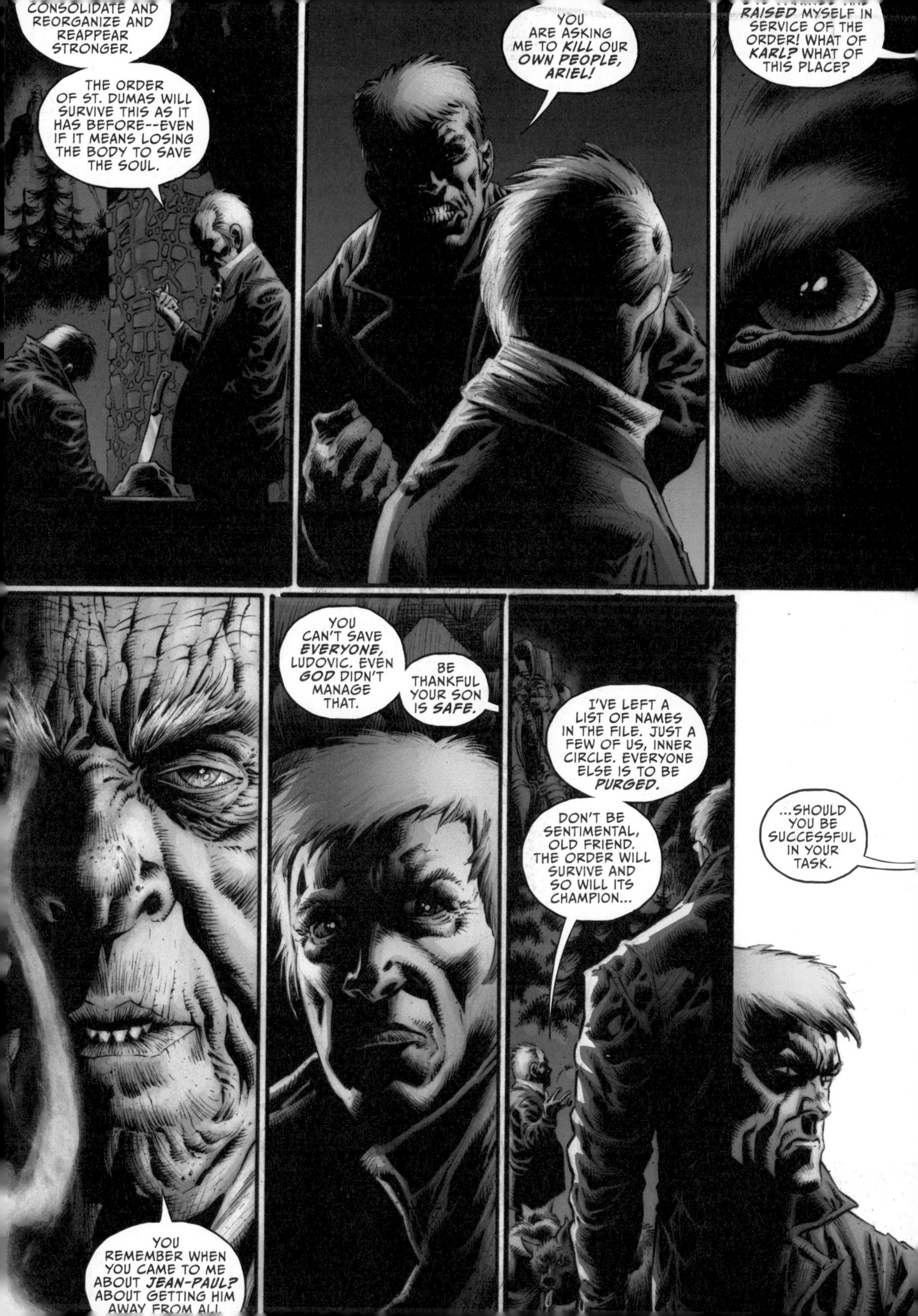
CONSOLIDATE AND REORGANIZE AND REAPPEAR STRONGER.
THE ORDER OF ST. DUMAS WILL SURVIVE THIS AS IT HAS BEFORE--EVEN IF IT MEANS LOSING THE BODY TO SAVE THE SOUL.
YOU ARE ASKING ME TO KILL OUR OWN PEOPLE, ARIEL!
RAISED MYSELF IN SERVICE OF THE ORDER! WHAT OF KARL? WHAT OF THIS PLACE?
YOU REMEMBER WHEN YOU CAME TO ME ABOUT JEAN-PAUL? ABOUT GETTING HIM AWAY FROM ALL
YOU CAN'T SAVE EVERYONE, LUDOVIC. EVEN GOD DIDN'T MANAGE THAT.
BE THANKFUL YOUR SON IS SAFE.
I'VE LEFT A LIST OF NAMES IN THE FILE. JUST A FEW OF US, INNER CIRCLE. EVERYONE ELSE IS TO BE PURGED.
DON'T BE SENTIMENTAL, OLD FRIEND. THE ORDER WILL SURVIVE AND SO WILL ITS CHAMPION...
...SHOULD YOU BE SUCCESSFUL IN YOUR TASK.

OUR REF: 122/FGH17:31/M4
YOUR REF: OC-S-456-8

SUBJECT: ACTIVE INCIDENTS AND CRIME ACROSS EUROPE AND CENTRAL/SOUTH AMERICA RELATED TO "THE ORDER"/"THE ORDER OF ST. DUMAS"/[redacted]/"THE FLAMING SWORD"/

DATA AND ANALYSIS.

OFFICER DESIGNATION [redacted]

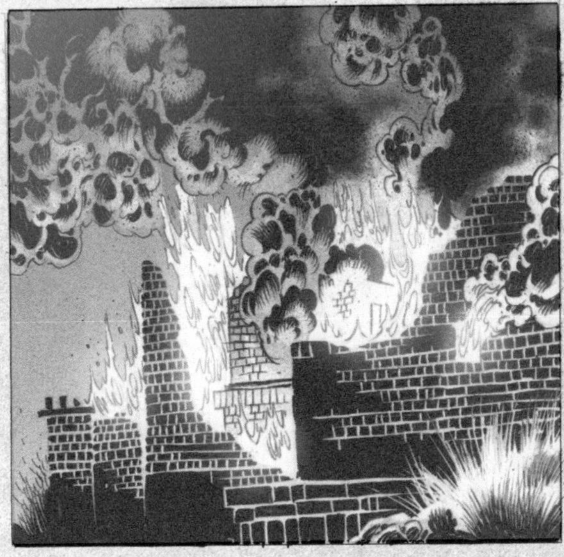

Following an initial red flag from CNI field office in JEREZ, SPAIN, Interpol analysts in cooperation with local agencies and [redacted] have been monitoring multiple incidents related to what we believe is the group known as "The Order of St. Dumas" (Henceforth ref to as the Order).

Since the original attack involving [redacted] at [redacted] in Tangier, we have seen a marked rise in incidents of violence across mainland Europe involving [redacted], which we believe to be staging locations frequently used by the Order.

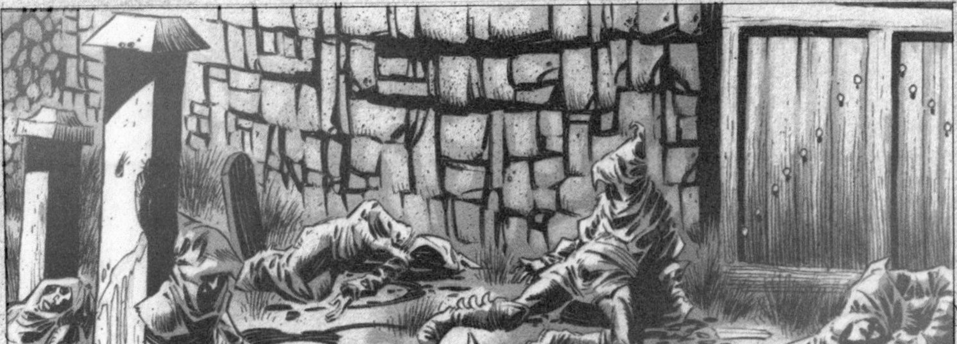

Our analysis is that in response to the leaks recovered from the Tangier incident from [redacted] the Order is attempting to eliminate its own ranks in the hopes that [redacted] will be among the eliminated. To this effect, the Order is using one or several field operatives acting under the name "AZRAEL"

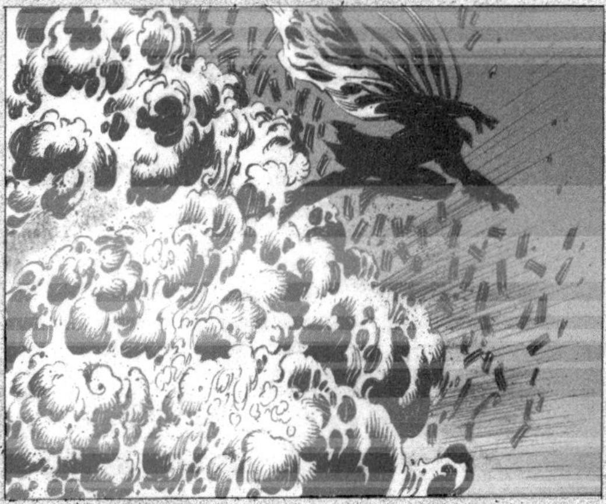

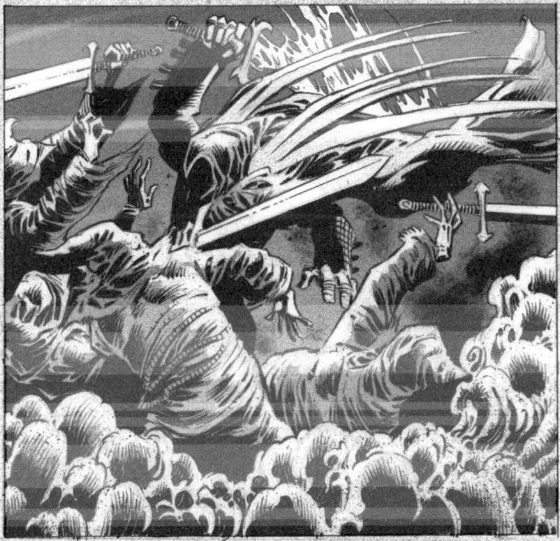

The analysis wing believes that once everyone except the leadership of the Order is eliminated, they will go to ground, into a period of extended hibernation. At this stage the Order's activity will become near impossible to trace.

The current scenario presents our best opportunity to attempt to flip assets at the Order, secure the Source [redacted] and/or apprehend the operative known as AZRAEL.

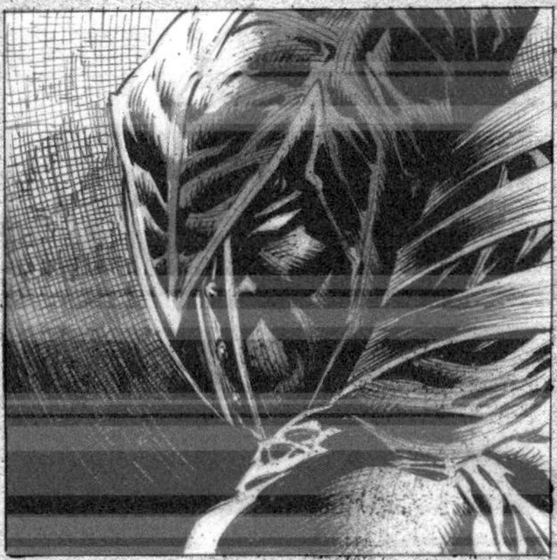

Our recommendation is to find and secure the location of [redacted] as soon as feasible. Recommend inter-agency assets be immediately mobilized to secure [redacted]. The risk of damaging the cover of operational assets is deemed acceptable.

Operative AZRAEL is to be considered an immediate threat. [redacted] has expedited a black-tag notice. All field agents to note.

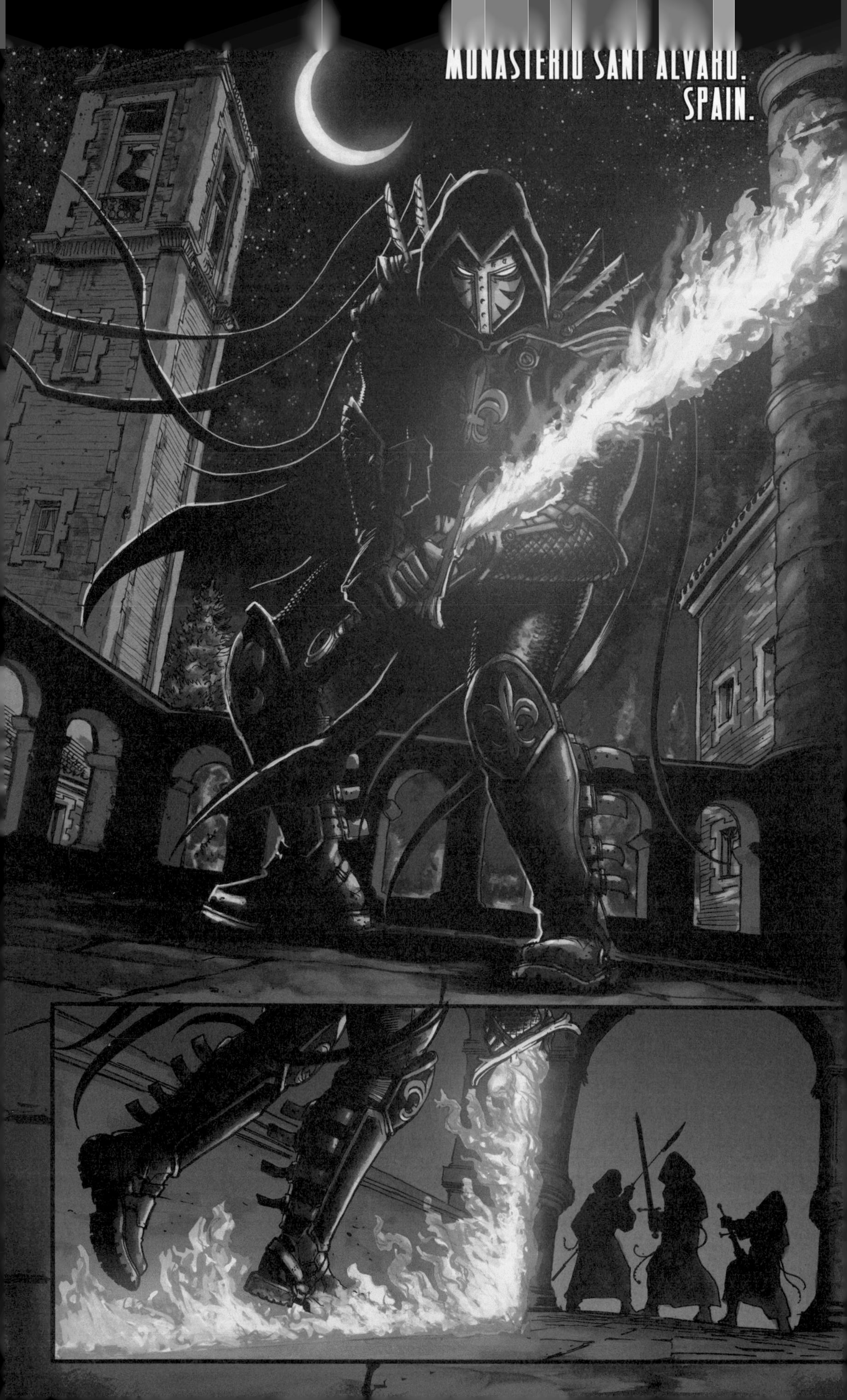
MONASTERIO SANT ALVARO.
SPAIN.

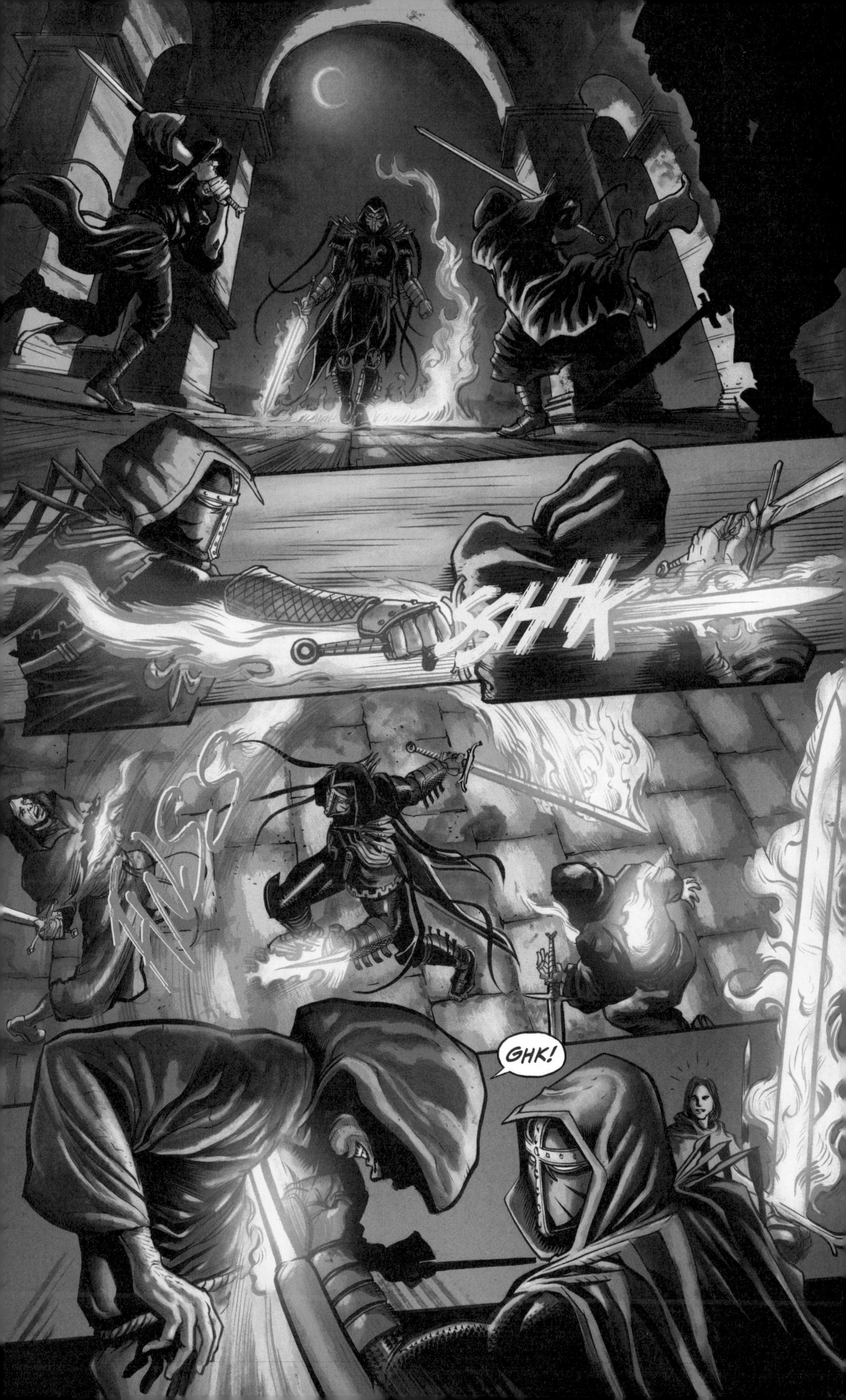
SHHK
GHK!

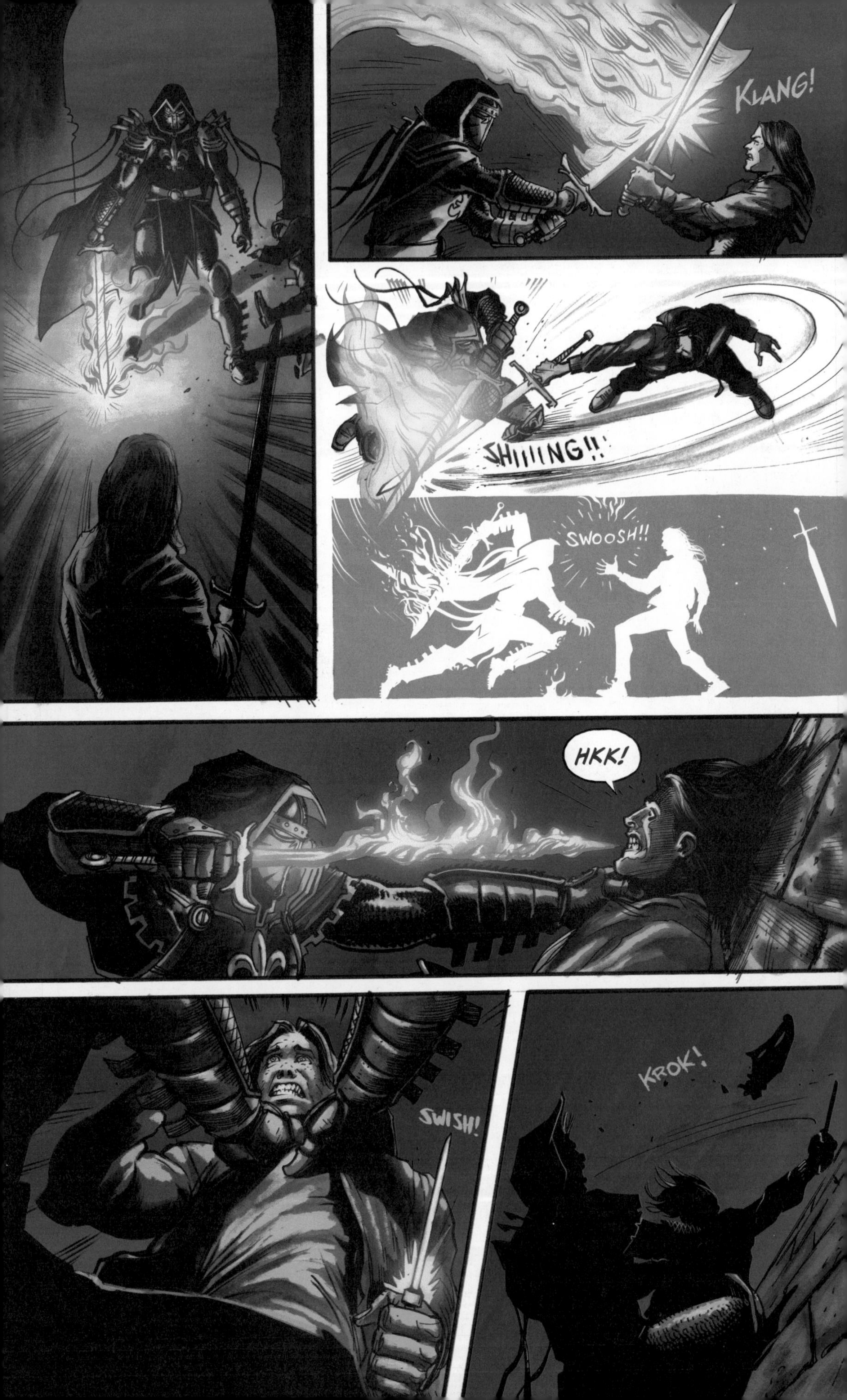
KLANG!
SHIIIING!!
SWOOSH!!
HKK!
SWISH!
KROK!

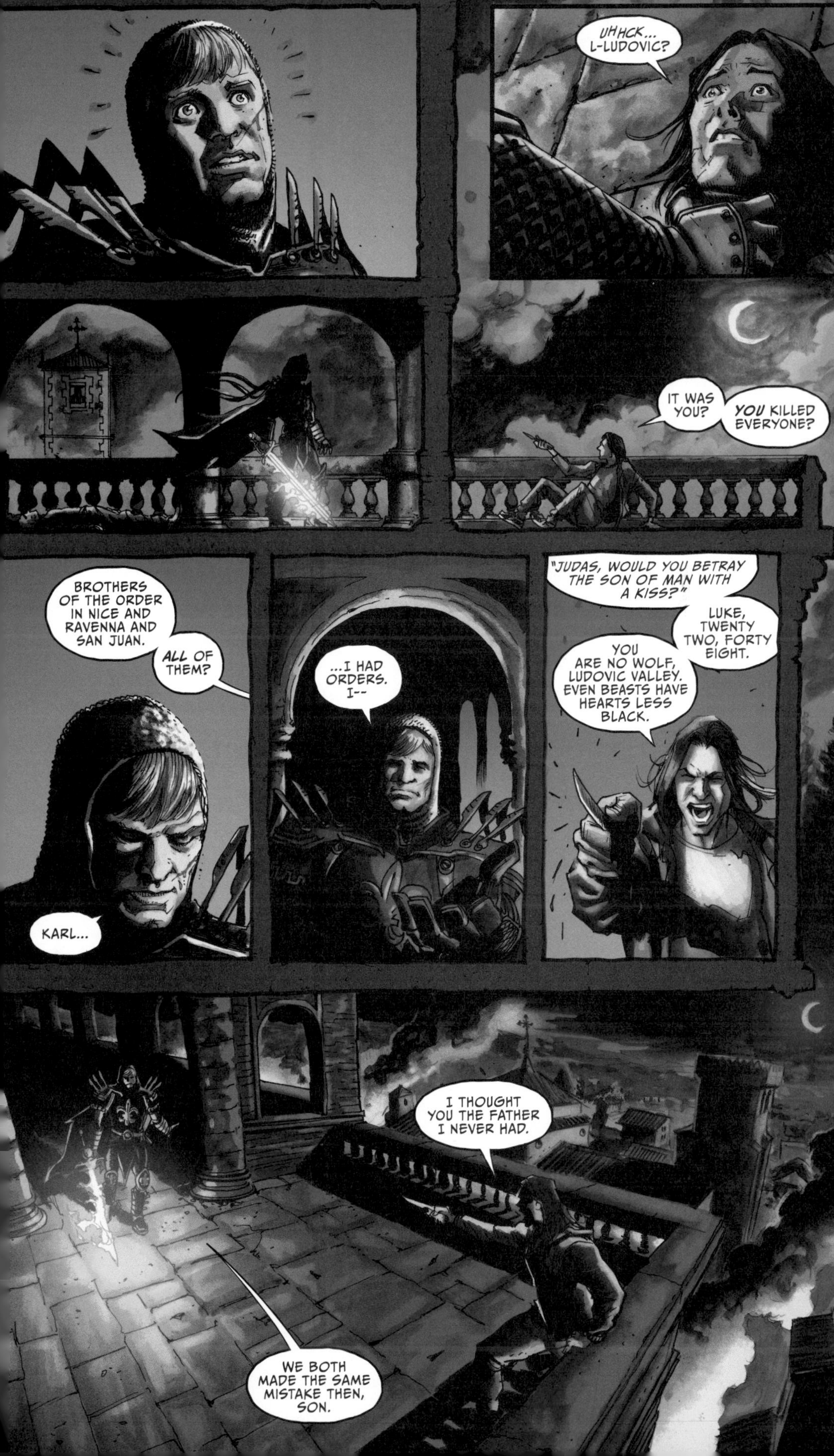
UHHCK... L-LUDOVIC?
IT WAS YOU?
YOU KILLED EVERYONE?
BROTHERS OF THE ORDER IN NICE AND RAVENNA AND SAN JUAN.
ALL OF THEM?
KARL...
...I HAD ORDERS. I--
"JUDAS, WOULD YOU BETRAY THE SON OF MAN WITH A KISS?"
LUKE, TWENTY TWO, FORTY EIGHT.
YOU ARE NO WOLF, LUDOVIC VALLEY. EVEN BEASTS HAVE HEARTS LESS BLACK.
I THOUGHT YOU THE FATHER I NEVER HAD.
WE BOTH MADE THE SAME MISTAKE THEN, SON.

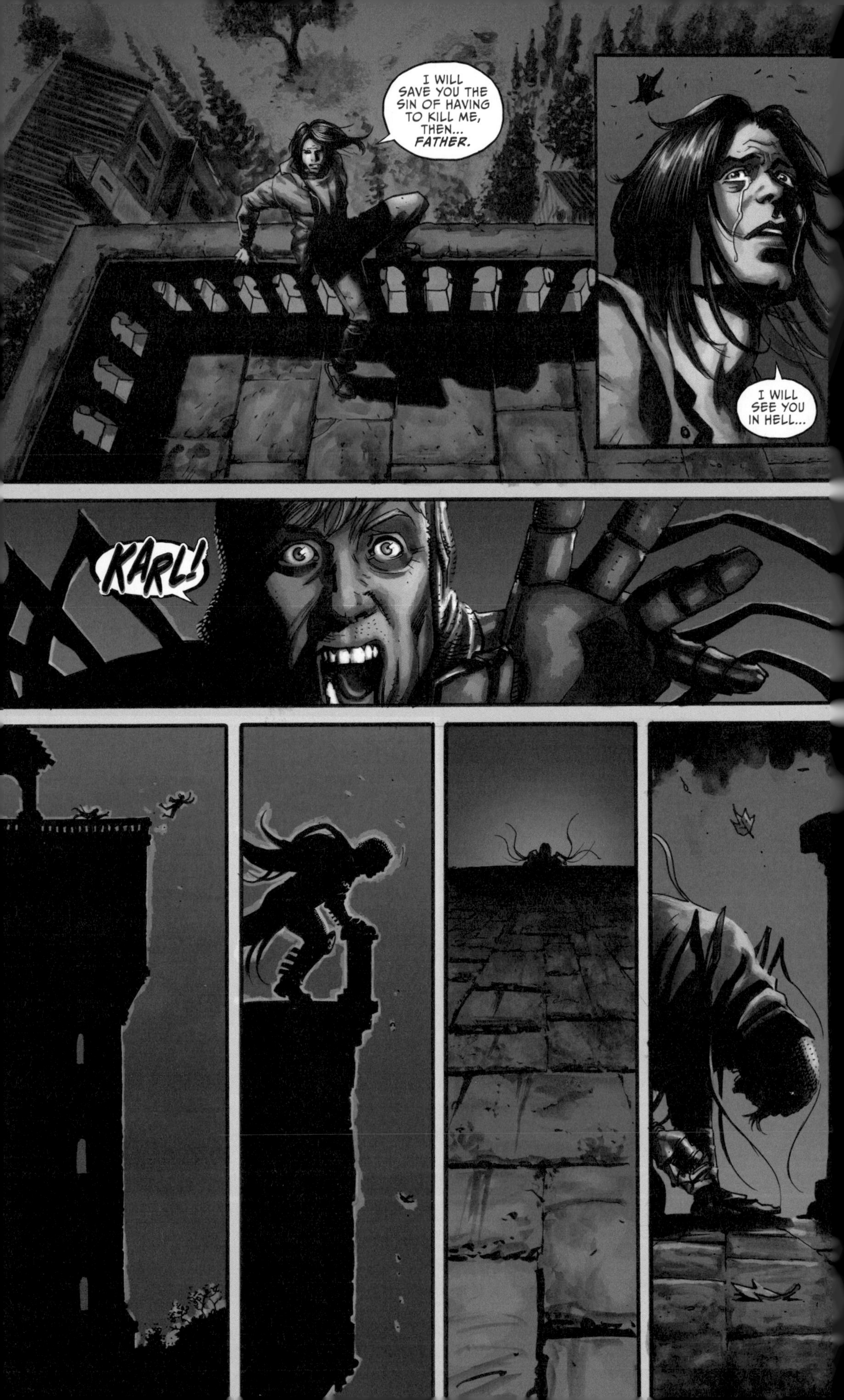
I WILL SAVE YOU THE SIN OF HAVING TO KILL ME, THEN... *FATHER.*
I WILL SEE YOU IN HELL...
KARL!

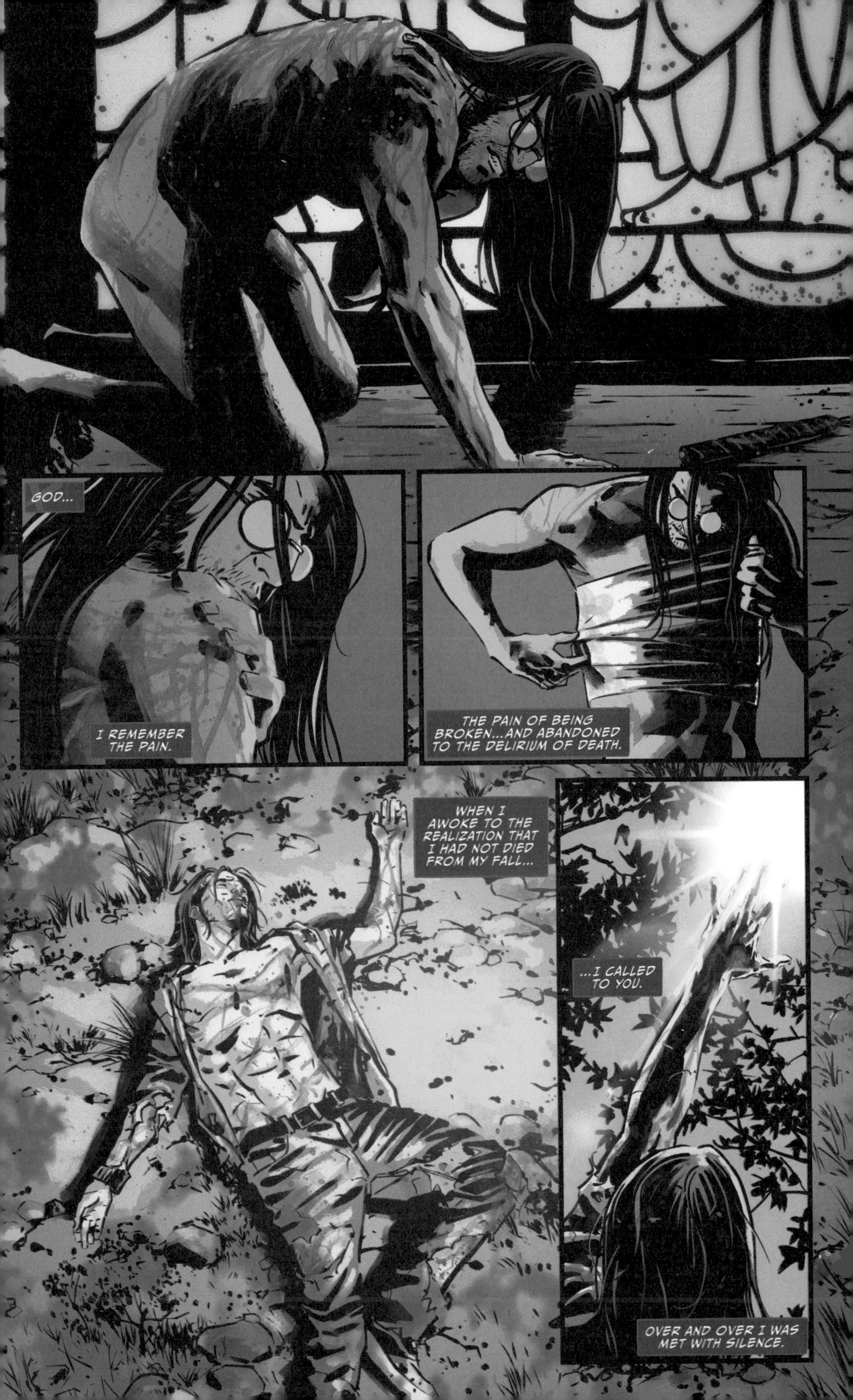
GOD...
I REMEMBER THE PAIN.
THE PAIN OF BEING BROKEN...AND ABANDONED TO THE DELIRIUM OF DEATH.
WHEN I AWOKE TO THE REALIZATION THAT I HAD NOT DIED FROM MY FALL...
...I CALLED TO YOU.
OVER AND OVER I WAS MET WITH SILENCE.

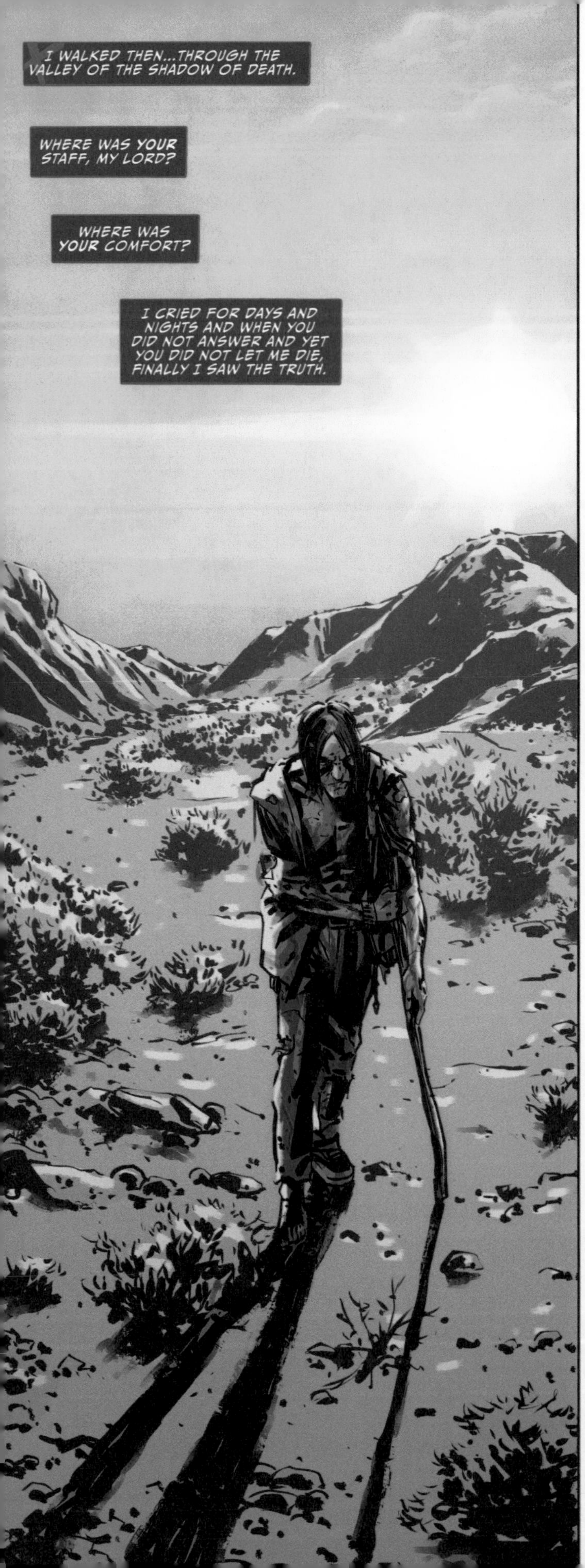
I WALKED THEN...THROUGH THE VALLEY OF THE SHADOW OF DEATH.
WHERE WAS YOUR STAFF, MY LORD?
WHERE WAS YOUR COMFORT?
I CRIED FOR DAYS AND NIGHTS AND WHEN YOU DID NOT ANSWER AND YET YOU DID NOT LET ME DIE, FINALLY I SAW THE TRUTH.

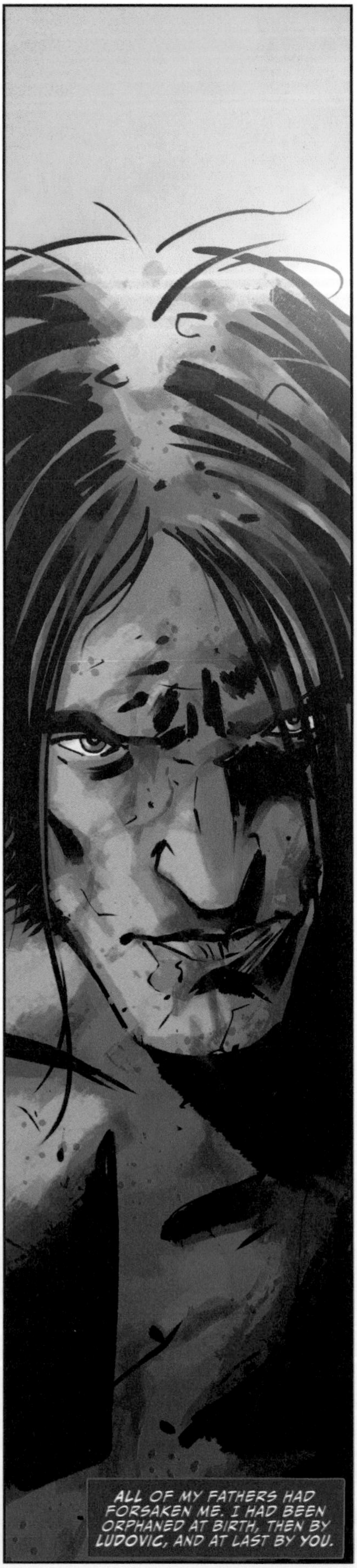
ALL OF MY FATHERS HAD FORSAKEN ME. I HAD BEEN ORPHANED AT BIRTH, THEN BY LUDOVIC, AND AT LAST BY YOU.

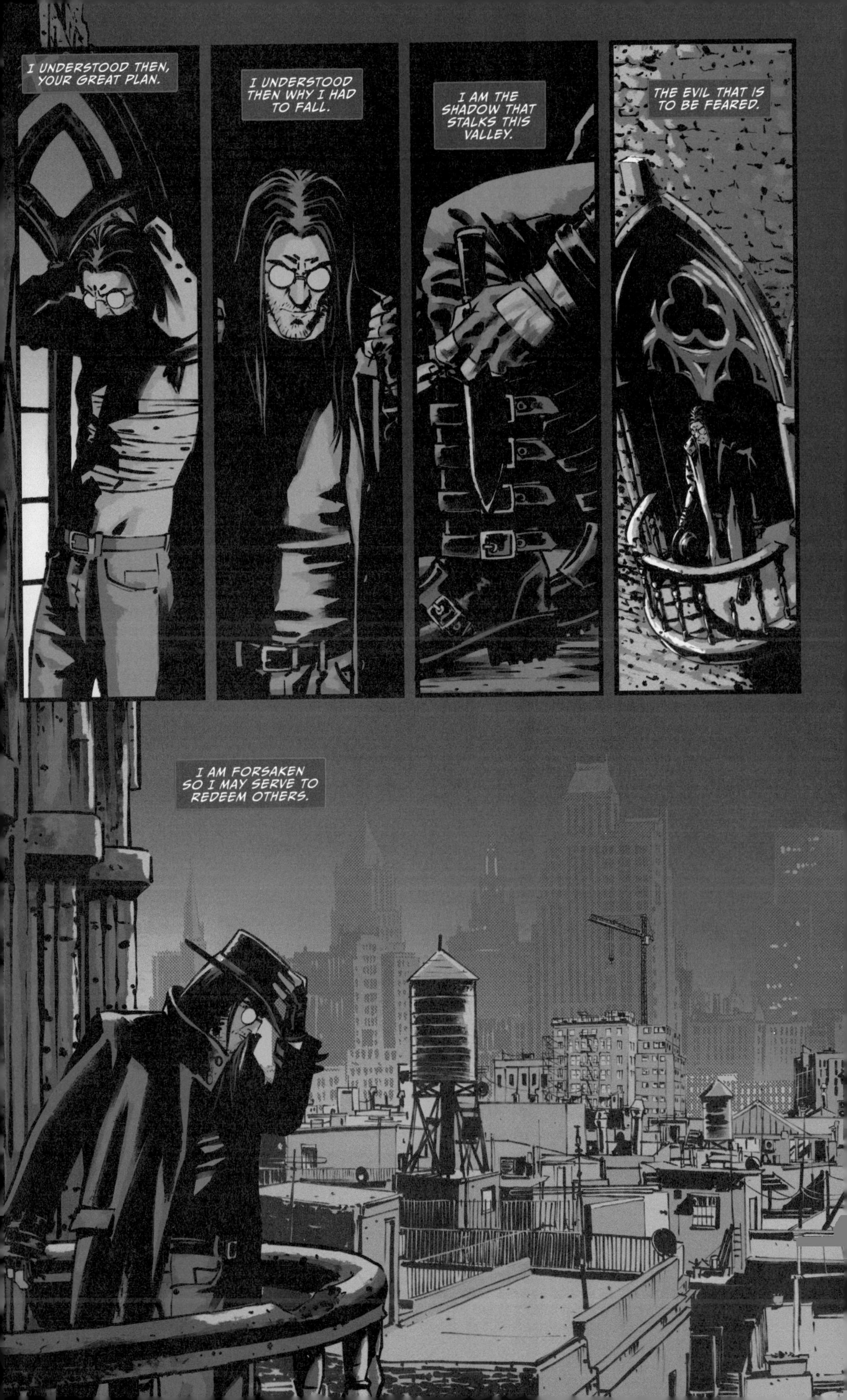
I UNDERSTOOD THEN, YOUR GREAT PLAN.
I UNDERSTOOD THEN WHY I HAD TO FALL.
I AM THE SHADOW THAT STALKS THIS VALLEY.
THE EVIL THAT IS TO BE FEARED.
I AM FORSAKEN SO I MAY SERVE TO REDEEM OTHERS.

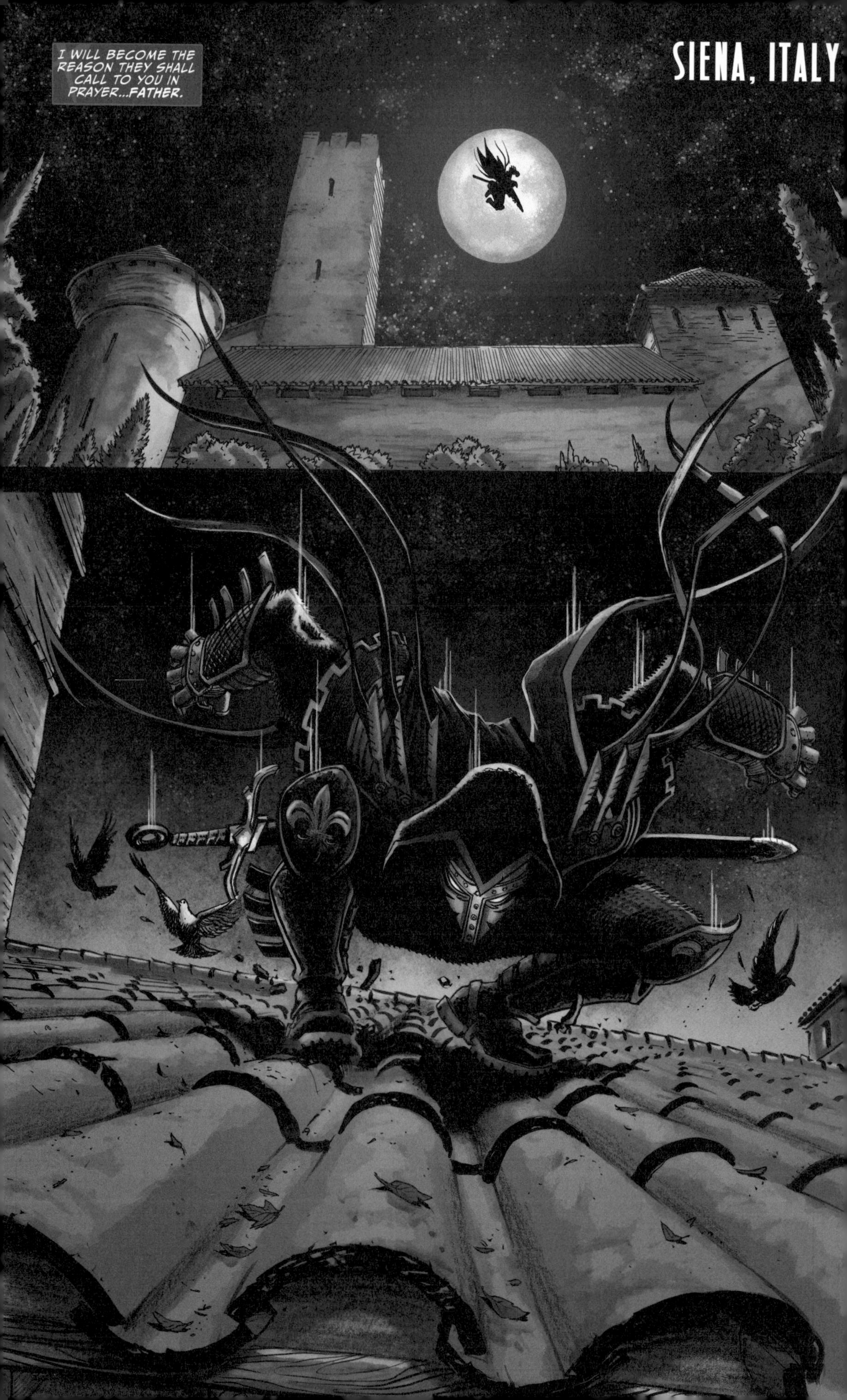
I WILL BECOME THE REASON THEY SHALL CALL TO YOU IN PRAYER...FATHER.
SIENA, ITALY

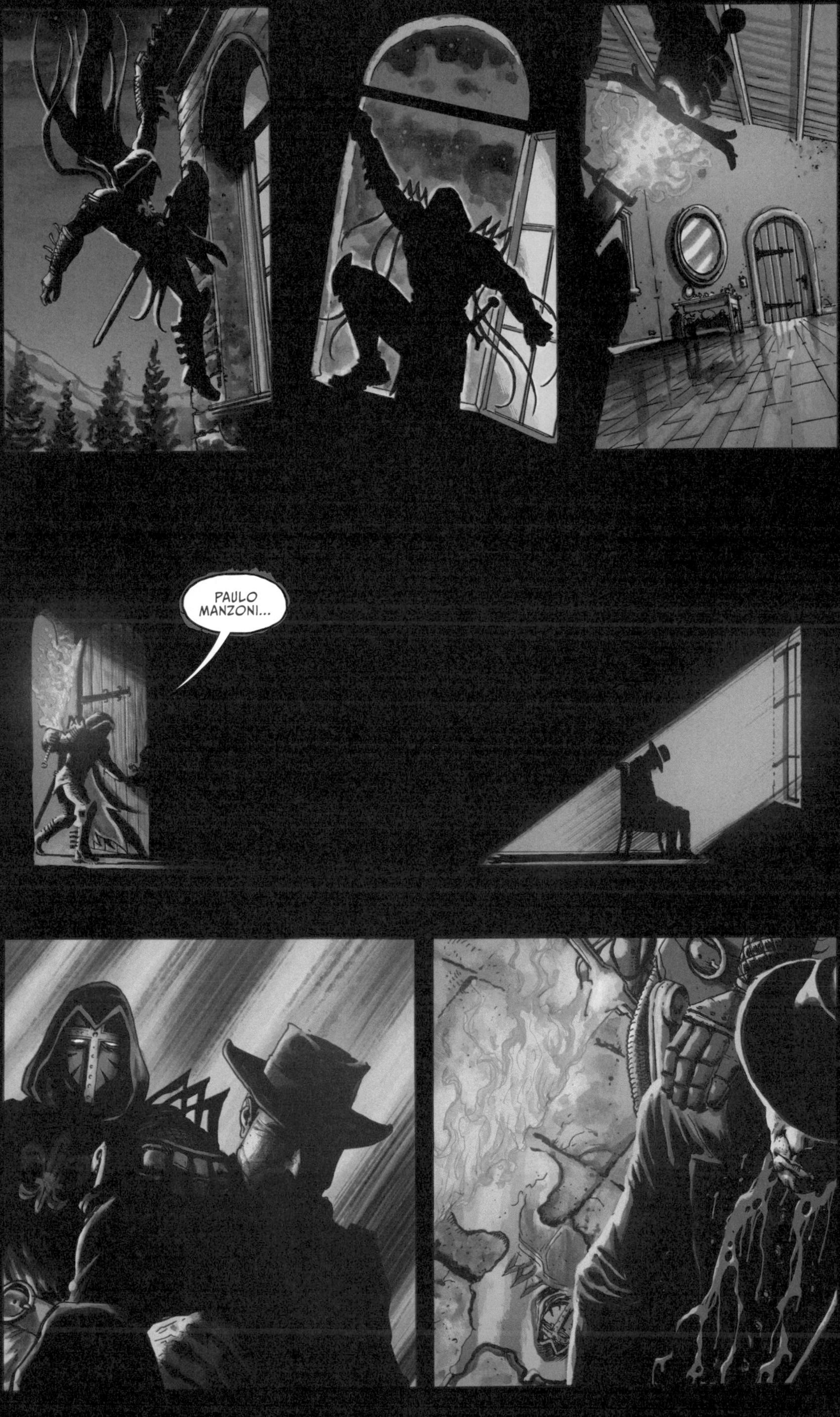
PAULO MANZONI...

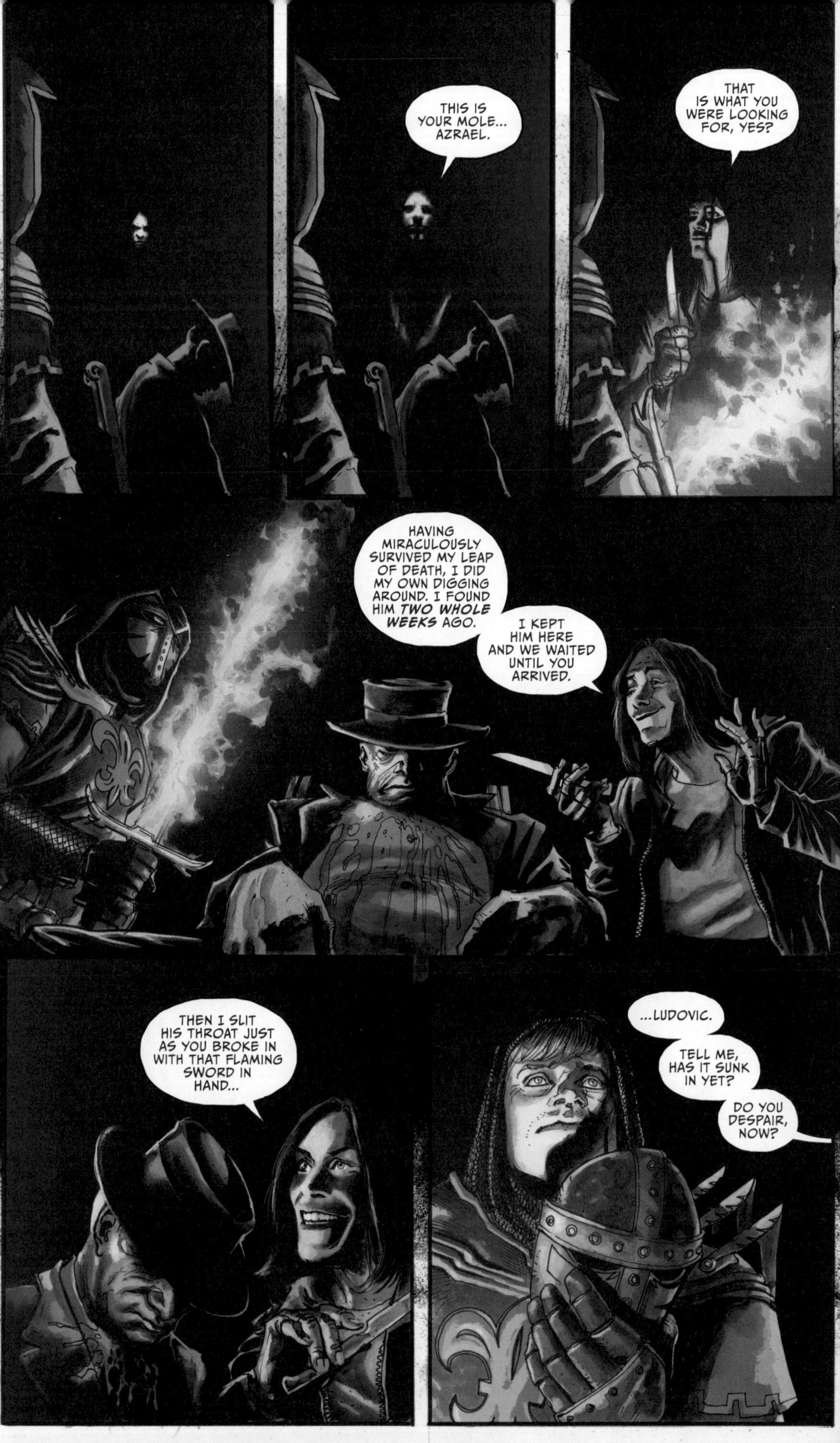
THIS IS YOUR MOLE... AZRAEL.
THAT IS WHAT YOU WERE LOOKING FOR, YES?
HAVING MIRACULOUSLY SURVIVED MY LEAP OF DEATH, I DID MY OWN DIGGING AROUND. I FOUND HIM TWO WHOLE WEEKS AGO.
I KEPT HIM HERE AND WE WAITED UNTIL YOU ARRIVED.
THEN I SLIT HIS THROAT JUST AS YOU BROKE IN WITH THAT FLAMING SWORD IN HAND...
...LUDOVIC.
TELL ME, HAS IT SUNK IN YET?
DO YOU DESPAIR, NOW?

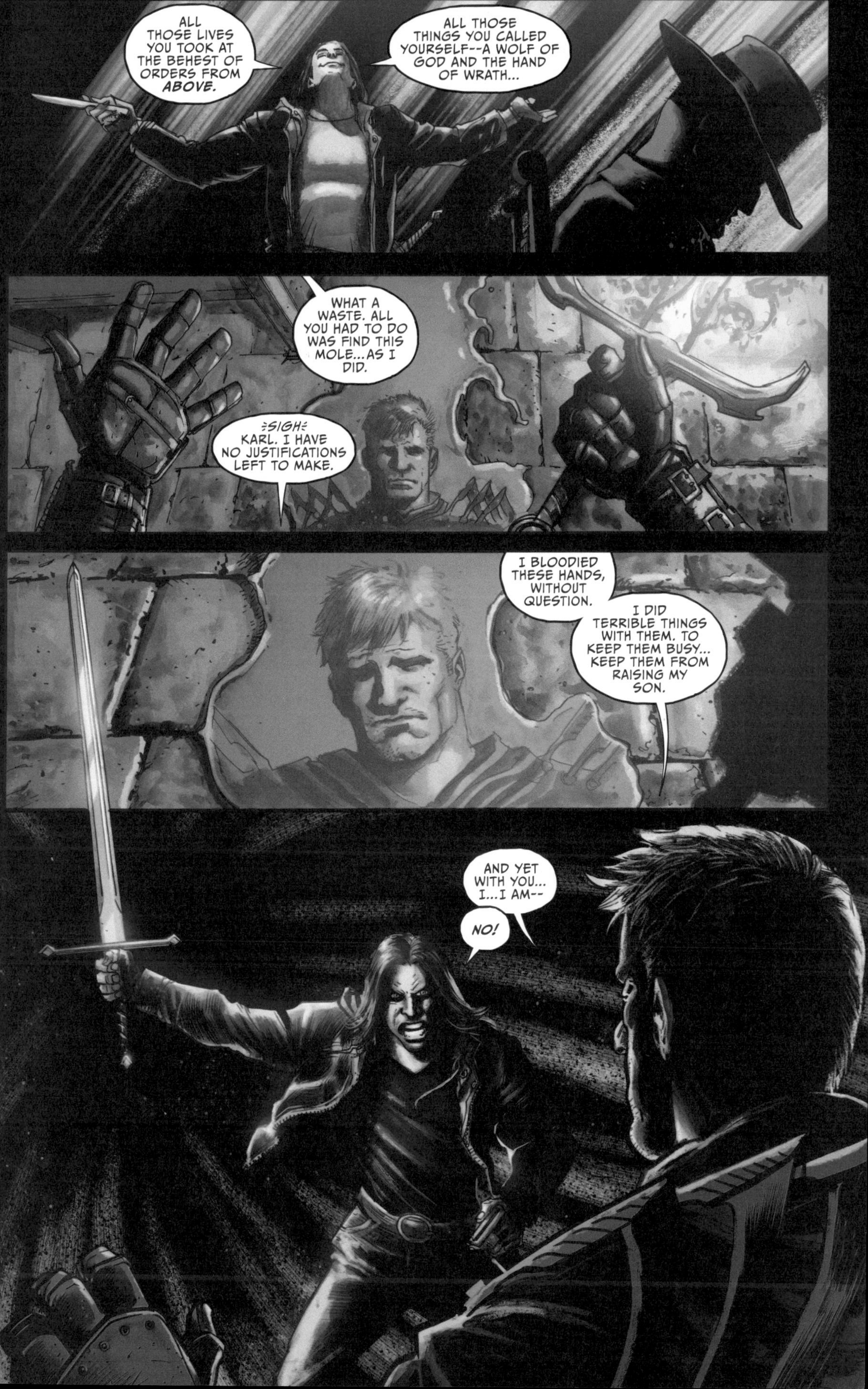
ALL THOSE LIVES YOU TOOK AT THE BEHEST OF ORDERS FROM *ABOVE.*
ALL THOSE THINGS YOU CALLED YOURSELF--A WOLF OF GOD AND THE HAND OF WRATH...
WHAT A WASTE. ALL YOU HAD TO DO WAS FIND THIS MOLE...AS I DID.
SIGH KARL. I HAVE NO JUSTIFICATIONS LEFT TO MAKE.
I BLOODIED THESE HANDS, WITHOUT QUESTION.
I DID TERRIBLE THINGS WITH THEM. TO KEEP THEM BUSY... KEEP THEM FROM RAISING MY SON.
AND YET WITH YOU... I...I AM--
NO!

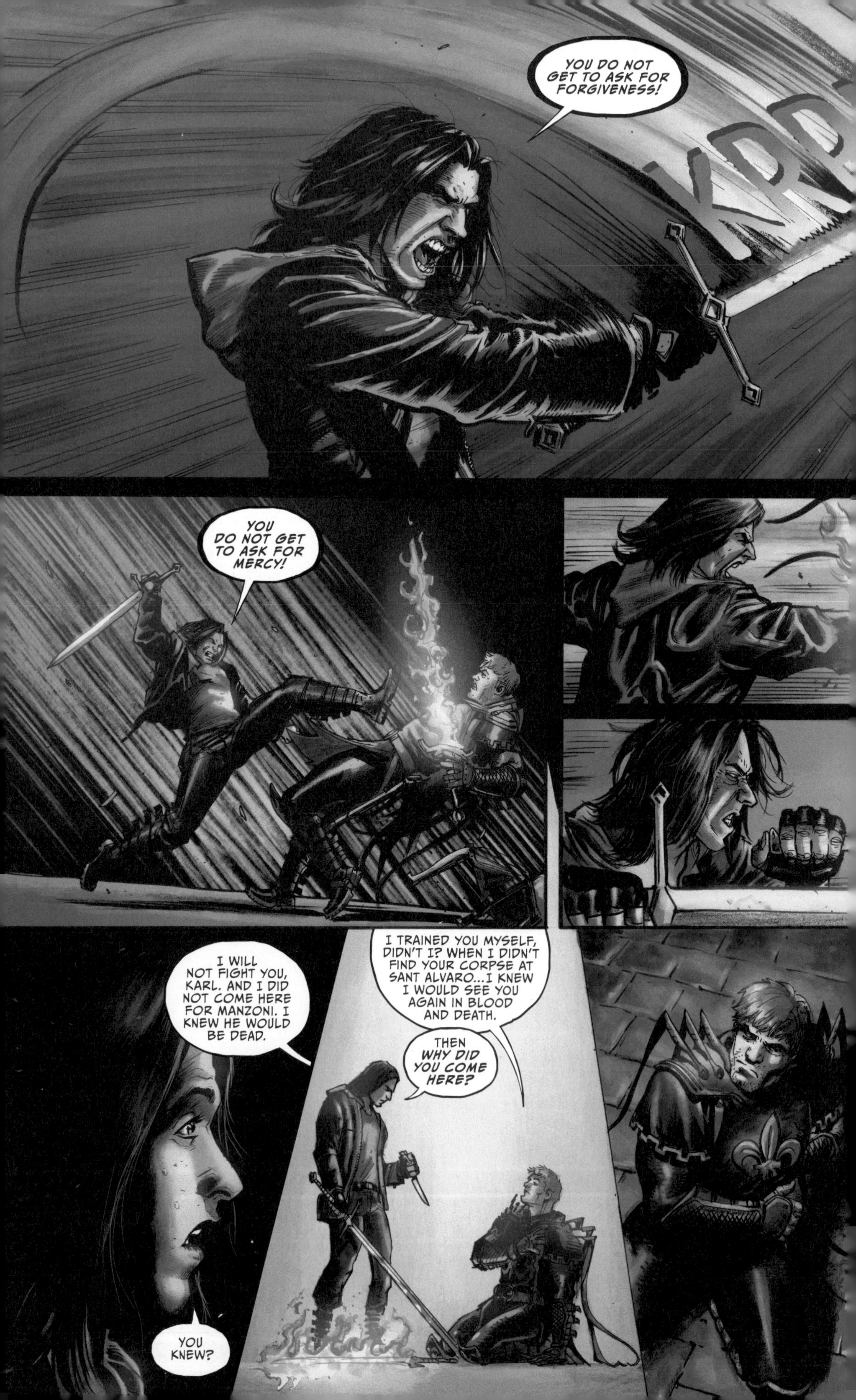
YOU DO NOT GET TO ASK FOR FORGIVENESS!
KRR
YOU DO NOT GET TO ASK FOR MERCY!
I WILL NOT FIGHT YOU, KARL. AND I DID NOT COME HERE FOR MANZONI. I KNEW HE WOULD BE DEAD.
YOU KNEW?
I TRAINED YOU MYSELF, DIDN'T I? WHEN I DIDN'T FIND YOUR CORPSE AT SANT ALVARO...I KNEW I WOULD SEE YOU AGAIN IN BLOOD AND DEATH.
THEN WHY DID YOU COME HERE?

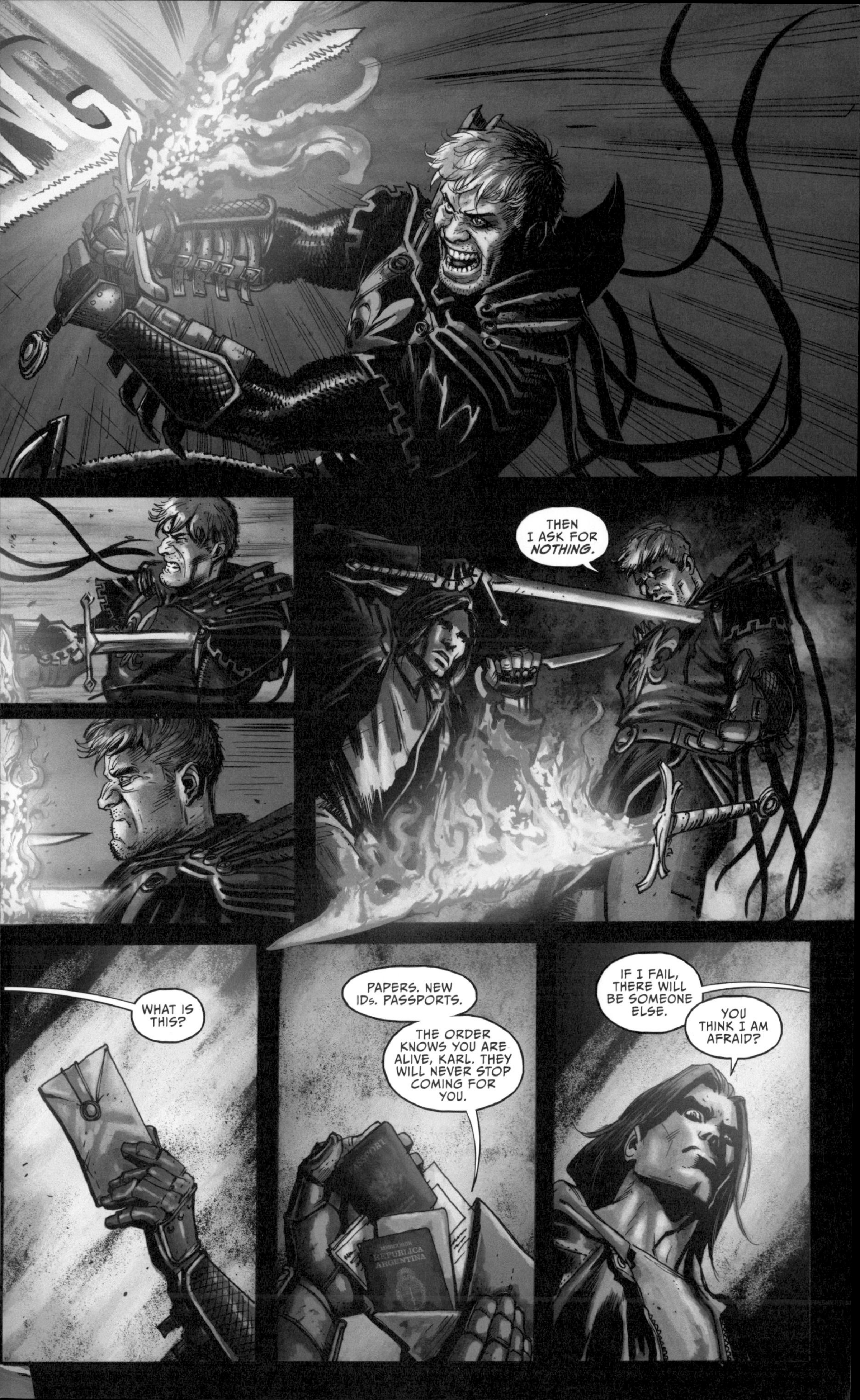
THEN I ASK FOR *NOTHING.*
WHAT IS THIS?
PAPERS. NEW IDs. PASSPORTS.
THE ORDER KNOWS YOU ARE ALIVE, KARL. THEY WILL NEVER STOP COMING FOR YOU.
PASSPORT
REPUBLICA ARGENTINA
IF I FAIL, THERE WILL BE SOMEONE ELSE.
YOU THINK I AM AFRAID?

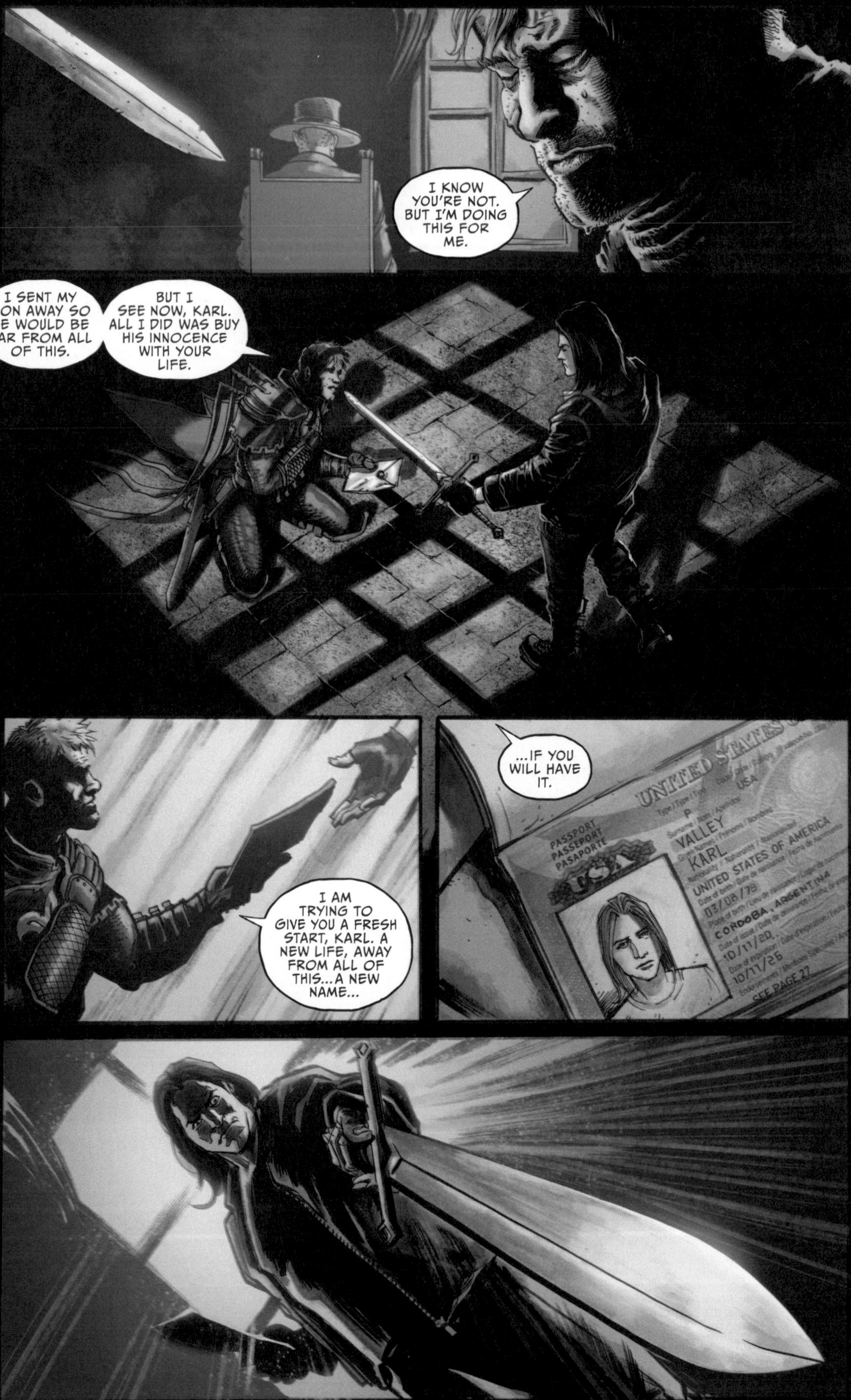
I KNOW YOU'RE NOT. BUT I'M DOING THIS FOR ME.
I SENT MY SON AWAY SO HE WOULD BE FAR FROM ALL OF THIS.
BUT I SEE NOW, KARL. ALL I DID WAS BUY HIS INNOCENCE WITH YOUR LIFE.
I AM TRYING TO GIVE YOU A FRESH START, KARL. A NEW LIFE, AWAY FROM ALL OF THIS...A NEW NAME...
...IF YOU WILL HAVE IT.
PASSPORT
PASSEPORT
PASAPORTE
USA
VALLEY
KARL
UNITED STATES OF AMERICA
03/08/79
CORDOBA, ARGENTINA
10/11/20
10/11/26
SEE PAGE 27

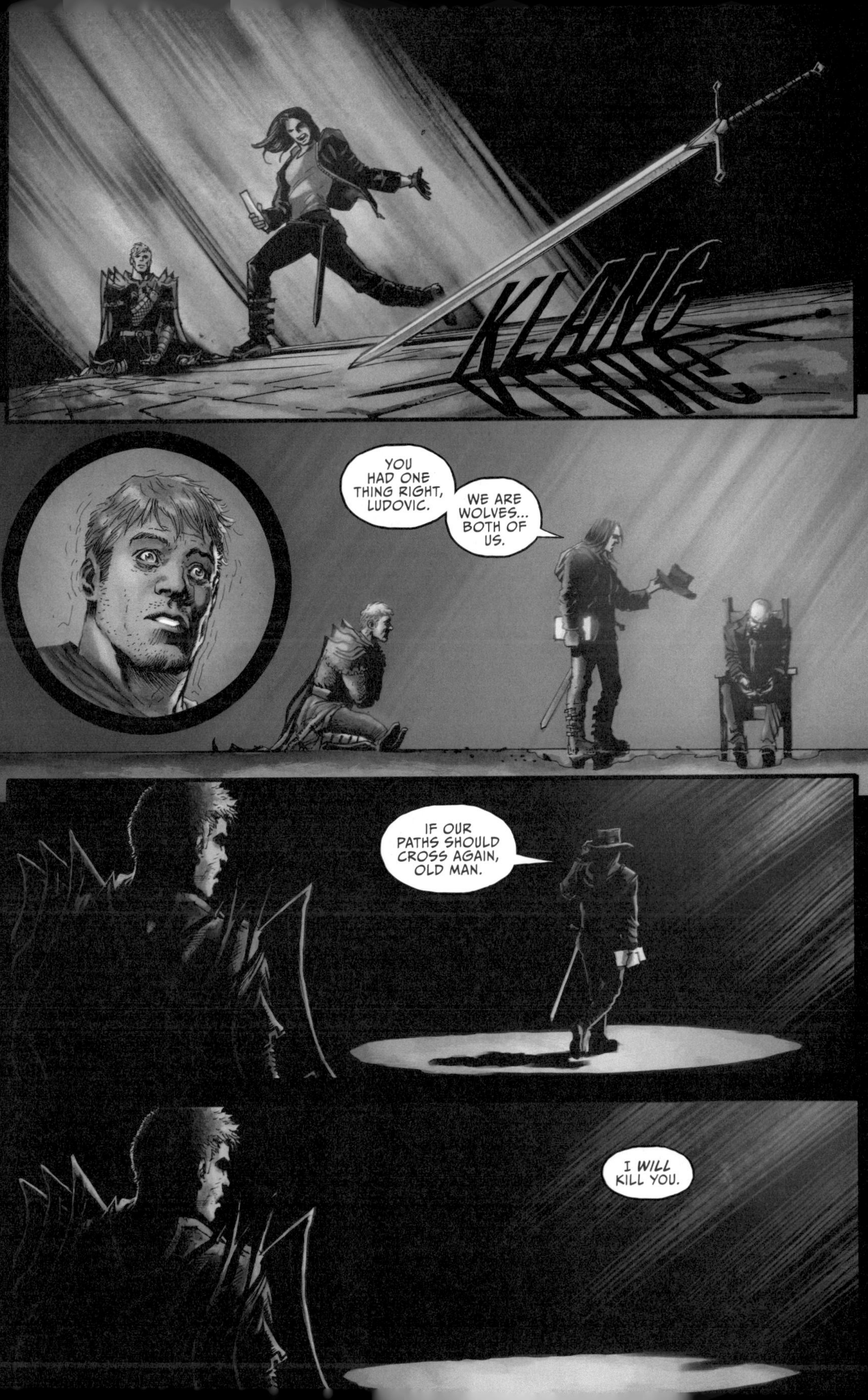
KLANG
YOU HAD ONE THING RIGHT, LUDOVIC.
WE ARE WOLVES... BOTH OF US.
IF OUR PATHS SHOULD CROSS AGAIN, OLD MAN.
I WILL KILL YOU.

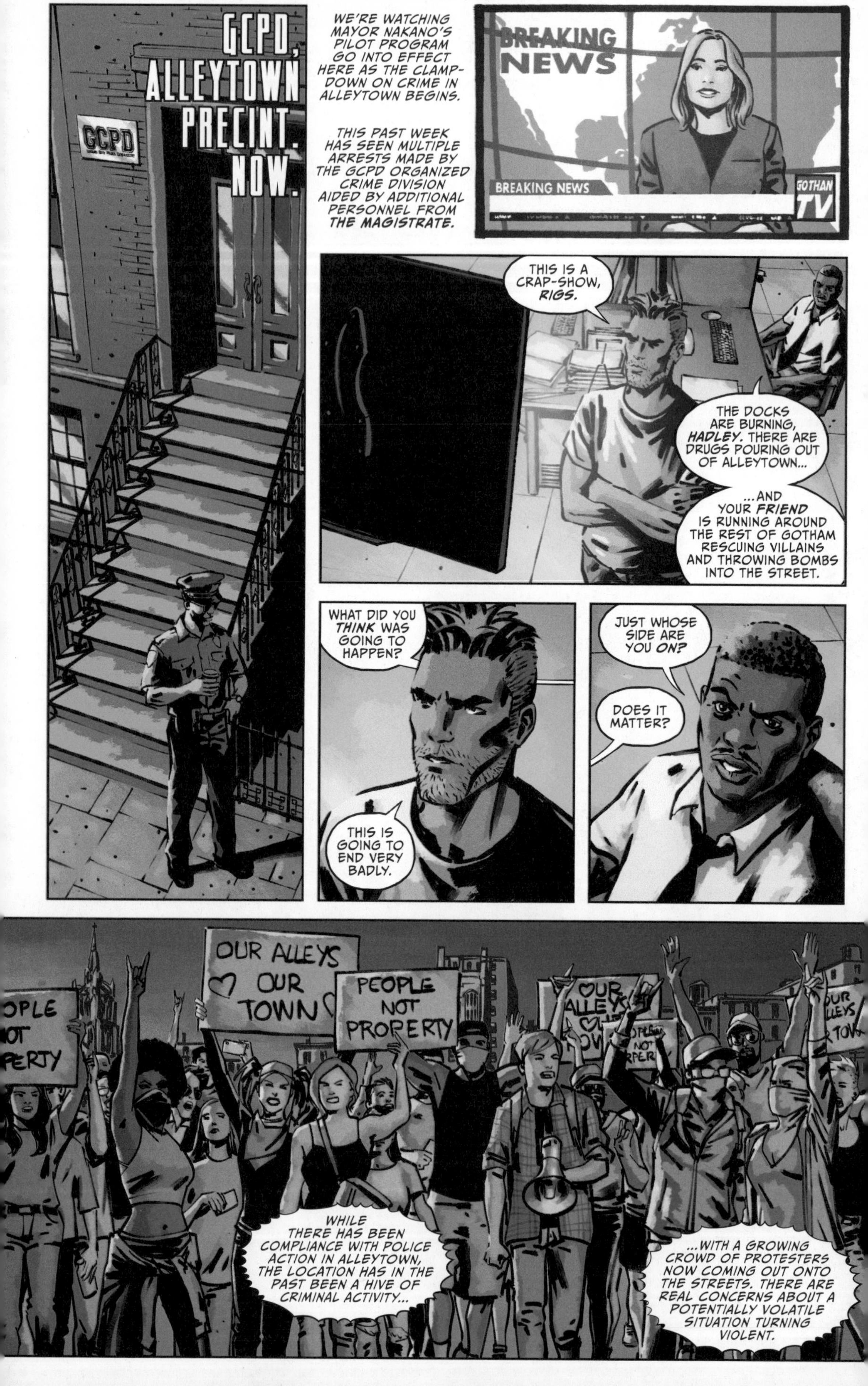
GCPD, ALLEYTOWN PRECINT. NOW.
GCPD
WE'RE WATCHING MAYOR NAKANO'S PILOT PROGRAM GO INTO EFFECT HERE AS THE CLAMP-DOWN ON CRIME IN ALLEYTOWN BEGINS.
THIS PAST WEEK HAS SEEN MULTIPLE ARRESTS MADE BY THE GCPD ORGANIZED CRIME DIVISION AIDED BY ADDITIONAL PERSONNEL FROM THE MAGISTRATE.
BREAKING NEWS
BREAKING NEWS
GOTHAM TV
THIS IS A CRAP-SHOW, RIGS.
THE DOCKS ARE BURNING, HADLEY. THERE ARE DRUGS POURING OUT OF ALLEYTOWN...
...AND YOUR FRIEND IS RUNNING AROUND THE REST OF GOTHAM RESCUING VILLAINS AND THROWING BOMBS INTO THE STREET.
WHAT DID YOU THINK WAS GOING TO HAPPEN?
THIS IS GOING TO END VERY BADLY.
JUST WHOSE SIDE ARE YOU ON?
DOES IT MATTER?
OUR ALLEYS ♡ OUR TOWN ♡
PEOPLE NOT PROPERTY
WHILE THERE HAS BEEN COMPLIANCE WITH POLICE ACTION IN ALLEYTOWN, THE LOCATION HAS IN THE PAST BEEN A HIVE OF CRIMINAL ACTIVITY...
...WITH A GROWING CROWD OF PROTESTERS NOW COMING OUT ONTO THE STREETS. THERE ARE REAL CONCERNS ABOUT A POTENTIALLY VOLATILE SITUATION TURNING VIOLENT.

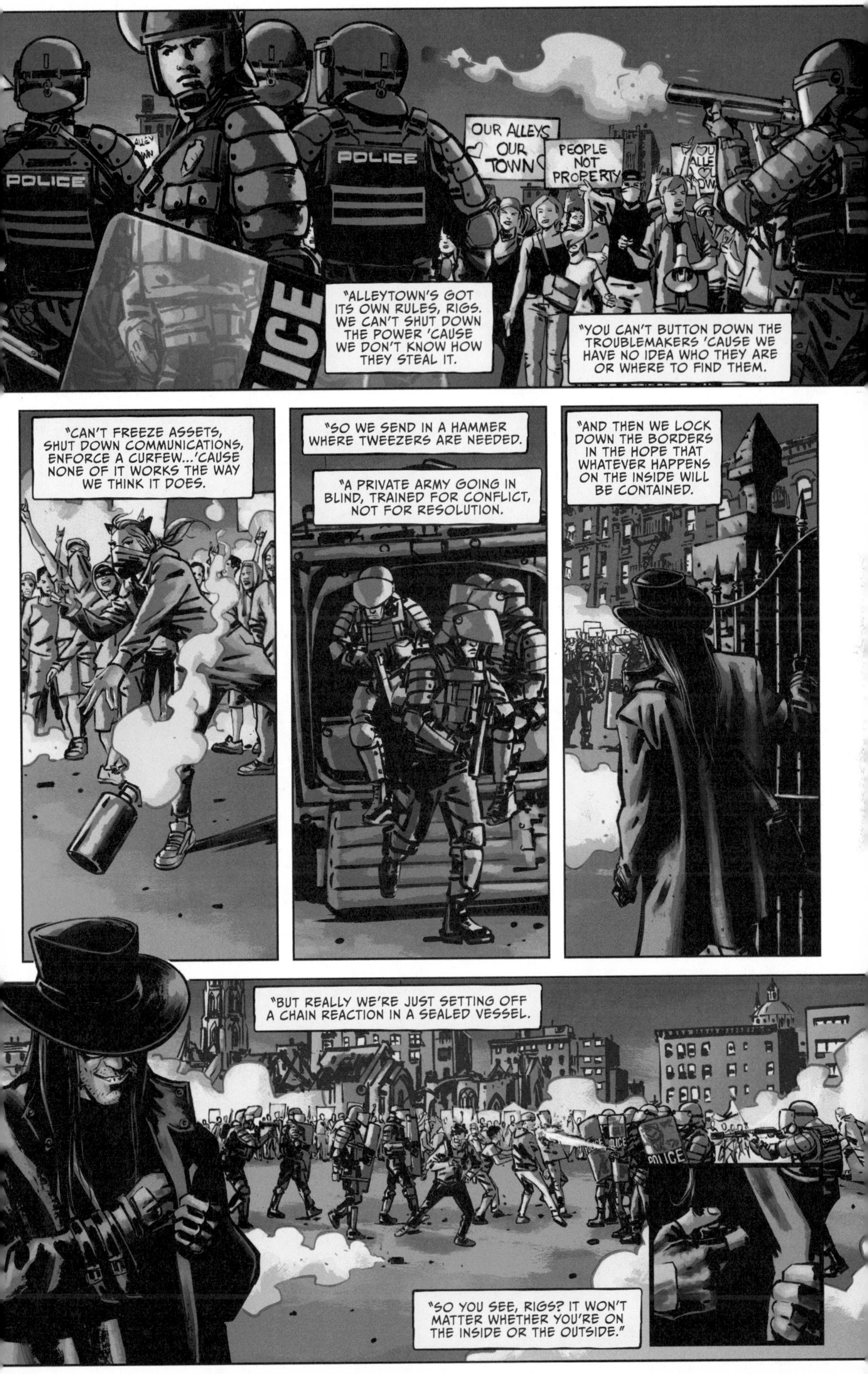
OUR ALLEYS OUR TOWN
PEOPLE NOT PROPERTY
POLICE
"ALLEYTOWN'S GOT ITS OWN RULES, RIGS. WE CAN'T SHUT DOWN THE POWER 'CAUSE WE DON'T KNOW HOW THEY STEAL IT.
"YOU CAN'T BUTTON DOWN THE TROUBLEMAKERS 'CAUSE WE HAVE NO IDEA WHO THEY ARE OR WHERE TO FIND THEM.
"CAN'T FREEZE ASSETS, SHUT DOWN COMMUNICATIONS, ENFORCE A CURFEW...'CAUSE NONE OF IT WORKS THE WAY WE THINK IT DOES.
"SO WE SEND IN A HAMMER WHERE TWEEZERS ARE NEEDED.
"A PRIVATE ARMY GOING IN BLIND, TRAINED FOR CONFLICT, NOT FOR RESOLUTION.
"AND THEN WE LOCK DOWN THE BORDERS IN THE HOPE THAT WHATEVER HAPPENS ON THE INSIDE WILL BE CONTAINED.
"BUT REALLY WE'RE JUST SETTING OFF A CHAIN REACTION IN A SEALED VESSEL.
"SO YOU SEE, RIGS? IT WON'T MATTER WHETHER YOU'RE ON THE INSIDE OR THE OUTSIDE."

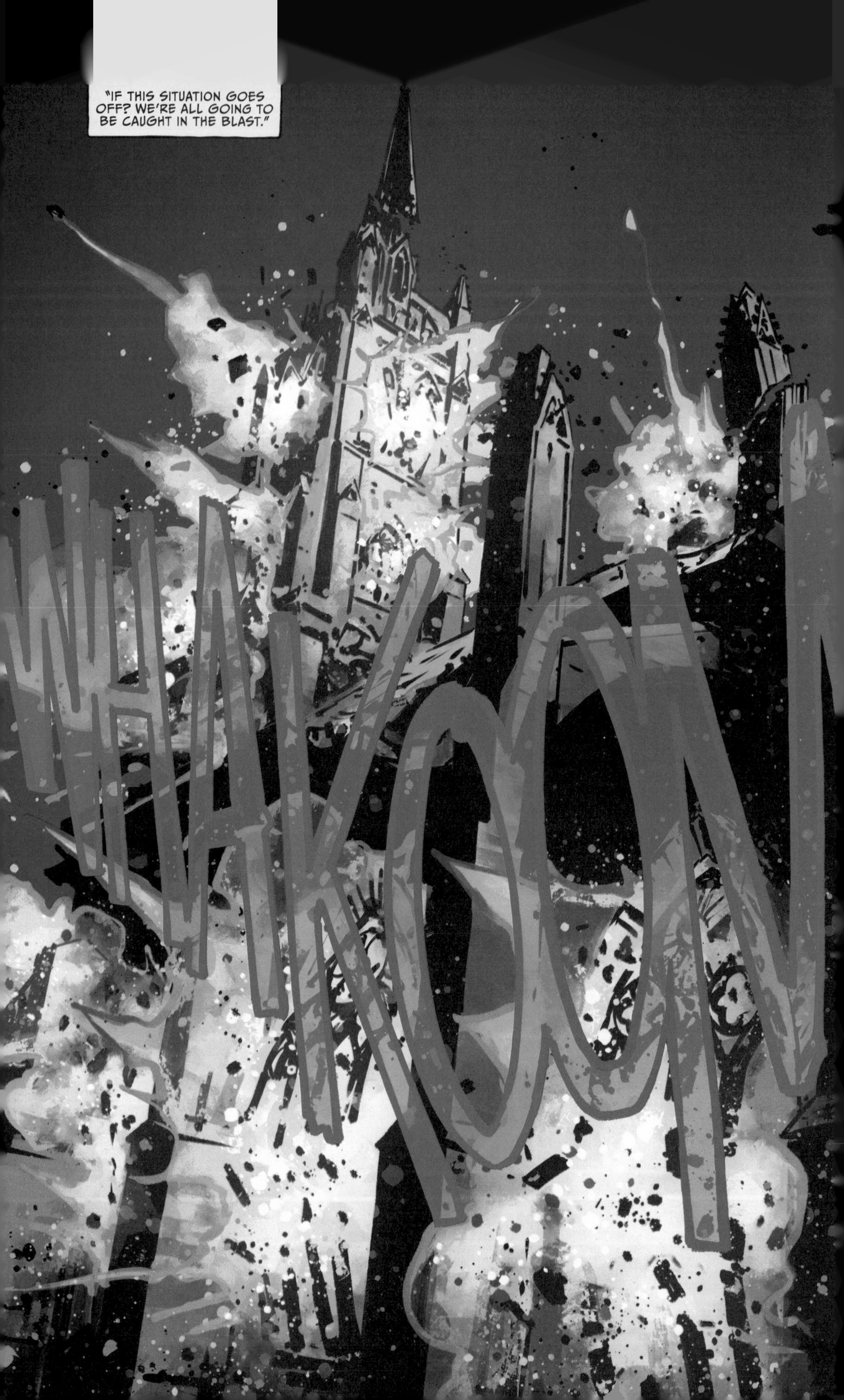
"IF THIS SITUATION GOES OFF? WE'RE ALL GOING TO BE CAUGHT IN THE BLAST."
WHAKOOM

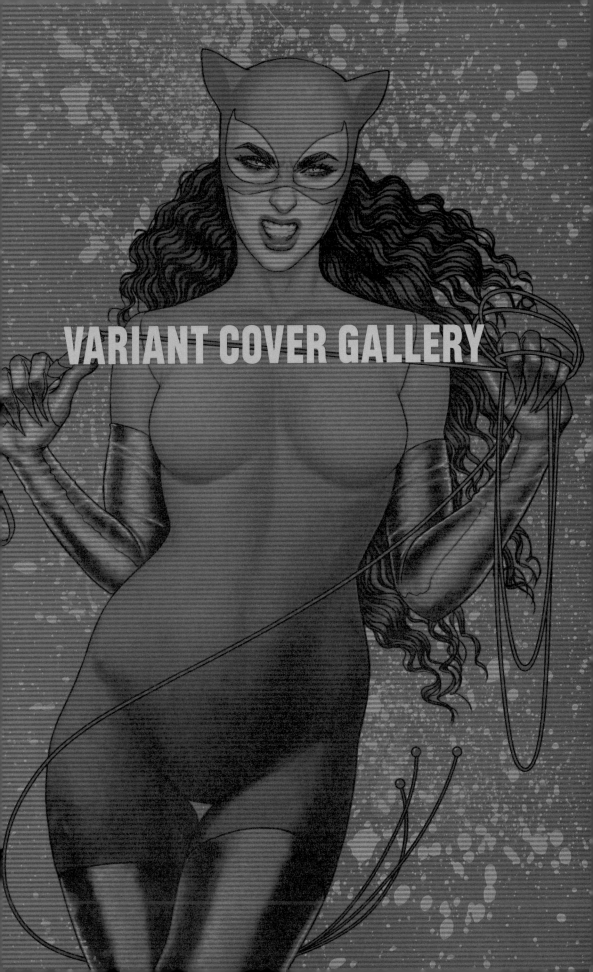

VARIANT COVER GALLERY

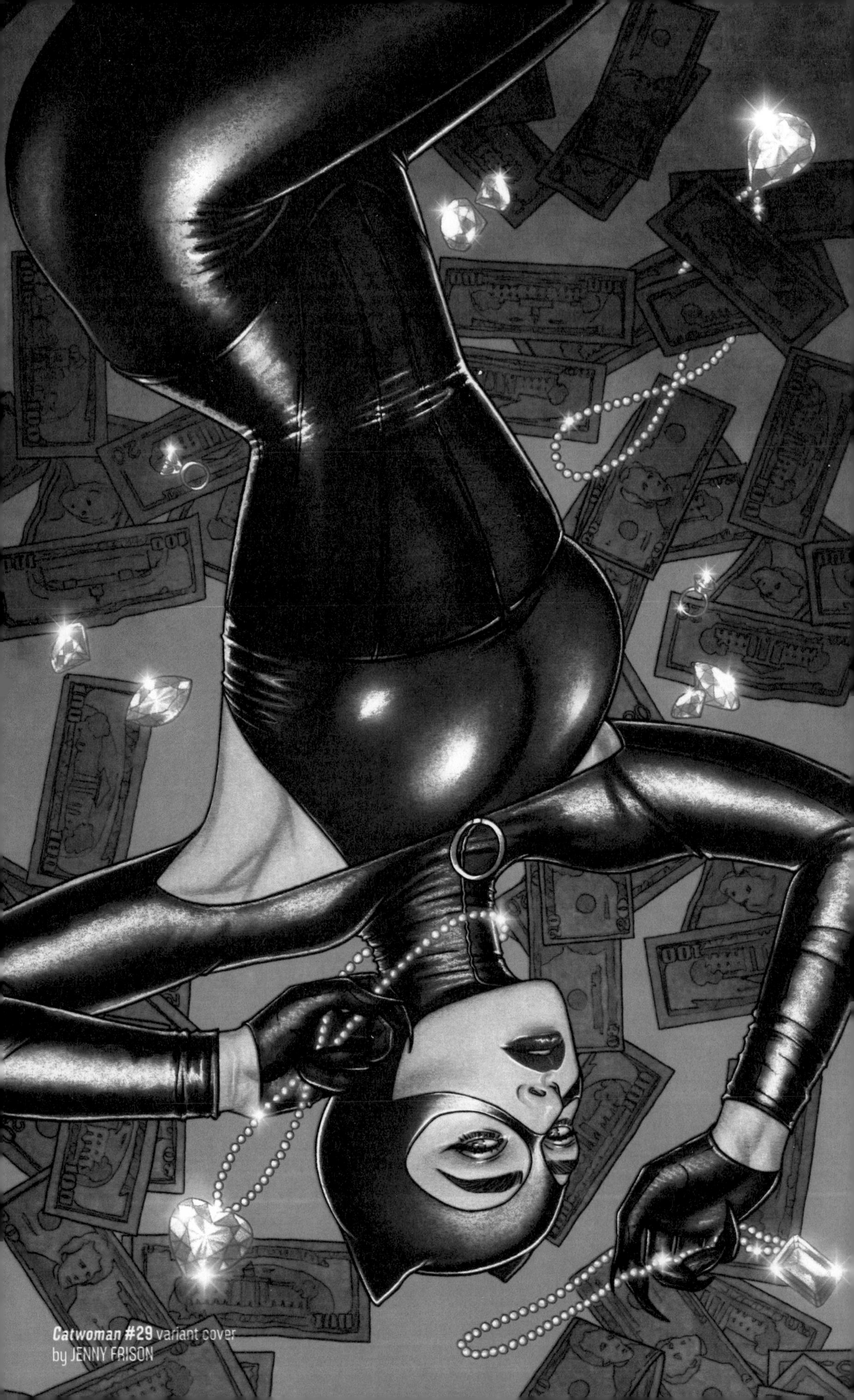

Catwoman #29 variant cover
by JENNY FRISON

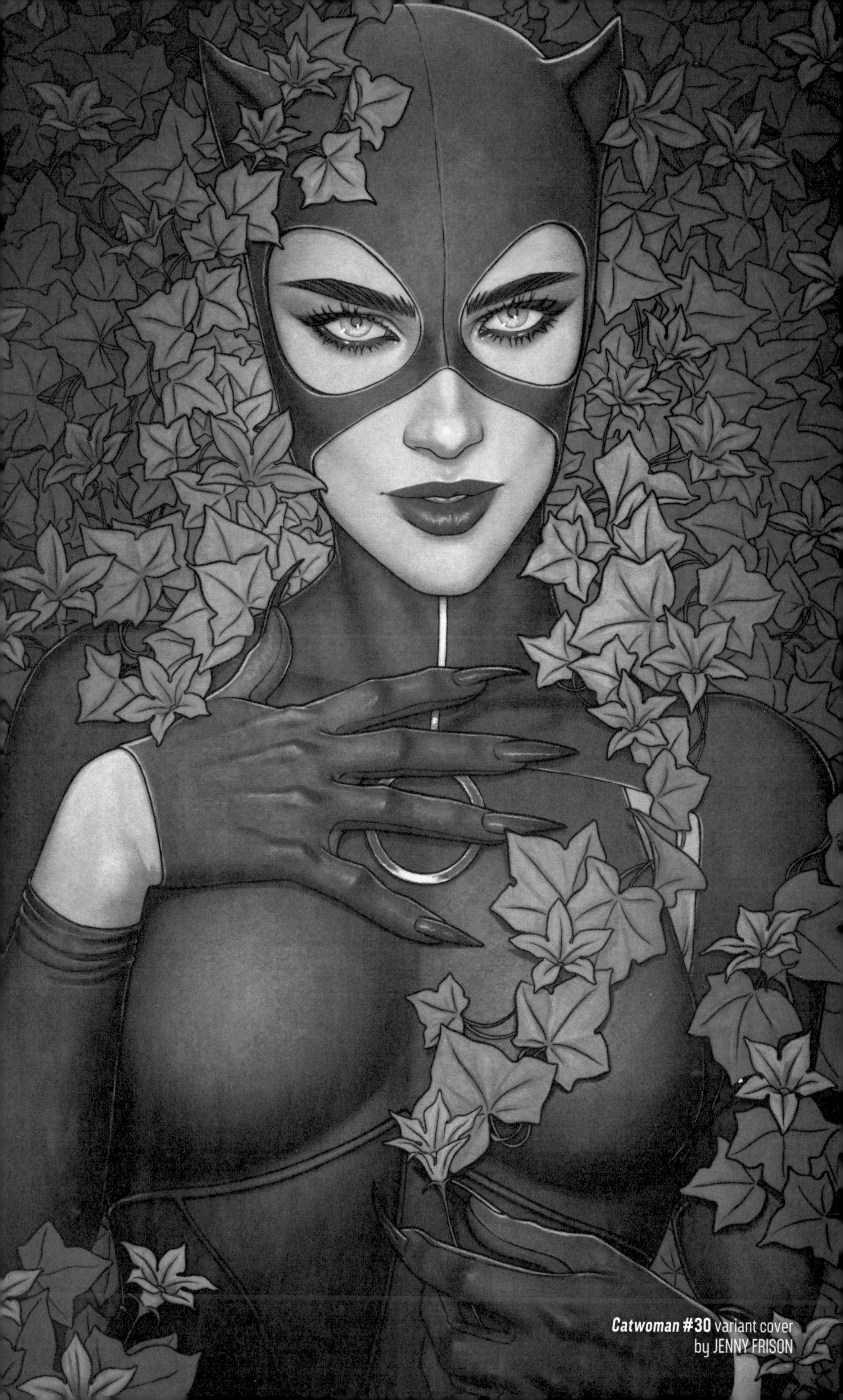

***Catwoman* #30** variant cover
by JENNY FRISON

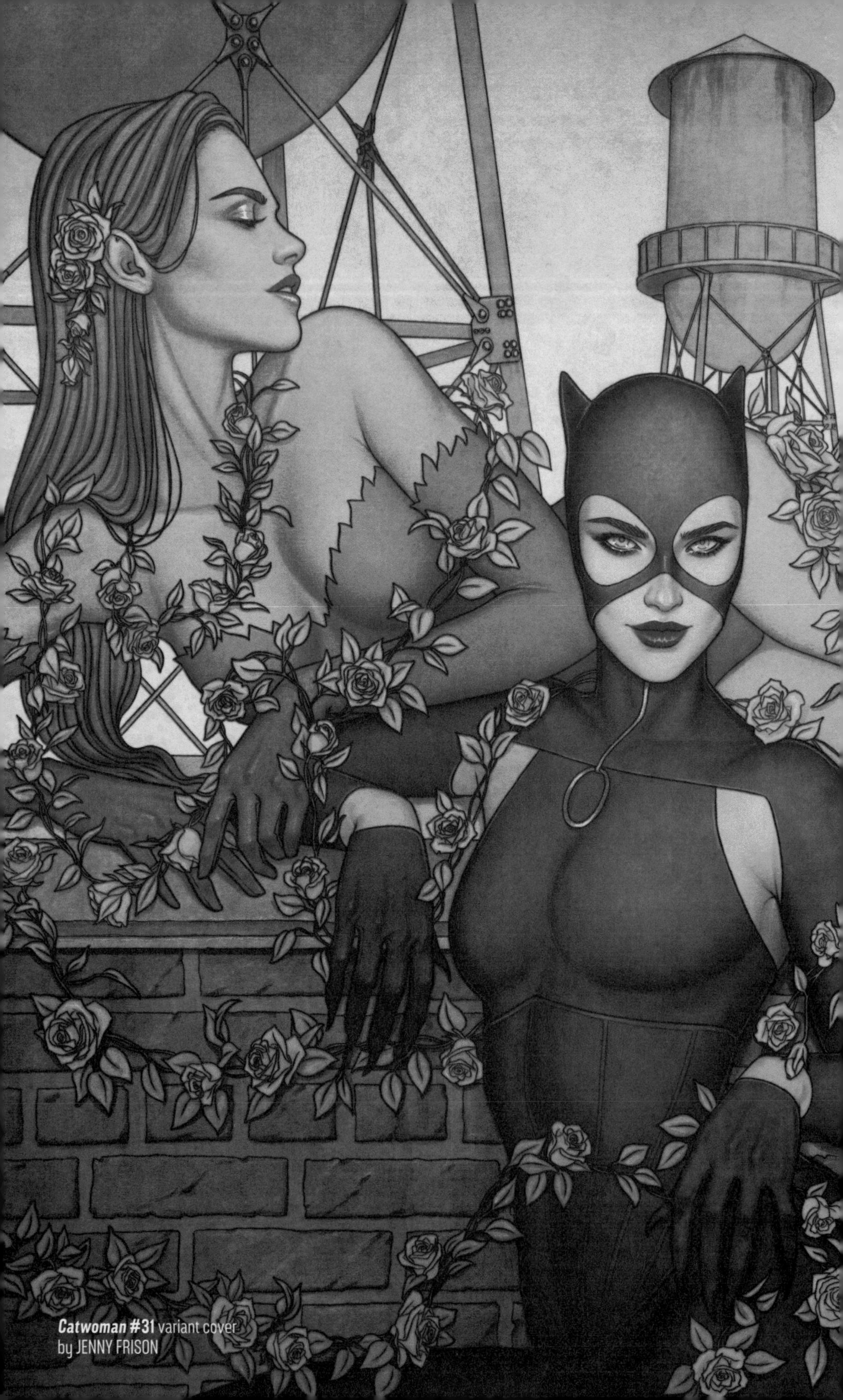

***Catwoman* #31** variant cover
by JENNY FRISON

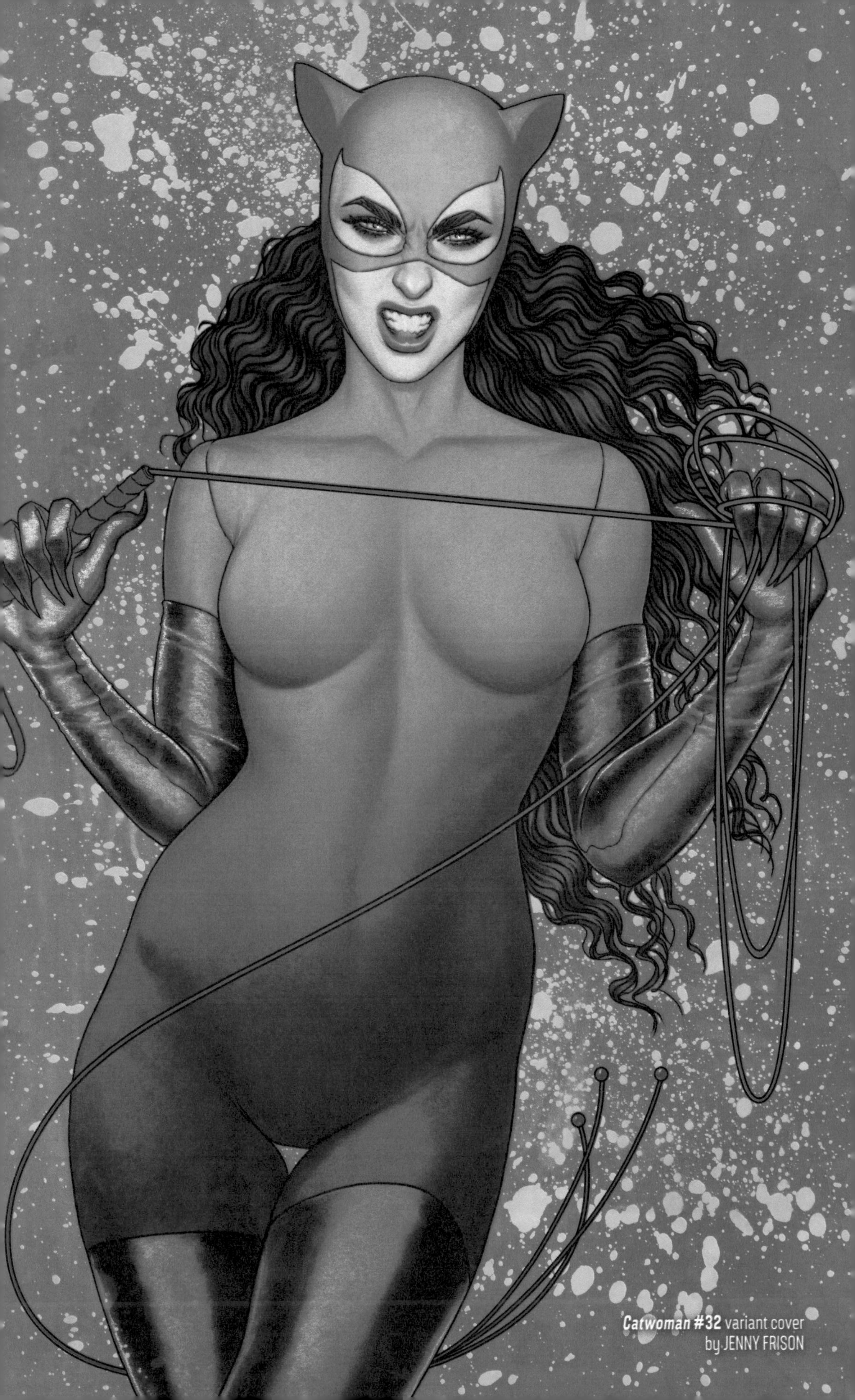

***Catwoman* #32** variant cover
by JENNY FRISON

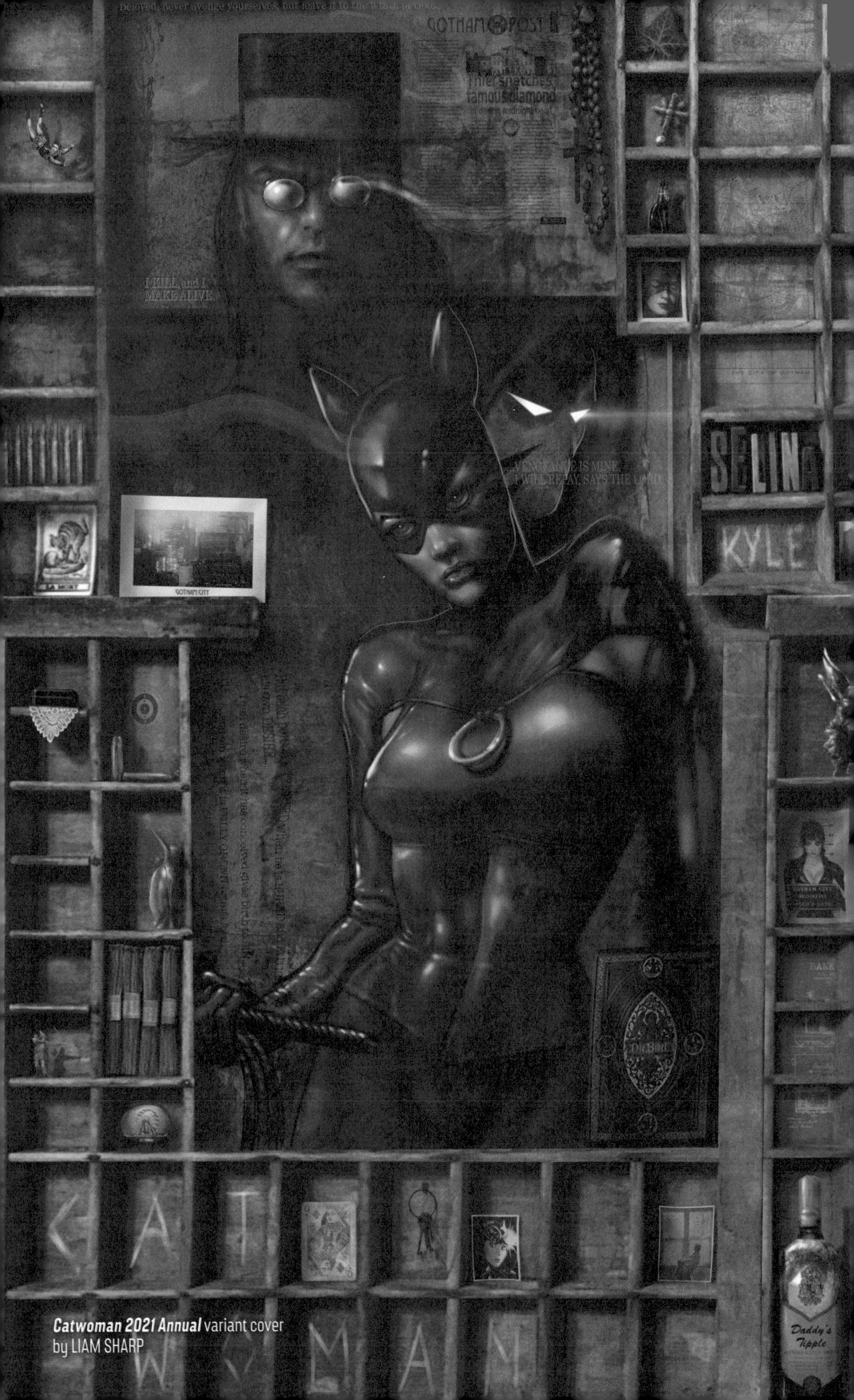
GOTHAM POST
Thief snatches famous diamond
I KILL, and I MAKE ALIVE.
VENGEANCE IS MINE, I WILL REPAY, SAYS THE LORD.
SELINA
KYLE
GOTHAM CITY
CAT
WOMAN
Daddy's Tipple

Catwoman 2021 Annual variant cover
by LIAM SHARP

CATWOMAN 2021 ANNUAL VARIANT COVER EASTER EGGS

CAN YOU SPOT THEM ALL?

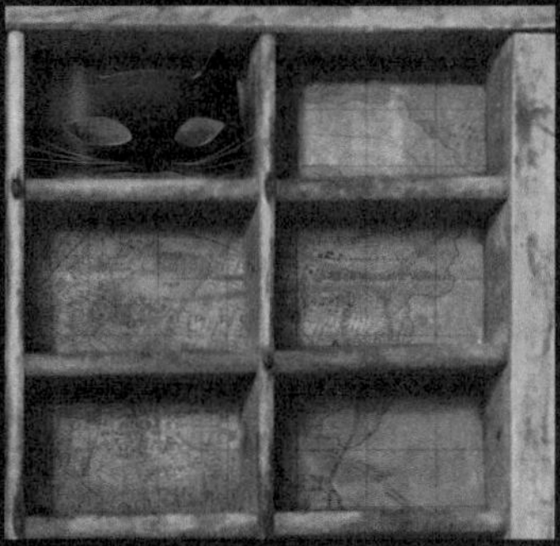

1. Diamond
2. Bell
3. Cat's-eye gemstone
4. Cat mask
5. Map of Gotham
6. Cutout trapeze artist
7. Newspaper report of jewel theft
8. Ivy leaf
9. Bullets
10. Tarot death card
11. Gotham City postcard
12. Wedding ring box
13. Target
14. The Penguin
15. Robin Hood
16. Money paid to Father Valley
17. Snow globe of carnival
18. Queen of diamonds

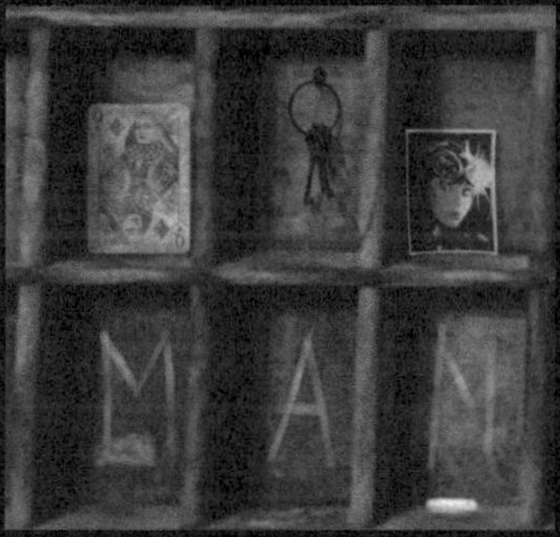
M
A
N

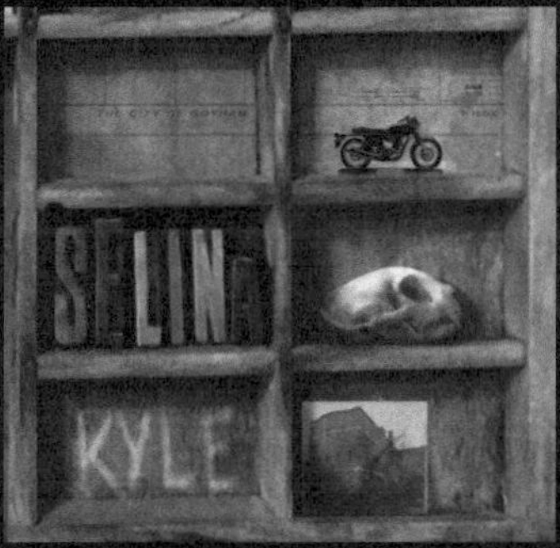
KYLE

19. Set of keys
20. Different costume
21. Mother sitting on edge of bath
22. Alcohol (referencing father's drinking problem)
23. Blueprint of bank safe
24. Floor plan of bank
25. Mug shot of Catwoman
26. Sword (of Azrael)
27. Avenging angel
28. Run-down children's home
29. Cat skull
30. Motorbike
31. Photo of Catwoman
32. Egyptian cat statuette
33. Cross
34. Rosary beads

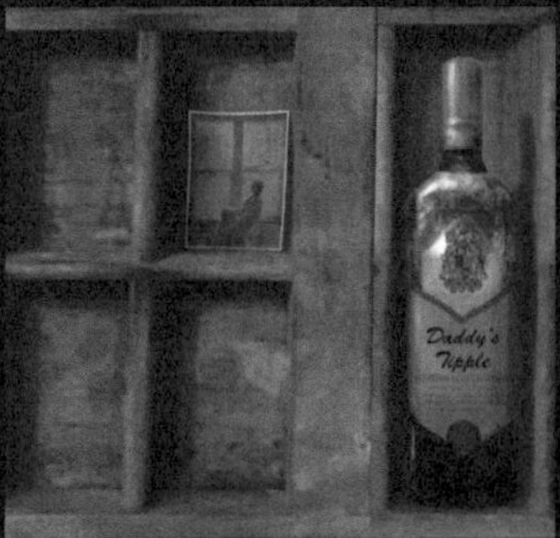
Daddy's Tipple

Character sketches
by EVAN CAGLE

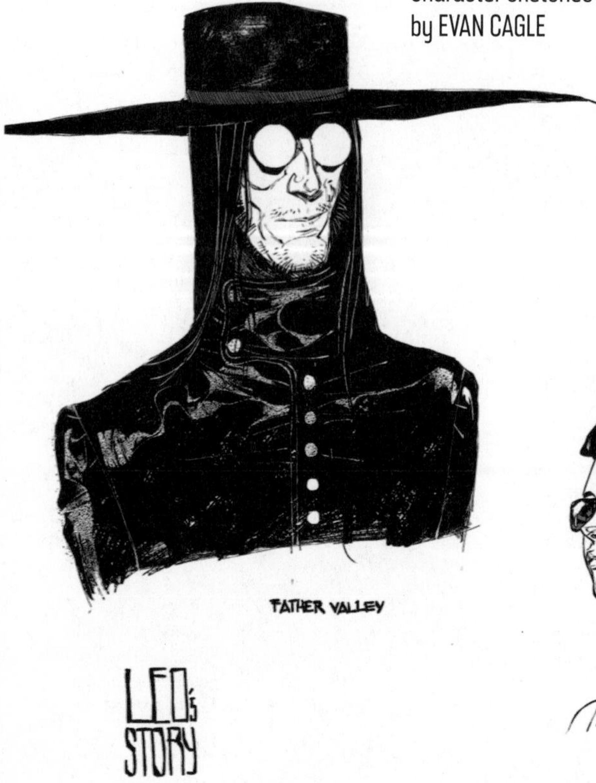
FATHER VALLEY
LEO's STORY

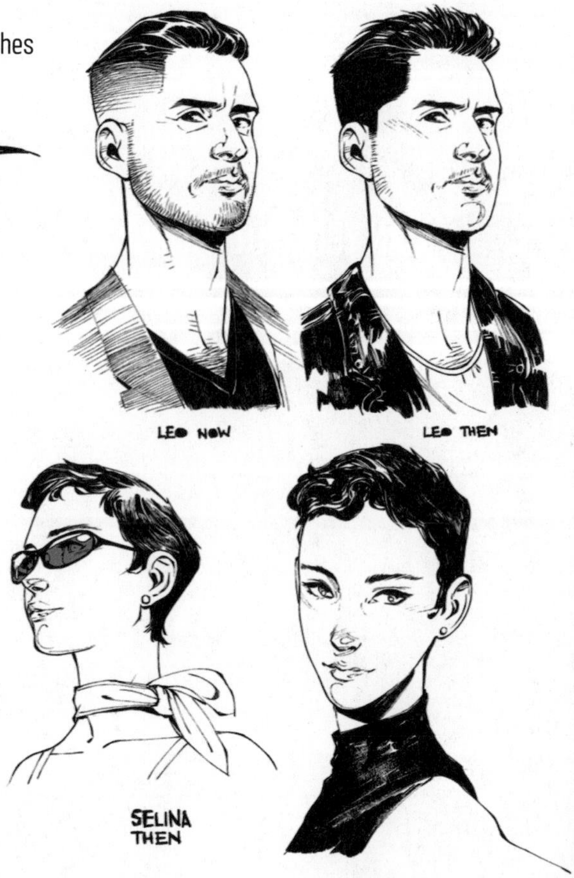
LEO NOW
LEO THEN
SELINA
THEN

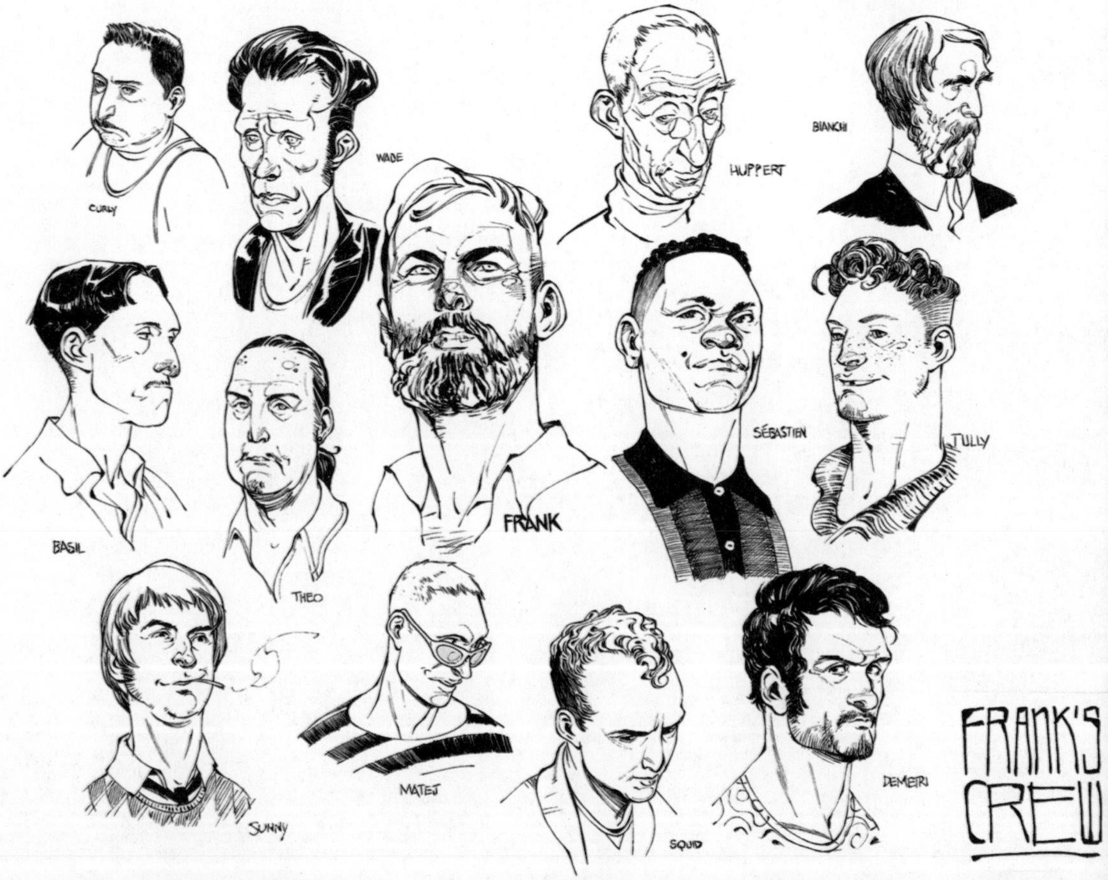
CURLY
WADE
HUPPERT
BIANCHI
BASIL
THEO
FRANK
SÉBASTIEN
TULLY
SUNNY
MATEJ
SQUID
DEMETRI
FRANK'S
CREW